ANTIMARKET ECONOMICS

ANTIMARKET ECONOMICS

Blind Logic, Better Science, and
the Diversity of Economic Competition

ROGER MANN

Westport, Connecticut
London

Library of Congress Cataloging-in-Publication Data

Mann, Roger, 1955–
    Antimarket economics : blind logic, better science, and the
diversity of economic competition / Roger Mann.
        p.   cm.
    Includes bibliographical references and index.
    ISBN 0–275–95466–8 (alk. paper)
    1. Economics—Methodology.   I. Title.
HB131.M36   1996
330—dc20   96–16272

British Library Cataloguing in Publication Data is available.

Library of Congress Catalog Card Number: 96–16272
ISBN: 0–275–95466–8

First published in 1996

Praeger Publishers, 88 Post Road West, Westport, CT 06881
An imprint of Greenwood Publishing Group, Inc.

Printed in the United States of America

The paper used in this book complies with the
Permanent Paper Standard issued by the National
Information Standards Organization (Z39.48–1984).

10 9 8 7 6 5 4 3 2 1

Contents

Tables and Figures

Preface

This book is a critical appraisal of conventional economic theory and practice and an argument for an alternative general theory and science of economics. Introspection and criticism in economics have a long history, and there has been a resurgence of interest in alternative economic thought in recent years. New theories and approaches have been and continue to be proposed. I am limited in the amount of text I can dedicate to these efforts, so I hope I have provided adequate credit and references for a reader interested in these perspectives.

In one sense, my goal is to combine many related criticisms, theories and approaches into one coherent theory. Antimarket economics links a variety of seemingly disparate economic ideas with each other and with market economics. Parts of public choice, game theory and institutional economics, the economics of expectations and information, market and government failure, the creative destruction of Schumpeter, new growth theory, differentiation and control of entry, rent-seeking, capture theory, and iron triangles all have a common thread. They all involve economic agents pursuing their self-interest by acting in ways that go against the assumptions or results of market theory.

Antimarket economics proposes that behaviors to escape or control market competition are a normal part of free enterprise, and the study of these behaviors should be an important part of the practice of economics. I have not yet tried to answer the question of how important. However, I propose that an improved general theory of behavior and change in free enterprise should include both market and antimarket forces.

I believe that the word *antimarket* will be a useful device for economics. It is easy to understand because the word *market* has such specific meaning for economists. We need a word to describe the opposing type of economic behavior. Indeed, I am not the first to use the word. The economic historian Fernand Braudel used *antimarket* to describe anti-competitive practices and institutions in his *The Perspective of the World* (New York: Harper and Row, 1986) and the term appears sparsely in other economic literature. My use of the term is somewhat different than Braudel's. There are not unique antimarket institutions; rather, there are antimarket behaviors, incentives and forces.

The second purpose of this book is to show that the practice of economics needs to be changed. The teaching of theory and logic in economics is the root cause of many of the problems identified in this book, and these problems extend into economic research despite decades of efforts to reverse this trend. Economists have been much more successful in promoting positivism than in producing it.

The use of deductive logic in market theory is not a proper use of logical methods. The logical argument for market behavior, economic equilibrium, and static economic efficiency is held together by conditions that were never based on facts. Worse yet, the theory fails a test of logical coherence because some of the assumptions are internally inconsistent, and the assumptions conflict with the result. The reasoning of market theory is only one of many possible lines of reasoning that could be applied to the types of conditions used by the theory, and the other lines of reasoning give very different results. These alternative results are the logical basis for antimarket theory.

This book is organized as follows. Chapter 1 is an overall summary. Chapter 2 critiques neoclassical economic practice and theory by appeal to scientific precedent and logic. Chapters 3 through 5 critique neoclassical theory by appeal to more empirical arguments. The scope of neoclassical economics is very narrow relative to the diversity of modern economic experience. Much of this diversity involves the conventional assumptions of neoclassical economics. Economic players can avoid or escape the rigors of market competition because many of the important assumptions of economic theory—information, property rights, entry, and cost structure—are actually endogenous. Modern economic diversity is a consequence of forces which have turned the narrow assumptions of market theory into complex and diverse phenomena.

Chapter 6 describes the scope and theory of antimarket economics. Chapters 7 through 9 provide more detailed description of antimarket behavior in innovation, government, and agriculture and suggest some implications. Innovation is conducted to obtain market control simply by being ahead of the competition or more formally through intellectual property rights. Most importantly, innovation creates technology, and this stock of technology is the basis for modern economic welfare. Chapter 8 covers the role of government as described by public choice theorists and their predecessors, and chapter 9 provides detailed analysis of two federal agencies in supporting market control.

Chapters 10 and 11 return to analysis of economic practice. Chapter 10 shows how biased quantitative analysis has been used to support rent-seeking antimarket behavior. Normally, the bias is not entirely intentional. Like most bias in science, it is a product of self-interest, poor science, and ideological preconceptions. Finally, the last chapter provides some recommendations for improvement in economic practice, which boil down to principles of empiricism and validation.

Although this book is about economics only, I am sure that many of the principles may be applied to scientific or research practices in other disciplines. Scientists often work in an economic and social environment that sustains the status quo. Progress is sometimes accomplished more slowly than necessary. The quest for better economics is made even harder by the fact that the economy changes. By the time we develop a better theory, the factual basis for the theory may have changed. This is why social sciences such as economics must be based on empiricism.

I am sure many economists will find my style of writing to be unconventional, perhaps unprofessional, and even biased. This book is meant to highlight what is wrong with economics, not what is right. The topic of antimarket economics involves some specific problems concerning free enterprise and the role of government in mixed economies. As part of its scope, antimarket economics highlights selfish behaviors to control others. Some of this discussion is not complimentary. It is also not completely original. I draw on my experience in agriculture and water to illustrate several of the major themes. Some readers will find that my viewpoint has been colored by this experience and this may be true. Still, I have been surprised by the amount of readily available documentation of antimarket behavior in many other industries.

I hope the book will set an example for some of the principles I espouse, especially the emphasis on empiricism and, more specifically, observation of economic actions, processes, and events. I have liberally added descriptions and interpretations of real events to provide empirical support for some of the principles, and I hope this makes the book more interesting to read.

This book includes no proofs but many hypotheses, no mathematics but many arguments, and little data but many facts. I hope to convince readers by argument and example that this is an appropriate form of creative economic expression. I may be wrong in some places, but I hope that readers find the arguments and conclusions to be compelling and appropriate overall. I would rather be provocative than unconditionally correct.

Modern economics is a highly logical and mathematical affair, and no economic theory seems able to escape mathematical exposition. By dispensing with the mathematical formalities, I hope to make this book simultaneously useful for economists, accessible to the economically astute public, and readable for both. Undoubtedly I will be criticized by economists for my lack of "rigor," and by the public by my lack of explanation. I have used footnotes and parenthetical references to provide a minimal explanation of economic terminology for noneconomists and to provide explanation for unique terms. A microeconomics textbook will be a useful accessory for any reader with only undergraduate training in economics.

I would like to thank the many people who assisted with the development of this book. The manuscript has benefitted from several anonymous reviewers who deserve some of the credit but none of the responsibility for the contents. I also want to thank my family for their enduring patience.

1

Introduction

Central to all scientific inquiry and discovery are certain dispositions: curiosity, a drive to experiment, and a desire to critically assess the validity of answers.

—Class of 2006 Kindergarten Information, San Ramon Elementary School, Novato, California.

Microeconomics, or neoclassical economics, is the single most influential paradigm of economics today, and market theory is the primary topic of teaching and research in microeconomics.* Market theory is a logical argument used to show how constrained economic incentives can lead to economic equilibrium and static economic efficiency. The efficiency associated with equilibrium is best summarized by the pareto principle, which states that in an efficient state, no one can be made better off without making someone else worse off.

Market theory works just fine—sometimes. Market theory does get support from the facts. Markets exist in free enterprise, some economic exchange occurs through near-perfect markets, and market exchange and competition do foster static economic efficiency.** This efficiency is a good argument for free enterprise. In other cases, economic inefficiency is a problem. Market theory

---

* A paradigm is a general pattern or method of developing knowledge and a way of viewing phenomena. Market theory is commonly known by its law of supply and demand. The theory is explained in some detail later.

** I use the term *free enterprise* to refer to the real economy of free agents, but free markets refer to the stylized markets of economic theory.

can then contribute to a solution. It is not the purpose of this book to detail the successes of market theory in promoting economic efficiency through free-market economic policy.

In some cases at some times—for some types of goods, industries, and economic phenomena—market theory does not explain what is going on. A large share of trade in modern free enterprise does not occur in competitive markets as defined by market theory. Microeconomics includes the comparative statics of imperfect competition, but comparative statics do not explain why imperfect competition exists.* Economic efficiency is at times sacrificed intentionally for other economic and social purposes such as innovation, private property rights, economic freedom, and equity. Market theory provides a limited basis for considering trade-offs between static efficiency and these other social values. A descriptive theory or group of theories is needed to explain the conflicts and forces that lead to imperfect competition.

This book argues against three related myths of neoclassical economics. These myths and the arguments against them are:

1. High standards of living in free enterprise economies are a result of economic efficiency created by free markets.

Conventional economics provides a theory of economic welfare based on efficient allocation, but modern economic welfare is based on what we have as well as how it is allocated.** Free enterprise fosters innovation and technical progress, but neoclassical economics alone does not explain why.

2. The economic theory of competitive markets provides a good general description of exchange, production, and resource allocation in free enterprise.

Market theory is a very incomplete description of economic activity because much activity is outside the scope of the theory.

3. Free markets normally tend toward a state of market equilibrium.

The logical argument used to get the result of static equilibrium and efficiency is at best weak. The market model fails the test of logical coherence

---

* Comparative statics is the method of comparing equilibrium results under two different sets of conditions. Imperfect competition is the study of trade with few or one buyers and/or sellers. Monopolies, duopolies, oligopolies (one, two, and a few sellers, respectively) and monopsonies (one buyer) are common topics.

** Economic welfare is the normative, or prescriptive, aspect of economic study. Economic welfare analysis in neoclassical economics is based largely on the pareto principle.

because the assumptions and the static equilibrium result are inconsistent with economic maximization. The existence and stability of market equilibrium is not likely because the driving forces that lead to it must also work to avoid it. Furthermore, we can observe the dynamics and results of free enterprise and we can observe behaviors which deviate from market competition. Perfect market exchange is normally an option available to economic players, but it is often not the option chosen.*

The purpose of this book is twofold. The first purpose is to propose and justify an economic theory that augments market theory as a general descriptive model of modern free enterprise. The theory also augments neoclassical economics as an economic paradigm by providing a general description of a common reason for dynamic change in economic competition.

Antimarket economics proposes that incentives and actions to escape or control market competition are a normal attribute of free enterprise, and the study of these actions should be a fundamental part of the practice of economics. An improved general descriptive and normative theory of free competition should include both market and antimarket behaviors and forces. Specifically, much technological innovation, product differentiation, control of information, development and protection of property rights, and influence of government occurs to intentionally or incidentally escape or control market competition. Antimarket behavior is the cause of some of the greatest virtues and the most intractable problems of modern mixed economies.

The second purpose of this book is to propose that the practice of economics should be substantially changed. Market theory is an incomplete theory of economic activity and welfare because it is the product of a tradition of poor use of scientific and logical methods. Mainstream economics divorced itself from science long ago, and this has led to a history of misleading theory, misguided policy prescriptions, and improper and even biased use of quantitative methods.

THE CRITICS

Neoclassical theory and conventional economic practice seem to have as many critics as supporters. Many critics have found that market theory is an incomplete and outdated representation of the basic functioning of free enterprise.

Economics has been caught up in the same "paradigm" ever since 1776 or thereabouts, a paradigm which still retains its grip on current thinking.[1]

---

* Players, a term commonly used in game theory, means anyone who participates in the economy. Consumers, firms, producers, buyers, sellers, and governments all qualify.

General economic theory has not really progressed beyond the stage of the natural philosophy of the Greeks, though of course it makes use of enormously more sophisticated mathematical tools.[2]

Economic theories meant to describe and explain reality often become frozen into dogmas that distort or falsify it.[3]

Many more economic criticisms are available in academic and specialized literature, such as evolutionary, institutional and environmental economics, public choice, political economy, and other fields. All critics are eventually faced with the perfectly fair challenge that they come up with a better theory. Many critics have taken the challenge and have tried to develop new theories to explain complex dynamics, disequilibria, and other phenomena. Despite these efforts, the critics have not displaced the old paradigm with a new or modified one, and economic criticism persists largely outside of the mainstream of economic teaching and practice.

Alternative paradigms have tended to dismiss or ignore neoclassical economics without recognizing the roles and values of markets and allocative efficiency in free enterprise. The concepts of market competition and static efficiency must clearly be part of any new or modified theory, but the markets of market economics are just one piece of the complex modern economy. There is a role for market theory and comparative statics in economics, but they have never been put into their proper context in the larger picture.

WHAT IS WRONG WITH CONVENTIONAL ECONOMICS?

It is probably true that neoclassical economics relies on logic more than any other science. In undergraduate economics classes, the logical argument for market equilibrium and efficiency is made verbally and graphically. Next, the study of economics in graduate courses is advanced by appeal to the rigorous logic of mathematics. Economists learn more about static efficiency and market structure by varying the assumptions. Next, economists learn about quantitative methods whose accuracy is always based on a variety of explicit or implicit assumptions and logical arguments. Modern economics applies these quantitative methods with computers. Consequently, economists are master logicians by training.

Scientists have frequently advocated a limited role for logical methods in science, a prescription that economists have been slow to recognize. In science, observation leads to theories, and more observation provides the confirmation of a hypothesis or theory. There is a role for logical methods in science, but logic has never been put in its proper context in economic practice. The logic of market theory is not based on objective observation of economic phenomena, and the role of positivism is largely reduced to the collection and manipulation of numerical data.* Neoclassical economics relies first on logical reasoning, second on the mathematical display of logic, and last on observation and analysis of real economic behavior.

The Logic of Market Theory is Faulty

Chapter 2 argues that the logical argument for perfect competition is not a proper use of logical methods at best and simply faulty at worst. The logical error of market theory is that only one type of logic—simple deduction —is used. As a test of logical coherence, it is also appropriate to consider whether the assumptions and result are reasonable taken as a set.**

The critical assumptions of market theory are as follows:

1. *Maximizing players*: Players maximize profit (firms) or utility (consumers).***

2. *Freedom of entry*: Anyone is free to be a player in the market game.

3. *Good information*: The information needed to play the game—prices, technology, and knowledge about the qualities of goods—can be readily obtained and used.

4. *Same product and numerous players*: Each product is sold by numerous sellers so that no player can affect prices.

5. *Well-defined rights*: Property rights are rival and exclusive. One player's use of a good precludes another's use of it, and players can be excluded from goods that are not theirs.

These assumptions are not logically independent or consistent, and the conventional result of market equilibrium is at odds with the very assumptions used to develop that result. These problems are related, and they provide a logical basis for an alternative dynamic theory of competitive behavior.

There are three logical errors in the reasoning of market theory. First, assumptions 2 through 5 are implicitly assumed to be independent of assumption 1, maximizing players. Maximizing players may seek to control entry, withhold or distort information, differentiate products, reduce the number of competitors, or change property rights. This is not a fatal error because the five assumptions could conceivably occur together. However, it seems reasonable that they will

---

* Positivism is the philosophy of science that emphasizes observation.

** The test of logical coherence checks to see if the outcome or proposition is free of logical errors.

*** A firm is a producer and a seller. Utility is satisfaction or happiness.

come into conflict.

Second, there is an internal conflict involving freedom of entry, well-defined property rights, and information. Economics has recognized that poorly defined rights—common property and contested rights, for example—can lead to inefficiency. However, well-defined rights can also lead to inefficiency when the right involves a unique good or new information. In this case, the well-defined property right can enable control of entry and result in monopoly. Mixed economies have recognized this problem. Owners of unique property are sometimes required to divest of their interest under antitrust or similar law. Market theory does away with this problem away by assuming many sellers of the same product.

Another manifestation of this logical error involves the creation of unique property and new information, that is, innovation. For the production process of innovation to be efficient, its products must have well-defined property rights, but if these unique products then have well-defined rights, they can be withheld from others as private property. To ensure freedom of entry, many types of information, including technology, must be available to all potential entrants, but property rights to new information enable market control. Therefore, if the theory is to allow for the production of new and unique things, well-defined property rights are inconsistent with freedom of entry. The theory of perfect competition can only cover the efficient production and allocation of existing, not new, goods.

I call this logical problem the *paradox of information*. The perfect information and open entry needed for perfect markets and static efficiency would stifle innovation. The practical result of the paradox of information is that, to protect incentives for the production of new goods and information, society must provide intellectual property and other proprietary rights, but these rights result in control of entry. Proprietary rights and intellectual property laws encourage business development and innovation by granting some market control. The existence and obvious worth of these laws are an indisputable example of why market theory is, at best, an incomplete framework for analysis of economic welfare in free enterprise.

Third, the result of the logical argument, equilibrium, is inconsistent with the assumption of maximization. If free markets do result in an equilibrium, there are no more trade opportunities to exploit. Players cannot make any more by playing the market game, but they still want to. Therefore, players must try to deviate from the equilibrium by assumption. Free enterprise does not naturally result in stable markets and economic equilibrium because market control can occur as a simple endogenous consequence of economic competition. With fixed resources and technology, this must create a pareto inefficiency. If no one can be made better off without making someone else worse off, then someone is likely to get hurt.

The logical argument for an antimarket economics is an extension of the logic of market theory. The potential for and expectation of market equilibrium must create a desire to control or escape market forces. At the theoretical equilibrium state, there are options that might result in improvements; there is upward sloping demand, waiting to be exploited, and new products or technology that might be more profitable. There is potential for control of entry, product differentiation, manipulation of information, and influence of property rights. At the theoretical equilibrium, there can be the means to pursue these options in the form of economic surplus, enabling institutions, technology, and social conventions that allow market control.

The Assumptions Are Normally Not True

Market theory often fails as an explanatory device because the assumptions cannot be confirmed. The assumptions of perfect competition were selected over time to ensure the desired result of equilibrium and efficiency, not because they were facts. Neoclassical economics is concerned with efficiency problems that occur when the assumptions of market theory are not true, and the logical method has been applied to the study of imperfect competition and market failure in some detail. However, conventional economics reasons under the premise that the assumptions of perfect competition are exogenous.* Therefore, market failure, or imperfect competition, occur because one or more of the exogenous assumptions of the theory are simply not true. For example, the conventional theory explains natural monopoly by appeal to declining average costs, a sort of technical aberration, and the models of imperfect competition reason with the number of buyers or sellers as an assumption. The method of comparative statics then shows the results of imperfect competition in terms of price, quantity, efficiency, and economic surplus, not how or why imperfect competition is developed or sustained.

The static result of neoclassical theories is a simple consequence of the invariance of the assumptions. Once it is admitted that the factors covered by the assumptions (entry, information, homogeneity of product, number of sellers and property rights) are actually variables, then many economic options become possible, and many more economic behaviors and associated problems must be considered. Entry, information, homogeneity and types of products, number of sellers, and property rights are all endogenous variables, and this enables dynamic change.** Much market control and market failure occurs merely because players make the assumptions untrue. Imperfect competition, innovation, and a variety of rent-seeking behaviors are a response to the rigors of market competition.

---

* *Exogenous* means determined completely outside of the system.

** *Endogenous* means affected by a given system. Endogenous is the opposite of exogenous.

Chapter 3 covers the problems of information in free enterprise. Market theory assumes that economic players have good information about prices and the characteristics of goods they buy. In fact, most goods must be produced before they can be sold, and most are not consumed until after they are purchased. Therefore, production and purchase decisions can not be based on knowledge. Producers must plan based on expectations of price and sales, and consumers must buy based on expectations about what they are getting. Second, many goods do not reveal the critical information. The important qualities of drugs, some foods, and many other goods are invisible. Third, the pertinent information is frequently closely guarded private property protected by law. Information is a variable, not a given, and it is also a good. There are costs and benefits associated with withholding, distorting, finding and understanding information.

Market economics begins with implicit assumptions about the nature of goods, but the true nature of many goods makes them hard to deal with in the market. Some goods are immobile, perishable, or otherwise create large costs in the process of trade. The nature of other goods makes it expensive to enforce their property rights. The problems of nonrival and nonexclusive goods are well known. More generally, property rights, like information, are a variable, and well-defined rights are a good that requires costs to protect and enforce.

Market economics starts with the assumption of freedom of entry. In many industries, freedom of entry is not allowed by law or is subject to government approval. In others, the information or technology needed to enter the industry can be withheld from others. In others, large initial costs and financial constraints limit entry. Entry is a variable, not a given, entry requires costs, and players influence the conditions and costs of entry to reduce market competition.

The Result of Market Theory, Being a State of Market Competition, Is Normally Not True

Furthermore, we can observe that the market model is not a good general theory for the modern economy. Market theory is not well substantiated by the facts because almost every business finds some means of protection from the extreme rigors of perfect market competition, and society allows and even encourages this behavior. Limited or minimum market control is a common and readily observable attribute of free enterprise. A variety of property rights, especially the right to limit physical access, labeling protections, proprietary information, and intellectual property, are used to control entry. Minimal market control can result in an equilibrium of a sort; a balancing of market forces, market control and social tolerance.

Substantial market control, though less common than minimal control, is a recurring feature of modern economies. The reasons for and problems of substantial market control are discussed throughout this book, but especially in chapters 7 through 10. Substantial market control is established in many industries by law. For example, substantial market control has recently been allowed for agriculture, labor unions, public utilities and transit, professional baseball, schools and hospitals, and certain joint newspaper publications.

Economic players frequently control information and the rules of property and exchange to violate the very conditions deemed necessary by market theory. In the conventional jargon, firms try to decrease the elasticity of demand and maintain a monopoly for their unique product. Businesses differentiate and strive to limit competitors' ability to sell that product through labeling and trademark protection.

Market theory limits players to control of their own affairs, and interaction with others occurs only through prices set by markets. Prices are often not set by the market as the theory finds because there are few sellers or buyers for the unique good. Generally, sellers set prices, or prices are negotiated. When prices are set by the market, sellers try to find ways to control them. Often, control of prices means control of others. Market theory argues that large numbers of similar players result in competitive markets, but freedom of assembly and the common interest of similar players result in a tendency toward collective market control.

The Scope of Conventional Economic Theories Is Limited

Market theory is limited in scope because it does not address the fundamental mechanics of change. Market theory is called static because it only considers the production and exchange of existing goods and resources. Static economic efficiency addresses the best allocation of resources and the best use of existing technology without considering why technology increases over time. Dynamic change is addressed largely in terms of how it affects the static result, but the reasons for dynamic change in relation to markets are not a part of the general theory. The practice of comparative statics stands in sharp contrast to the accelerating pace of technological change in modern economies. Economic competition in free enterprise creates a variety of new things, but neoclassical economics does not explain why. Creation and the variety that follows is a response to relatively poor returns in market competition.

The topic of market theory is resource allocation by markets because this is the only allocation allowed by the theory. Neoclassical economics tends to focus on one market structure at a time. In fact, economic players buying or selling a good usually face many trade options at the same time, each quite different from the stylized perfect market, but in different ways (chapter 4). Players even create new options for exchange, and the options may not be anything like the competitive trade of market theory.

Conventional economics covers a limited range of voluntary trade, but some exchange is incidental or unintentional. Some economic exchange is extramarket. It occurs outside of markets. Some exchange, as allowed by civil law, is completely involuntary. Anyone may be forced to participate. Sometimes, economic players seek to change property rights through involuntary exchange. In antimarket economics, these activities are explicit economic alternatives to participation in markets.

The theory of the firm, central to neoclassical economics, cannot be generally substantiated. Some of this problem is merely a consequence of the diversity of products, costs, trade options, and business structures that have been spawned by competition (chapter 4). Timing problems, contracts, and government create major economic problems and opportunities for firms. The theory of the firm ignores many types of costs and, subsequently, the variety of business decisions. Marginal costs, so critical to the theory of price, are often indeterminate, and the common presumption of increasing marginal costs is not defensible.* Even when marginal costs are determinate, they are often irrelevant. Pricing is most often determined by expectations, average costs, marketing strategies, and financial needs, not marginal costs. Market theory does not consider the preeminence of expectations, financial feasibility and wealth in determining pricing and sales strategies.

Neoclassical economics does not consider the significance of survival as an economic motive. Survival is a real problem for much of the world. For many players, immediate survival often takes precedence to profit or utility maximization. The priority of survival in combination with limited options causes economic players to behave in ways not predicted by the theory. For example, lower prices can cause desperate players with limited options to supply more rather than less as the theory predicts.

Social values, often expressed through government, result in a variety of economic constraints and opportunities not considered by the theory. The conventional economic problem is the efficient allocation of scarce resources, but this definition simply ignores other important social values that play a large role in economic policy and have been used to justify or rationalize market control for over a century. For example, the social value of private property supports the belief that new information and products developed by private initiative should have protection.

Market theory misses many of the crucial arguments for free enterprise. Values such as economic freedom and private property, not efficiency, are often viewed as the major reasons for free enterprise. Conflict between static economic efficiency and other economic and social goals is an important problem of mixed economies, but mainstream economics is unable to make a balanced contribution to these debates because of its myopic fixation with logic and efficiency.

Even more important, the conventional theory of economic welfare is faulty. Economic welfare is based on the stock of goods as well as the efficiency of

---

* *Marginal* means incremental, the value for the last unit produced or bought or sold, whichever pertains.

their allocation, but neoclassical theories take the existing stock of goods as given. The promise of market control can increase long-term economic welfare by increasing investment, technical progress, and economic stability at the expense of immediate efficiency. Privacy of information and control of entry are required to create and preserve economic motives for business development, investment, and innovation. Technological progress, protection of property rights to information and ideas, and market control all go hand in hand.

Market theory is limited in scope by not fully considering the complex roles of government in the economy. Market theory fails as an explanatory device when government tries to make markets behave like those of market theory, but fails, or when government forces economic players to behave unlike market theory for other reasons. Market control often involves the manipulation of production, resources, and trade by government. Price or quantity in some sectors is substantially determined by government bureaucracies, agencies, or commissions, not markets. Intervention in the banking, telephone, trucking, and airline industries has recently been diminished. Agriculture is the topic of chapter 9. Many industries are heavily regulated. Environmental regulations substantially affect the cost structure of many industries. Government regulation of production or trade practices, not market competition, is the most important economic problem for many businesses, and economic competition often involves the influence of government.

THE ROLE OF ANTIMARKET ECONOMICS

Rather than serving as an alternative, antimarket theory complements and builds on free market theory. It augments market economics as a description of economic behavior and economic welfare in free enterprise. Antimarket theory is more general than market theory in that there are no a-priori assumptions except, perhaps, maximization. Firms compete in any way expected to be profitable, and a variety of important economic decisions and behaviors occur outside of the competition of the marketplace. If the current general theory of free enterprise is the static neoclassical theories of market and imperfect competition, I propose that market/antimarket theory is a better alternative.

The theory of antimarket competition is discussed in more detail in chapter 6. Antimarket economics proposes that market competition, downward sloping demand, market failure, and many institutional factors create pervasive incentives to escape, avoid, control, remove, or undermine market competition. These incentives result in many important economic phenomena, including market control, economic crime, property rights disputes, product differentiation, technical innovation, and government intervention. In market economics, everyone is a winner. In antimarket economics, there are usually winners and losers.

A major incentive for monopoly and other market control is that most fundamental of economic phenomena, downward sloping demand. Downward sloping demand makes market control profitable, and control of entry makes it possible. The potential for static market equilibrium as described by market theory is also a fundamental incentive for market control. Competitive pressures encourage the allocation of resources to activities that are alternative opportunities to markets.

In a complex legal and technical environment, participation in conventional markets is just one of many possible alternatives for exchange and use of resources. Firms can usually buy and sell at competitive prices, but the competitive market is merely one of many trade options. The rules and penalties do not necessarily constrain other behavior. They may even encourage it. The range of options is limited only by law and creativity. Law is subject to influence and control, while creativity knows no bounds. There are alternatives to perfect markets, each is selfishly evaluated, and market trade is frequently not selected because it is not the best option.

Antimarket theory proposes that the conventional assumptions of market theory cannot be interpreted as constraints; they must be interpreted as endogenous variables. The nature and types of goods that can be sold, freedom of entry, information, number of players, costs, business structures, property rights—all of these are human artifacts that are created and changed by actions that respond to competitive pressures. The nature of goods, laws, and many other factors affect the costs and benefits of these actions.

In market/antimarket theory, the normal state of free enterprise is dynamic competition between market and antimarket forces. Market forces do exist, and they foster efficiency in production and allocation of existing goods and resources, but forces just as fundamental to free enterprise destabilize markets. Perfect markets create incentives for antimarket behaviors, such as market control to obtain economic rents, *and* economic rents created by market control create incentives for market behavior, such as free entry that will eliminate the economic rents.

This dual system of seemingly contradictory incentives is a major cause of endogenous dynamic change in free enterprise. In the long run, market/antimarket dynamics lead to an evolving economy of increased diversity, specialization, and variety. Market competition selects the players who can exploit existing resources and markets most effectively. Sometimes, however, a new niche is created by combining or creating technology, laws, goods, or other pieces of the human environment. Someone must be first, but success attracts other players who imitate each other to the point of market competition, and the new niche becomes a new part of the economic environment.

One economic option is to create new options. Antimarket economics considers the benefits and costs of the creation of new products and trade options from the private perspective. Innovation as antimarket behavior is discussed in chapter 7. The potential for profit from new products becomes a better opportunity as returns in existing markets decline with competitive pressure. Rather than direct resources to unprofitable competition in existing markets that approach equilibrium, players invest in ideas and actions that can be protected from market forces. The incentive for innovation is the promise of market control later. Market control is obtained merely by being ahead of the competition, or it is granted by property rights. By protecting innovation through intellectual property laws, society encourages this form of escape from market forces.

Property rights are among the most important institutional factors that enable market control, and part of the process of business development is to develop and protect these rights. We know these rights as intellectual property, proprietary information and labeling, trademarks, and brand names, among other terms. In addition, the right to limit others' physical entry onto real property keeps competitors from observing production techniques or obtaining other useful information. Contracts are often used to obtain or retain market control through nondisclosure requirements, sales exclusives, and many other terms.

Many U.S. laws recognize the facts of market control and, true to the findings of market theory, seek to require market-like behavior. Antitrust law, as the term is typically used, regulates private market control. Conventional examples of illegal market controls include predatory pricing and buy-outs; price collusion, fixing, and discrimination; and restrictions on entry, access, or mobility of goods, information, or resources. Consumer protection laws limit deceptive labeling, advertising, and other unfair marketing practices. However, these laws are not hard constraints. Rather, they are just one factor in the benefit-cost analysis used by players to evaluate their options. The decisions of players with respect to laws are affected by the probability of success and the chance and size of benefits or costs such as fines. Laws can create options, not constraints.

The Worth of Antimarket Theory

Conventional methods emphasize a comparison of equilibrium states—the practice of comparative statics—with little concern for what forces may disturb equilibrium to start with. Part of the worth of antimarket theory is simply to recognize that players incidentally or intentionally destabilize markets as an endogenous consequence of the competitive process.

Market theory argues that economic freedom leads to an optimal state. If free markets work perfectly and efficiency is the only thing that matters, there is no practical economic purpose for economists or government. But other values matter, and economics has recognized that free markets can be inefficient when there are underlying technical relationships unlike the assumptions required for stylized markets. Market failure has focused on technical problems, such as technical externalities, public goods, and increasing returns to scale. To this list, we must add costs of exchange and information, uncoordinated planning, survival problems, and financial obligations. Sometimes, the assumptions of free market theory can only be obtained at a substantial cost, and sometimes, they cannot be obtained at any reasonable cost.

Antimarket economics goes a step further by recognizing that market failure can occur without any underlying technical problems. Market control, biased information, and imperfect property rights often occur just because someone has the incentive and ability to make them occur. Market failure can be an endogenous consequence of the competitive process, the existence of wealth, and/or the powers vested in government. Market control is not an aberration of free enterprise; it is a normal consequence of selfish motives and the costs and benefits of options.

Modern technology is the basis for much of our high standard of living. New technology is created in the private sector not by perfect markets, but by a desire and ability to generate economic rents using control of entry. To preserve incentives for technical progress, modern societies must allow private players to restrict access to new information and technology. Market competition creates allocative efficiency, but it also drives resources away from existing markets when the option of innovation and/or market control is possible. Therefore, the basis for modern economic welfare is market competition for existing goods *and* the competition for market control that can be obtained for new ideas; that is, market/antimarket dynamics.

More generally, the stability and growth of business is based on property rights that protect the incentive and ability to control entry and reduce competition. The incentive to take risks, develop new products, and find better ways of doing business are diminished without protection of these property rights. This protection may result in static inefficiency, but this is part of a normal trade-off between static efficiency and investment and growth.

There are long-term trade-offs between innovation of valuable products and business development, on one hand, and static efficiency on the other. The proper balance between these two forms of economic welfare is a major economic problem of modern free enterprise. The blanket protections provided for patents and copyrights illustrate the lack of effort applied to this important policy issue. Intuitively, there is potential for improvement.

The Relationship of Antimarket Economics to Some Other Theories

Antimarket theory is discussed in relation to some other economic fields in chapter 6. A variety of economic studies under the labels of public choice, capture theory, and rent-seeking have shown that laws are often used to gain market control and competitive advantage. Government makes the laws that regulate trade, contracts, marketing, production, entry, information, and property, but government can be affected. When maximizing economic players seek to change or control the variables of competition, they must often work through government. The means to obtain market control in mixed economies include the ability to influence government either directly or through public perception.

The antimarket view of innovation is closely related to the theory of creative destruction as first defined by Joseph Schumpeter. More recently, the new growth economists have argued on the similar notion that technological growth is endogenous. Schumpeter recognized that innovations can disturb economic equilibrium, that innovation is a temporary source of monopoly profit, and that an innovation is followed by the classical competitive pressures of market theory. However, Schumpeter did not fully explain that market control, not the innovation itself, is the source of profit and the true incentive behind innovation. Innovation without market control is likely to lose money, and profit and personal financial gain drive modern innovation.

Schumpeter and the new growth economists are primarily concerned with the dynamic process of innovation. Antimarket economics is more general in that antimarket behaviors can result in a variety of destabilizing actions and dynamic processes. Innovation disrupts equilibrium, but so can collusion, mergers, government intervention, court decisions and influence of information, perceptions, and expectations, and all of these are endogenous to the competitive process.

Game theory has made a valuable contribution to economics by providing a variety of alternative models of economic competition under a variety of unconventional assumptions, especially involving information, strategies and number of players. Much of game theory, however, is also logic. In the real world, the rules of the game are constantly subject to influence by the players.

THE PROBLEM OF GOVERNMENT

Control of markets by government is usually initiated with good intention, but perfectly rational forces then seek to influence government in their own interests. Intervention created to correct market failure or promote other social goals often evolves to suit those with the most to gain or lose. Intervention then becomes a vested interest. After a time, the original economic reasons for intervention become rationales. The government and beneficiaries sustain their interests by arguing that their relationship is in the public interest.

Antimarket behavior through government is discussed in chapter 8. Government often provides the institutional means to control competition or otherwise obtain unusual profits. The profits created by government intervention provide the incentive and capability to sustain and enforce government's role. The beneficiaries influence the political process through politicians, lobbies, political contributions, and other gifts, perks, promises, and pay-offs. Government provides support to beneficiaries through low-priced sales, high-priced purchases, the distribution of tax monies, and/or establishment and enforcement of market control. The bureaucracy implements the subsidy or market control and assists with rationalization of the system. The bureaucracy gains by expansion of its programs, and politicians gain by financial support or the indirect purchase of votes.

Government intervention often results in the betterment of a few at the expense of many, and the total cost to the many far exceeds the total benefit to the few. The result is a public bad, analogous to the public good of conventional theory. Taxes to pay for a single government project or program are spread over large numbers of individuals so that each has little incentive to resist that program, but benefits are concentrated into the hands of a few so that each beneficiary has a large interest in supporting the program. Similarly, market control can increase prices to many people by just a little, while concentrating the increased revenues into the hands of a few.

By supporting this type of activity, government can simultaneously contribute to inefficiency, inequity, and increased concentration of wealth and power. Furthermore, intervention can reduce incentives for innovation by creating profit in existing rather than new goods. Therefore, rent-seeking through government intervention can reduce static efficiency and innovation at the same time. Government intervention can disrupt the market/antimarket dynamics that foster efficiency and progress. Market control in free enterprise tends to be eliminated as competitors enter the market, but market control enabled by government often works by prohibiting entry on a sustained basis.

U.S. agriculture, discussed at length in chapter 9, has used extensive government intervention to control markets at a substantial cost to U.S. taxpayers and consumers. Manipulation of public perception and a large vested interest have allowed the system to continue for decades. The intervention has reduced private incentives to develop new types of crops and markets. The 1996 Federal Agriculture Improvement and Reform Act has reduced, but not eliminated agricultural market control, and the Act was possible only because free markets and subsidies independent of prices are temporarily more profitable than the market control they replace.

Many of today's most pressing economic issues involve policies justified and supported in the past with economic arguments. Economic arguments and quantitative analysis are often used to rationalize government intervention in the economy (chapter 10). Especially, biased benefit-cost and input-output analysis have both been used extensively to advocate misguided public spending initiatives. Finally, we return to where we started. A poor balance of scientific methods leads to faulty logic, theory and analysis.

TOWARD BETTER ECONOMICS

Economics has progressed to the point that these problems are sometimes recognized, and some improvements have been suggested, but economic theory has fallen far behind the more complex debates of today. As society grapples with difficult issues involving government and the economy, economics still clings to a basic theory and approach that is too simple to make a balanced contribution. Economics has not progressed fast enough to help, and this slow pace of improvement is the consequence of economics' emphasis on logic and mathematics at the expense of scientific procedures, especially observation and confirmation.

Chapter 11 discusses how economics can be improved. Economics must be changed to reflect a more diverse and balanced application of scientific methods. Conventional economics often approaches quantitative economic analysis with three tools: economic theory, economic data, and quantitative methods. Often, economic theory is not validated by observation. Good theory must be based on observation of economic actions, process, and events, and economic practice must become more oriented to the observation of economic behavior and less oriented to logic, mathematical process, and numerical analysis. The logic of the market allocation of widgets must be replaced by the observation and facts of production and exchange of real goods and services, and quantitative analysis should be confirmed using commonly accepted scientific principles.

It is doubtful that any one economic theory can provide a sound, permanent, or general basis for economic thought. There is too much variety in economic structure and behavior to justify a single general economic theory constrained by general premises about technology, costs, and behavior. Rather than have one general theory, economics needs a large number of theories tailored to small segments of the economy, and each theory should be clearly dated.

Many of the concerns of economics are the sole topic of other disciplines. Economics should utilize other sciences for behavior and production theory. Economics should become a multidisciplinary study involving psychology, sociology, business, marketing, technology, institutions, and evolutionary process.

The voluntary exchange of goods and services is more clearly the sole province of economic theory and practice. Economics needs a more sophisticated theory and study of trade. Trade has at least four identifiable components: negotiation, contracting, buyer obligations, and seller obligations. The modern economy is characterized by separation of the location and timing of the four components. Trade options differ in the characteristics of their trade components, and these differences affect the extent to which each option differs from perfect competition. Modern exchange is very complex and diverse and deserves its own empirical discipline. Economics should develop more detailed procedures for observing and evaluating the contractual, financial, and physical characteristics of exchange; especially trade options, the search for buyers and sellers, development of information and terms, negotiation, the expectations involved, the physical transfer, and the results in terms of the fulfillment of expectations and economic welfare.

NOTES

1. Mark Blaug, *Economic Theory in Retrospect*, Third Edition (Cambridge: Cambridge University Press, 1978), p. 720.

2. Nicholas Kaldor, *Economics without Equilibrium*, The Arthur M. Okun Memorial Lecture Series, Yale University (Armonk, NY: M. E. Sharpe, 1985), p. 11.

3. Leonard Silk, *Economics in the Real World* (New York: Simon and Schuster, 1984), p. 15.

2

Market Theory Reconsidered

The origin of discoveries is beyond the reach of reason.

—W.I.B. Beveridge, *The Art of Scientific Investigation*

Market theory might be summarized as follows: a market is a form of voluntary trade between buyers who demand and sellers who supply a good. For a variety of behavioral and technical reasons, quantity demanded generally declines while quantity supplied increases with the good's price. When supply and demand are combined in free trade, the result is static market equilibrium at which there exists a market clearing price for exchange. No one can be made better off without making someone else worse off because all potential trades in the mutual interest of buyers and sellers are realized. This optimum is called *Pareto-efficient*. Static economic efficiency and economic welfare, or surplus, are maximized at the equilibrium state.

Market theory boils down to a simple logical argument for the existence and worth of market exchange. Economists are taught to regard market theory as a useful description of the process of trade between buyers and sellers in free enterprise and to use it as the basis for reasoning and analysis of economic problems. For example, economic research is frequently based on the assumption, not the observation, that prices and quantities are caused by supply, demand, and markets, as shown by the theory. The study of economic welfare is focused almost exclusively on the efficiency of production and exchange as suggested by the theory.

THE NATURE OF SCIENCE

Much has been written in recent years about the practice of economics as science. The literature has been prescriptive as well as descriptive, critical as well as supportive. Rather than restate and summarize these efforts, this section addresses particular problems of science of relevance to later arguments.[1]

Science is "the organized accumulation of systematic (reliable) knowledge for the purpose of intelligent explanation/prediction."[2] What science does is an iterative and creative process that uses empiricism (the use of the senses, or observation) and reasoning (the internal process of thought) to arrive at understanding of cause and effect phenomena. Positivism requires empiricism and empiricism relies on observation.

Logic is formal reasoning. The practice of logic goes by many names: deduction, inference, extrapolation, and reasoning are all related terms. Logic might best be defined as any thought process that starts with a premise, given, or fact and arrives at a conclusion. Deductive reasoning is "inference in which the conclusion follows necessarily from the premises." Inductive reasoning reasons "from particulars to generals or from the individual to the universal."[3]

Logical positivism has been used to refer to the standard combination of logic and empiricism that characterizes modern science. It has served science well when there are indisputable facts to start from. This has been especially true in physics, chemistry, astronomy, and related hard sciences. Facts, which are verifiable observations, can be demonstrated with a high degree of certainty. When logic is based on facts, one possible source of error is eliminated, and when logic arrives at a conclusion that can be validated by observation of facts, a check on the result is possible.

The conclusions of logic, along with any facts and logical process used to arrive there, may result in a theory. Webster's defines theory as "the analysis of a set of facts in their relation to one another" or a "general principle or body of principles offered to explain phenomena."[4] Both of these definitions imply that theories must be based on facts or observed phenomena. A theory does not require much logic to be a good theory, but it does require facts. According to Darwin, "Science consists in grouping facts so that general laws or conclusions may be drawn from them."[5]

A good theory must be able to be judged by comparison to some facts. "Theories are 'scientific' if they are falsifiable in principle or in practice and not otherwise."[6] A theory must be constantly re-evaluated in light of more facts; science returns to observation to see if inference is correct. Better methods of observation may be justified; experimentation may be used to filter out effects of unknowns, and new devices may be developed to observe or measure. To discourage the practice of salvaging bad theories by making them untestable, "refuted theories may be amended to avoid future refutations but only if these amendments increase the empirical content of the theory, that is, render it more falsifiable or testable."[7] The final result is a theory refined and confirmed by observation.

Sometimes theories become facts. The idea that the world was a globe was once only a theory. We don't know who first reasoned that the world is round or why. Perhaps this person noted the shape of the moon or sun or observed a ship slipping over the horizon. But once the idea developed, experiments were devised. Plans were made and executed to observe the angle of the sun's shadow at different places at the same time, and ships were sent on uncertain experiments to circumnavigate the world. Technology—first rapid communications and later spacecraft—made direct observation possible. The theory of a global world was elevated to the status of fact by the lack of any observations to refute the theory.

More often, a theory cannot become a fact. Once it is shown that a theory is wrong just once the question: What is its worth? arises. This is clearly the position of economic theories and many other theories of human behavior. An economic theory is a generalization, not a fact, and economists should be very concerned with the measurement and description of its worth.

Verification, falsification, validation, and confirmation are terms commonly used to describe the process of checking a theory. Verification means the establishment of truth. A theory cannot be proven by an observation, but it can be falsified if it is shown to be wrong once. "Nothing can ever be exhaustively verified but a single falsification suffices."[8,9] It is a verified theory that the world is quite close to being a globe.

A theory can only be strictly verified in a closed system where no new processes can occur to change the system and therefore require changes to the factual or logical basis of the theory. The world is a globe, but it would not be correct to say that the world will always be a globe. An asteroid could enter our closed system in the future and change the world's shape. All economic systems, except perhaps the global economy, are quite open in comparison. Therefore, most economic theories cannot be strictly verified. Verification also requires that "all the components of the system are established independently and are known to be correct."[10]

Validation denotes the establishment of legitimacy. It implies a standard of social acceptance, not truth, and is therefore less restrictive than verification. Validation is an argument for empirical adequacy where adequacy is a judgment. Confirmation is the process of checking theoretical results against observed results.

While the concepts of positivism that lead to the formulation and checking of scientific theories are useful, there are also limitations in their application to economics. All economic theories have been falsified at some place and time, but this does not mean that they should be rejected for every time and place. Many economic phenomena are continuous, not true or false. In economics, falsification, validation, and confirmation must be relative concepts. The closer theoretical results are to observed results, and the more cases in which they are close, the stronger the case for validation. In modern science, there are often competing theories, different models, or quantitative representations of the same theory. In this case, a theory or model may be validated if it demonstrates practical worth by giving the best prediction or explanation.

A theory that gives the best predictions or explanations may be validated, but this may not be the only factor leading to social validation. Because validation is social acceptance the psychological and social factors of preconception, power, politics, and prejudice in fact affect which model is validated. Logic may be used to reason for the theory. To rationalize is "to justify by reasoned argument a view which in reality is determined by preconceived judgment."[11]

WHEN LOGIC AND THEORIES GO WRONG

Most sciences suggest a limited role for logical methods, and many scientists have noted that logic can lead to erroneous theories. For example, "reason seldom can progress far from the facts without going astray," and "logical reasoning has often prevented the acceptance of new truths." As early as the 1600s, Francis Bacon noted that "the present system of logic rather assists in confirming . . . errors founded on vulgar notions . . . and is therefore more hurtful than useful." F.C.S. Schiller, a philosopher, stated in 1917 that "among the obstacles to scientific progress a high place must certainly be assigned to the analysis of scientific procedure which logic has provided. . . . The great men of science have usually been kept in salutary ignorance of the logical tradition." Other authors found that "reason has obstructed the advance of science owing to false doctrines based on it," and "science differs from the non-scientific metaphysical speculation that preceded it, in attempting to give a rational explanation of the natural world, which is firmly supported by observed facts."[12,13,14]

There are uncountable ways in which logic can go wrong. Table 2.1 lists eight common types of logical arguments that are improper, and four types of tests that should be applied to logical arguments to check their validity and worth.

Several examples demonstrate how errors of logic and lack of proper confirmation can lead to improper conclusions and counter-productive actions. There was once a cholera epidemic in Russia that brought doctors to the homes of the afflicted. The populace observed the disease and the doctors, concluded that doctors caused cholera, and killed them. Often the search for cause and effect relationships must start with simple association. In this example of false cause, the inferred association was exactly opposite from the truth.

Bad science tends to persist until someone is harmed by it. Often, a potential for substantial harm is the incentive to initiate a sustained challenge. Two recent cases from psychology illustrate this point. In one case, the technique of recovering memories with hypnosis was put to stringent tests only after it was used to implicate people in criminal activities.

Table 2.1
Logical Fallacies and Tests for Reliability

Logical Fallacies	Problem Definition
Special Pleading	Information that may refute the argument is ignored
Affirming the Consequent	Conclusions based on unsubstantiated premises
Attacking the Person	Argument rejected or accepted because of the status of the person arguing
Appeal to the People	Argument accepted or rejected because a large number of persons accept or reject it
Appeal to Authority	Argument or conclusion accepted because the experts accept it
False Cause	Attributing the wrong cause to an effect, usually by spurious correlation
Argument by Analogy	What is true for one case is also true for a similar case
Composition and Division	What is true for the part is true for the whole, or vice versa

Tests for Reliability	Favorable Test Result
Correspondence	The result is consistent with prior knowledge
Logical Coherence	The outcome or proposition is free of logical errors
Clarity	The outcome or proposition is not ambiguous or vague
Workability	The result solves the problem or issue addressed

Source: Summarized from Don Ethridge, *Research Methodology in Applied Economics: Organizing, Planning and Conducting Economic Research* (Ames, IA: Iowa State University Press, 1995), p. 47.

The technique was shown to be unreliable. In another case, the technique of facilitated communication (FC) was developed to help severely disabled individuals communicate. Typically, a facilitator held the hand of the disabled person who pointed to a chart of letters to create language. When this technique was first developed and applied, remarkable success was reported. Severely disabled persons were writing explicit statements, poetry, and letters. Then, FC was used to assert charges of molestation against family members, and the technique was only then put to experimental tests. It was quickly discovered that the words thought to be created by the disabled person were actually the product of the facilitator who intentionally or subconsciously directed the disabled persons' communications. Furthermore, it was discovered that the disabled persons often did not even look at the chart of letters, making selection of letters impossible. FC persisted through a network of advocates and adherents even after lawsuits were brought against the creators of the technique.

Facilitated communication and recovered memories both illustrate important principles of why science goes bad and how bad science persists. In both cases, the techniques were not put to strict scientific tests before being released for public use. Once released, they developed followings of people who made a livelihood from them or developed an emotional attachment to them. They both persisted until someone had reason to challenge them.

Conflicting theories tend to coexist more in the social and behavioral sciences than in any other sciences. Value judgments influence perceptions of what is true and false. Value judgments involving people tend to be strong compared with those involving physical sciences. People develop emotional attachments to theories that can explain human suffering or provide hope for improvement. Theories in the social and behavioral sciences are often rationalized, and economics—the study of the behavior of people in relation to the material world—is a social science.

THE ECONOMIC TRADITION

The pre-eminence of market theory in economics is sustained by some evidence and several varieties of bad science. A logical argument without factual support and confirmation is not a science. The assumptions of market theory are as often wrong as true, the logical argument for market equilibrium is faulty in several ways, and the result is not substantiated by reference to facts. The logical approach keeps neoclassical economics from being a scientific discipline and has stifled the field from fully appreciating and exploring the rich dynamics and diversity of free enterprise. Even worse, the logical approach sometimes allows economic rationales to be used in biased support of public policies and programs.

Students of economics master the mathematics of logical problems, but they learn little about other scientific methods and process; taxonomy, creativity, opportunism, and especially, observation in all its forms are relatively neglected in economics. The teaching of economics is largely unconcerned with the observation of facts, and economics students are not taught how to observe or interpret them.

The errors of economics endure through teaching that typically relies almost wholly on economic logic. First, the premises of technology and behavior are provided, but they are not usually backed up with facts. The student of economics has been led away from science because there has been little or no discussion of the extent to which the underlying premises or the results are in fact true, and students are not taught how to find out if they are true in particular cases.

Then, the logical process used to derive supply and demand functions is shown. The premises that underlie market trade are provided and explained, and the logical process behind market equilibrium and static economic efficiency is developed. Again, economics students are not being taught good science because they are not being taught good use of logical techniques. If they were, they would be taught to look for alternative lines of reasoning that could lead to different results. They would determine whether the logic of market theory is internally consistent and consistent with the results.

Finally, economics students arrive at the conventional results of market theory. If economics were a science, students would be taught how to confirm the results by reference to facts. Economic confirmation has often used econometric analysis, but econometrics can not prove anything. Analysis of economic data does not reveal the actions that resulted in that data, and economic empiricism is reduced to probability theory.

Observation of economic institutions and their actions and behavior is not a basic component of the practice and study of economics. One author finds that "to the outsider the most puzzling fact about academic economists is their indifference to the world of business. . . . It is difficult to exaggerate the degree to which academic economists, in their devotion to the abstract, theoretical analysis, have isolated themselves from the world of business."[15]

It is appropriate to ask how economics came to be where it is and why it remains there. Some have traced many of the problems of economic methods to David Ricardo, whose approach has resulted in "a reliance on tendencies and assumptions and an indifference to empirical confirmation."[16] "The abstract deductive method. . . nowadays elaborated with vast displays of almost totally irrelevant mathematical rigor, was that of deducing conclusions or predictions from a small number of allegedly obvious, common-sense assumptions."[17]

The belief that a self-regulating market mechanism would tend to equilibrium and optimality was originally developed in detail by Alfred Marshall, who was a highly recognized mathematician turned economist. But Marshall said, "I had a growing feeling in the later years of my work that a good mathematical theorem dealing with economic hypotheses was very unlikely to be good economics. . . . The application of exact mathematical methods to those [economic facts] that can [be expressed in numbers] is nearly always a waste of time while in the large majority of cases it is particularly misleading."[18]

One historian goes so far as to suggest that "the axioms of equilibrium theory were originally chosen to secure the desired result, in other words, the assumptions required for proving the existence of a unique and possibly stable general equilibrium."[19] "Indeterminacy of equilibrium was eliminated. . . stability of equilibrium was insured by placing various restrictions on the underlying functions."[20] In this view, the assumptions of market theory have never been based on facts. Rather, the creators of market theory may have started with the assumption of market equilibrium and deduced the conditions needed to attain it.

There are four reasons why market theory retains its pre-eminent role in economics. First, it works well in some cases, although it is not the role of this book to detail those successes. Second, the logical methods of economics are self-sustaining. Third, market theory provides a rationale for many types of private and public goals and policies. Fourth, many people make a living from market theory.

Logical Methods Are Self-Sustaining

The logic of economics is self-sustaining in several ways. The introspective nature of logic precludes discovery. "Deductive analysis cannot significantly help in discovering which particular kind of ignorance, or erroneous expectations, may be operative."[21] The mathematical approach to deductive reasoning also detracts from examination of the underlying assumptions. "Unreal assumptions are not relaxed—their unreality is intensified and camouflaged by mathematics."[22]

Economists sustain themselves with their own logical rationales for the theory. Consider this quote from an economics textbook: "Perfect competition frequently works as a theoretical model of economic processes. The most persuasive evidence supporting this assertion is the fact that, despite the proliferation of more 'sophisticated' models of economic behavior, economists today probably use the model of perfect competition in their research more than ever before."[23] This quote, slightly modified, could well have been provided by medieval flat-world proponents: "The flat world model frequently works as a theoretical model of the shape of the world. The most persuasive evidence supporting this assertion is the fact that, despite the proliferation of more 'global' models of the world's shape, geographers today probably use the flat world model in their research more than ever before."

Economists are distracted from the economic facts by the sheer devotion of resources to market theory and mathematics. The extensive use of mathematics in economics has distracted economists from other scientific methods, especially, the collection of new factual information. "The emergence. . . of a superfluity of mathematics stems not from the increase in the absolute quantity of mathematics at our disposal, but from the ever greater injection of mathematics into a fixed quantity of material."[24]

Mathematics is the logic of numbers. The rise of statistical, quantitative, and computer methods in economics lends the image, if not the substance, of science to economic research. Sometimes personal computers make things worse. Computer modeling is a logical device. It does not observe or reveal errors of assumption. The low cost of personal computer logic and mathematics increases the relative cost of observation and validation. Also, computers facilitate presentation at the expense of substance. With the personal computer, results can be displayed quickly in easy-to-interpret graphics, and high-quality reports can be produced easily.

Electronic data and information are becoming more accessible, but this should not be confused with observation and the collection of new information. Electronic databases do not generate new data; they increase the availability of existing data. To make things worse, data are normally observed and obtained under circumstances that require explanation and qualification. When stripped of context and appropriate background information, data can be misused. Modern data-retrieval techniques create unprecedented opportunities for information and data to be misinterpreted.

Market Theory Is a Convenient Rationale for Free Enterprise

Market theory provides a rationale for many private and public actions in the economy. In one view, market theory helps defend economic freedom in the self-interest. "Self-interest is successfully masquerading as a technical imperative. Ideology has appropriated the costume of value-free positive economics."[25]

Self-interest benefits from the rationale provided by the theory, and economics benefits by association with the success of free enterprise. The use of market theory has been encouraged by association. The success of capitalist economies and the central role of market theory in economics suggests that free markets must be doing the job. First, market economics finds that exchange in Western, free economies occurs through markets that tend to market equilibrium. Second, the theory shows that market equilibrium and subsequent market allocation is efficient, and this is good. In free enterprise economies, things are relatively good. By association, economics implies that the high standard of living in Western economies is due to the efficient allocation of resources through free markets.

As a historical proposition, the display of economic theory as fact frequently distracts people from the true nature of their economic systems. Economic theories, whether market or Marxist, have always been to some extent a rationale for the existing economic order. Market theory provides a convenient rationale for free enterprise; an efficient and harmonious exchange relationship, disturbed only by outside factors which result in a quick adjustment to a new but again perfect equilibrium.

From time to time, market theory conflicts with private economic interests. For example, intellectual property rights are often criticized because they provide market control. Apparently, market theory has not caused enough harm to force a substantial change, perhaps because much economic policy is not based on market theory anyway. As will be shown, some quantitative techniques of economics have threatened substantial harm, and this has resulted in challenge and improvement.

Economics Has a Vested Interest in Market Theory

Thousands of economists, publishers, and others make a living from economic theory. University jobs are dependent on ability to teach the theory. Journal publications, where the theory is constantly reinvented, are needed for tenure. Market theory is in demand because it purports to explain prices, quantities, revenues, costs, profits, and similar monetary measures, and these measures are in great demand by public and private interests.

Economists are just as sincere about economics as any other disciples are about their discipline. They are trapped by their logical, introspective training and societies' need for economic rationale. At the same time, many if not most economists recognize that economics could be improved. In particular, institutional, evolutionary, and experimental economics; industrial organization; and others have worked to change the fundamental principles and practice of economics. Despite their efforts, these fields remain outside of the mainstream.

A LOGICAL CRITIQUE OF THE PERFECT COMPETITION MODEL

Even more striking than the critique of the logical and mathematical tradition is that the basic logical argument is very weak. The theory of perfect competition fails the test of logical coherence in that the assumptions are internally inconsistent and the conventional result is at odds with the very assumptions used to develop that result. "A valid argument is one that does not contain obvious errors of logic."[26] By this definition, market theory is not a valid argument. Strictly speaking, the deductive reasoning that leads to equilibrium and efficiency is valid, but deductive reasoning is not the only appropriate thought process to fairly apply to this problem.

For free markets to result in equilibrium and static economic efficiency certain assumptions are required. Again, these assumptions are as follows:

1. Players are maximizers; firms maximize profits, and individuals maximize satisfaction (*maximization*).

2. All resources and players are freely mobile; there is freedom of exit and entry (*freedom of entry*).

3. Players have perfect knowledge of the relevant economic (prices) and technological data. (*perfect information*).

4. The product of any one seller is the same as the product of any other seller (*same product*).

5. Each participant in the market is small in relation to the entire market, so that he or

she cannot affect the product's price (*numerous players*).

6. Property rights are well defined (*well-defined rights*).

These assumptions or conditions, plus the additional assumptions about technology and consumers that determine the slope of supply and demand functions, plus some selective logic result in the static market equilibrium. Equilibrium is often defended by mathematical or graphical arguments by starting from a position of disequilibrium and showing how market forces lead to equilibrium prices and quantities.

Interactions Between the Assumptions

Several interactions between the assumptions should be noted. Economic theory has often relied on the law of diminishing returns in production—which, of course, is no law at all—to show that free enterprise results in many sellers (Assumption 5) because average cost per unit begins to increase at a small output level compared with the entire market size. However, there is no reason to believe that increasing average production costs must lead to many sellers because a producer is not necessarily the same as a seller. The conventional firm of market theory is a producer and a seller, but real firms often find it efficient to separate these functions. One big seller can own all of the small producers and establish a monopoly. The best average cost function for the seller is then flat, not upward sloping. Therefore, Assumption 5 is needed even if increasing marginal production costs result in many small producing units. In general, firms separate their buying, producing, and selling activities to realize a variety of economies and strategic goals, and firms become complex organizations, not simply producer-sellers.

If marginal and average production costs decline with production (increasing returns to scale), the implication is that there should be only one producing unit to obtain the cost efficiency associated with economies of scale. If this one producing unit was also one seller, however, it could drive all other firms out of business on the basis of cost and obtain a monopoly. This natural monopolist then restricts sales and raises price along the market demand curve leading to inefficiently small output and high price.

The conventional solution to natural monopoly allows one firm to have the monopoly, but price is regulated to be near average cost. Another solution also allows one producing unit to obtain the economies of scale, but many sellers are also required to ensure competitive pricing. This approach is essentially that taken in the deregulation of telephone services. Each of many sellers is able to use the same facilities to provide phone service.

Another important interaction between the assumptions is that freedom of entry matters more to the extent that products are not the same. If a firm has a unique product and allows no one else to sell it, then this creates an efficiency problem. But if there are many sellers of a similar or same product, then blocking entry to sale of one firm's product doesn't much matter to the market.

Finally, the theory of the second best states that if one assumption is not true, then the other assumptions may not be desirable for efficiency purposes. If one assumption cannot hold, then the most efficient, best-possible solution may include violations of the other assumptions.

Why the Logic Fails

A problem of market theory is that the theory uses only one logical approach. The theory starts from the assumptions and applies deductive reasoning to arrive at the conclusion. This application is not itself faulty, but there are other forms of reasoning that should be applied for the following reasons: (1) it is well known that the assumptions are not strictly true; and (2) the argument implies that the assumptions and the result are going on simultaneously. They must occur together to maintain the equilibrium state, so as a matter of logical coherence, it is appropriate to see if they are otherwise independent and internally consistent. Therefore, it is appropriate to see if any alternative and equally reasonable logic could lead to a different conclusion.

In this case, several alternative and reasonable lines of thinking lead to the conclusion that the assumptions may not be true. The assumptions should not be taken as givens because unbiased reasoning must lead to their re-examination. One general argument against market theory is that the assumptions are internally inconsistent. There are two different arguments of this type: Argument 1 finds that the assumptions of perfect information, freedom of entry, and well-defined rights are not consistent—they cannot all be true. Argument 2 finds that maximization may conflict with all other assumptions.

Argument 3 finds that the conventional line of reasoning is incomplete. The equilibrium result of downward sloping demand, stable equilibrium, and economic surplus is logically inconsistent with the maximization assumption. The static result of market equilibrium means that some economic players have the resources (economic surplus), the motive (profit maximization), and the incentive (downward sloping demand, among other things) to escape or control markets.

The deductive reasoning of market theory argues in this way: If A (maximization) and B (Assumptions 2 through 6), then C (equilibrium). Argument 1 finds that B is not a feasible set if creation, innovation, or production of new things are allowed. Argument 2 reasons that, given A, then not B and therefore not C. Argument 3 finds that, starting with C and allowing for any feasible alternative to B, then not B and therefore not C. All three arguments support each other. If Argument 1 is true, all of the assumptions cannot be true. Argument 2 provides another reason why the assumptions may not be true. Argument 3 is supported by Arguments 1 and 2 because Argument 1 finds that there must be a feasible alternative to B, and Argument 2 finds that there may be.

Argument 1. The assumptions of information, well-defined property rights, and freedom of entry are inconsistent. Well-defined property rights are necessary for efficient trade. It must be possible to exclude others from a good if it is to be sold to them. If there are many sellers of the same good, as the assumptions of market theory require, then market trade and competition force price to cost. But sometimes one seller obtains property rights to a unique good or resource. Then, the property right of exclusion enables control of entry, and monopoly is possible. The property right of exclusion is only desirable when the assumptions of many sellers and same product also hold.

The logical conflict arises when it is recognized that the creation of new things is a productive activity. Technical knowledge, for example, is produced at a cost and sold either directly or as embodied in new types of goods. For this new information to be produced and sold efficiently, it must have well-defined property rights. Most importantly, it must be possible to exclude others from it. If new ideas cannot be private property, the incentive to create them is diminished because anyone can use the ideas for nothing. To have incentive to invest in creation, information creators must be able to withhold entry from others.

But creation—almost as a matter of definition—results in a unique good. For markets to function efficiently, no player should be able to exclude others from the market by control of entry. Because unique ideas cannot be both withheld as private property and not withheld as perfect information, the assumptions of market competition are in conflict when creation is allowed as a productive activity. I refer to this conflict as the *paradox of information*. The practical implications of this problem are taken up in chapters 3 and 7.

Note that I have inserted an additional assumption—that new ideas are created at a cost—into the argument. Market theory works only because it covers the allocation of existing goods only. The creation of new types of goods and new information is not covered by the theory.

Argument 2. Maximization is inconsistent with the assumptions of freedom of entry, perfect information, same product, numerous players, and well-defined rights. Maximization is potentially inconsistent with the other five assumptions. Profit maximization may provide incentive for players to restrict or control entry, to distort and control information, to make products dissimilar to other firms' products, to reduce the number of competitors and increase control over price, and to control and change property rights. These actions are not economic aberrations; we can observe that they are part of the everyday reality of economic behavior.

Freedom of entry refers to the ability of players and resources to move freely between economic activities and enterprises. This assumption is required to obtain the result of static economic efficiency because players must be free to enter or exit markets to make deals in their own self-interest. If they were not free, they obviously could not make efficient choices—those that maximize satisfaction and profit.

Freedom of entry is inconsistent with maximizing players because players may maximize by controlling resources or other players. The theory of monopoly explains why control of entry maximizes profit. In fact, we often observe that players do block entry. Critical information or technology is not available to potential entrants, existing players strategize against new entrants, or entry is discouraged by use of law.

Slavery is perhaps the most extreme example of the real conflict between profit maximization and freedom of entry. Freedom to leave the work force is denied. Slavery is a recurring feature of free enterprise, and not just in the Third World. In a recent case, a suburban Los Angeles sweat shop was charged with holding seventy Thai immigrants against their will to make garments for the U.S. market. Some of the clothes were sold in prominent retail outlets such as Sears, Macy's, Montgomery Ward, and Neiman-Marcus.

The assumption of *perfect information* is required to obtain the result of static economic efficiency because players must know what goods, resources, and technology are available and what their prices are to make best use of them and realize the most efficient trades. Market theory presumes that the pertinent information is freely provided to all.

Perfect information is inconsistent with maximizing players because some choose to withhold or distort information in their own self-interest. The true perfect market, by definition, provides a high level of display of goods to buyers and other sellers, so it is difficult to hide or distort information. In fact, players can withhold or distort information because the pertinent information is simply not revealed by the good, or it is not revealed until after the good is purchased (chapter 3). "The essential role of this extreme assumption regarding knowledge, expectations, and certainty was successfully overlooked by the followers" of the logical method.[27]

The assumption of *same product* is required to obtain the result of static economic efficiency because it ensures that there will be competition between sellers. However, the condition is inconsistent with maximizing players because maximization results in downward sloping demand, and this demand provides incentive to differentiate and develop unique products. Product differentiation is the process of making a product be or appear to be different from others' products. Clearly, there is incentive in free enterprise for firms to differentiate their products and thereby obtain some control over price to make profit.

To the credit of economics, the roles of advertising and differentiation are sometimes noted in the classroom to explain why free enterprise provides such varied products to the benefit of its participants. Some differentiation is innovation, resulting in better products and more consumer satisfaction. The recognition of differentiation is a first step to understanding the reason for and results of innovation. Both involve players attempting to escape from competitive markets, but conventional theory seems incapable of divorcing the logical argument for static economic efficiency from a more general and comprehensive view of market escape and technical progress.

The assumption of *numerous players* is also required to obtain the result of static economic efficiency. Competition is required to keep one or a few players from controlling markets and prices, either as buyers or sellers. All firms and consumers are price-takers, not price-makers, and efficiency in production is thereby ensured.

However, the assumption is inconsistent with maximizing players because there is incentive to collude or eliminate competitors and reduce the number of players. In the conventional result of market theory, some players could be better off by colluding, restricting output, controlling prices, or otherwise acting like one seller or buyer, but they are constrained from doing so merely by assumption. In addition, problems of price expectations, investment, and uncoordinated planning result in additional incentives to reduce the number of players and control production or prices. The uncoordinated activities of numerous firms can lead to substantial static inefficiencies in investment and supply, and these inefficiencies have created incentives for market control. These facts are discussed in detail in chapter 5. Control of others to reduce the effective number of competitors is a recurring feature of free enterprise.

The assumption of *well-defined rights* is also inconsistent with maximizing players. Perfect goods have well-defined property rights, but self-maximizing players sometimes seek to change property rights completely outside of the market system. For most goods, the benefits of ownership can be obtained by physical control; therefore, we have theft. Physical control can also be obtained through the courts or government. Property rights to many types of information and businesses are uncertain. A substantial public and private industry sells the establishment, protection and enforcement of property rights.

Argument 3. Maximization is inconsistent with economic equilibrium. Consider the static market equilibrium. This situation implies a stable, unchanging situation where each player is unable to gain any additional economic surplus. However, they are unable to only because the assumptions force them to. Equilibrium is taken as a final result of the logical argument, and the lack of additional deduction is part of the problem with the theory.

This problem can be demonstrated with a simple allegory. Suppose a farmer has a bull which he wishes to keep in a small pasture. He decides that a small fence will be sufficient to keep the bull inside the pasture, so he builds the fence and leaves. The bull, however, sees things differently. The grass on the other side of the fence becomes relatively attractive as his pasture is depleted. He may see other opportunities on the outside. He sizes the fence up and tries to learn about it. Finally, he breaks through the fence and is free. In this story, our farmer is the economist, the bull is maximization and the fence is the assumptions of market theory. The farmer's logic was faulty because he assumed that the fence was inviolate; he did not consider the bull's incentive to remove the fence or the relative strength of fence and bull.

Market theory implies that static equilibrium and economic surplus will not change unless outside forces change demand or supply. But the driving force is maximization. Economic players must, by assumption, seek means of escaping or improving on the market equilibrium. Static economic efficiency results in a condition where no one can be made better off without making someone else worse off, but self-maximizing players do not care if they make someone else worse off. If stable equilibrium were defended in court, it would lose. The motive (maximization) and the weapon (economic surplus) are there, and stable equilibrium is only maintained because Assumptions 2 through 6 must hold and because new and unique things cannot be created. Markets can be escaped by diverging from the assumptions required for static efficiency or by creating new options for use of resources.

The theory of production that drives price to average cost exemplifies the major problem of the theory. If firms accept the theory of supply with identical firms, they must expect to make no profit in the long run. Why would any firm passively accept this result? In fact, they do not, and the struggle to avoid or control the very process that leads to equilibrium and efficiency in supply begins. The story of economic history and dynamic change is one of economic players dissatisfied with the market forces that tend toward market equilibrium. Antimarket economics includes the study of how they act on this dissatisfaction.

In another variant of production theory, some producers are better situated than others. In agriculture, for example, farms with the best climate and soils can expect to make a profit in perfect competition. Market theory accounts for this profit through conventional upward sloping supply and producer surplus. The logic of market theory, however, ceases without accounting for how the profit is spent. Producers still want more profit, and they may be able to invest the profit they have already made in advertising, market control, innovation, or lobbies. Of course, market theory largely rules out these types of activities by assumption.

These problems of logic demonstrate that market theory cannot be a tenable general theory of economic behavior in free enterprise. Assumptions 2 through 6 are not part of economic logic because they are general observations based on fact; rather, they were included in order to ensure the desired result of static equilibrium and economic efficiency. The modern economy is anything but static, and a better general theory must recognize that economic competition provides incentive to deviate from the results, the assumptions and even the scope of the market model.

NOTES

1. See, for example, Roger E. Blackhouse, ed., *New Directions in Economic Methodology* (London: Routledge, 1994); Alexander Rosenberg, *Economics: Mathematical Politics or Science of Diminishing Returns* (Chicago: University of Chicago Press, 1992); Glenn L. Johnson, *Research Methodology for Economists Philosophy and Practice* (New York: Macmillan, 1986); Daniel M. Hausman, ed., *The Philosophy of Economics: An Anthology* (Cambridge: Cambridge University Press, 1994); Mark Blaug, *The*

Methodology of Economics or How Economists Explain (Cambridge: Cambridge University Press, 1982); Mark Blaug, *Economic Theories: True or False?* Essays in the History and Methodology of Economics (London: Edward Elger, 1990).

2. Don Ethridge, *Research Methodology in Applied Economics: Organizing, Planning and Conducting Economic Research* (Ames, IA: Iowa State University Press, 1995), p. 47.

3. *Webster's New Collegiate Dictionary* (Springfield, MA: Merriam, 1981), pp. 293, 583.

4. Ibid., p. 1200.

5. W. I. B. Beveridge, *The Art of Scientific Investigation* (New York: Vintage Books, 1950), p. 123.

6. Mark Blaug, *Economic Theory in Retrospect*, Third Edition (Cambridge: Cambridge University Press, 1978), p. 697.

7. Mark Blaug, "Confessions of an Unrepentant Popperian," in *New Directions in Economic Methodology*, ed. Roger E. Blackhouse (London: Routledge, 1994), p. 111.

8. There are numerous definitions of the terms *validation* and *verification*. This text uses the definitions put forth by Naomi Oreskes, Kristin Shrader-Frechette, and Kenneth Blitz, "Verification, Validation and Confirmation of Numerical Models in the Earth Sciences," *Science* 263 (February 1994): 641–646.

9. Blaug, "Confessions of an Unrepentant Popperian," p. 111.

10. Oreskes, Shrader-Frechette, and Blitz, "Verification, Validation and Confirmation of Numerical Models in the Earth Sciences," p. 642.

11. W. I. B. Beveridge, *The Art of Scientific Investigation* (New York: Vintage Books, 1950), pp. 113, 120.

12. Ibid., pp. 109, 112.

13. Ibid., pp. 110–112.

14. Mark Blaug, "Comment 2," in *Economics in Disarray,* eds. P. Wiles and G. Routh (New York: Basil Blackwell, 1984), p. 53.

15. Dudley H. Chapman, *Molting Time for Anti-Trust: Market Realities, Economic Fallacies and European Innovations* (New York: Praeger Press, 1991), pp. 93, 95.

16. Ibid., p. 101.

17. Terrence Hutchinson, "Our Methodological Crisis," in *Economics in Disarray*, eds. P. Wiles and G. Routh (New York: Basil Blackwell, 1984), p. 3.

18. Marshall's quote is from Nicholas Kaldor, *Economics without Equilibrium,* The Arthur M. Okun Memorial Lecture Series, Yale University (Armonk, NY: M. E. Sharpe, 1985), p. 59.

19. Ibid., p. 13.

20. Blaug, *Economic Theory in Retrospect*, p. 700.

21. Hutchinson, "Our Methodological Crisis," p. 4.

22. Guy Routh, "What to Teach Undergraduates," in *Economics in Disarray*, eds. P. Wiles and G. Routh (New York: Basil Blackwell, 1984), p. 241.

23. C. E. Ferguson and J. P. Gould, *Microeconomic Theory,* Fourth Edition (Homewood, IL: Richard D. Irwin, 1975), p. 223.

24. Michio Morishima, "The Good and Bad Uses of Mathematics," in *Economics in Disarray*, eds. P. Wiles and G. Routh (New York: Basil Blackwell, 1984), p. 64.

25. Robert Kuttner, *The Economic Illusion: False Choices Between Prosperity and Social Justice* (Boston: Houghton Mifflin, 1984), p. 2.

26. Oreskes, Shrader-Frechette, and Blitz, "Verification, Validation and Confirmation of Numerical Models in the Earth Sciences," p. 642.

27. Hutchinson, "Our Methodological Crisis," p. 3.

3

Information, Property Rights, and Transactions Costs

The model of perfect competition frequently fails because the assumptions are simply not true, and conventional criticisms of market theory have often focused on this fact. As one author noted, "The importance of general equilibrium theory lies precisely in showing how stringent the conditions must be for 'free markets' to secure the results for welfare that are so naively attributed to them."[1]

Market failure is the inability of free markets to provide goods efficiently as described by market theory. Market failure occurs when the facts conflict with the assumptions of perfect competition. Some theories of market failure involve imperfect property rights, natural monopoly, and transactions costs. We can readily observe nonrival and nonexclusive goods and other imperfect property rights, a tendency to monopoly in some industries, and imperfect information and large trading costs that create problems. Mixed economies have developed strategies to deal with these problems. Usually, the proposed solution involves government intervention.

This chapter expands on the problems of information, property rights, and transactions costs in four ways. First, more types of inherent problems are developed. The enduring nature of many goods and economic processes bring them into conflict with the assumptions of market theory. Second, the assumptions are not merely true or false; they are often continuous variables. Third, they are not independent of or exogenous to the competitive process; they are endogenous. Fourth, the variables of information, property rights, and transactions costs are often associated with private costs and benefits. Economic incentives and capabilities can make the assumptions less true merely because, from the perspective of private players, it is economical to make them less true. There are costs and benefits associated with reducing, removing, escaping, or avoiding the assumptions of perfect competition. Even if markets tend to equilibrium, there are private costs and benefits associated with deviating from the equilibrium state.

Two important assumptions required for perfect markets and static efficiency, which are not verified by facts, are well-defined rights and perfect information. Aside from the fact that these assumptions do not hold, there is also the contradiction involving them. The property right of exclusion can enable market control. This chapter sets the stage for an understanding of incentives and capabilities to obtain property rights to unique economic information.

NONRIVAL GOODS AND POORLY DEFINED RIGHTS

For free markets to function efficiently, it is necessary that goods have certain characteristics. First, one's use of a good precludes any other person from using it; it is *rival*.[2] For nonrival goods, it is their very nature that once produced, their services can be provided to more persons at no incremental cost. Such goods are nonrival. Take for example, scenery. To a point, my enjoyment of scenery does not reduce another's enjoyment of it, at least until I stand in front of him. For existing nonrival goods, there is no economic rationale for excluding anyone from using them because the additional use has no cost.

Congestible goods are nonrival at low levels of use but become increasingly rival with more use. In the country, I don't care about the presence of other drivers, and perhaps I'm even glad to see another driver every once in a while. In the city, a large numbers of cars reduces the value of roads to each driver.

Efficiency requires that owners of rival goods can exclude others from them. A good is *exclusive* if it is easy, if not costless, to exclude others. For some goods, it is impractical or expensive to exclude others from using the good; these goods are nonexclusive. The costs required to collect payment on the basis of services rendered or, alternatively, to provide services on the basis of payment are prohibitive. Fisheries are the classic example. It is very expensive to enforce property rights on the open ocean and enforcement is often incomplete.

In conventional economics, trade involves just the buyer and the seller. *Externalities* occur when trade or production has incidental effects on third parties, and externalities create an efficiency problem when the third party is excluded from the trade process. If the externality is harmful, those harmed cannot participate in the trade to reduce the amount of harm, and the good involved and its externality are overproduced. If the externality is beneficial, those who incidentally benefit cannot be made to pay because they cannot be excluded from the benefit, so the good and its externality are underproduced.

Often, the inefficient externality is nonexclusive because of transactions costs associated with the large number of persons being affected. Trees produce oxygen, shade and scenery, all beneficial externalities, but it would be impractical to collect payment from everyone who receives these benefits, so trees tend to be directed to uses such as lumber because a price can be obtained.

Imperfect property rights create problems for free markets. Rival nonexclusive goods cannot be produced efficiently because once the good is produced, anyone may take it and no one needs to pay to use it. Sometimes, the very nature of things makes it inefficient or prohibitively expensive to assign and enforce private property rights to them, and markets cannot produce or allocate them efficiently. By definition, there are costs to correct the problem.

Rules of property are a social institution, usually defined by law. Property rights are made exclusive when exclusion is allowed by law, but law is not a necessary condition for exclusion. Law is not necessary to the extent that people believe in the value and justice of private property rights as a commonly held value. This social value, and other commonly held beliefs about the fairness of trade and property, play a large role in the conventions of property and, in the larger picture, how economic exchange compares to the model of perfect competition.

Nor is the law sufficient for exclusion, because it must still be enforced. Enforcement of property rights would not be needed if property rights were perfect. Enforcement is part of the cost of property rights, and more cost gets more benefit in terms of more secure rights. In fact, physical possession provides much of the benefit of ownership. Property can be protected by hiding, by physically withholding, or by threat of force.

Property rights are not perfect simply because it is in the self-interest of some players to change them. The economic value of things is all the incentive needed for players to want to change property rights. Therefore, we have theft. 'Possession is 90 percent of the law' as the saying goes. Physical possession often provides evidence of ownership as well as its benefits.

Furthermore, we have laws that allow the involuntary exchange of goods and their property rights. Civil law allows anyone to try to claim the property of others, and eminent domain allows for taking with compensation. Juries, legislatures, and government agencies, not markets, sometimes determine the extent and allocation of property rights. Most property rights are attenuated by a variety of rules involving the use or sale of the good. Sometimes, the nature of a good is quite rival and property rights could be exclusive, but government is unwilling or unable to clearly assign or enforce property rights. Many property rights are *uncertain*. The law may explicitly allow for uncertainty in the extent and duration of property rights. Imperfect property rights as a form of government failure are discussed in chapter 8.

From this discussion, it should be clear that property rights are a variable, not a given, and the ability to maintain or change property rights is affected by the nature of the thing, law, and social convention. The unique nature of property rights to a rival good is that they are normally binary. By law and the nature of possession, it's usually all or nothing.

Rivalry and exclusion are related in that rival goods create an incentive for their users to exclude others from them. Also, exclusion for rival goods is desirable from the perspective of efficiency. It is not efficient to exclude any user from a nonrival good, but sellers of nonrival goods have incentive to exclude users so that a price can be charged. A price cannot be charged for a nonrival nonexclusive good, and this is efficient because the incremental cost of providing the good is zero.

Information can be a most valuable kind of good, and information can take on any of the features of property previously described. Some information is rival because its value to one player is reduced by its use by another. Therefore, there is incentive to exclude others from it. Other information, such as the location of open markets or the price of gasoline, is nonrival. It won't hurt one player to provide this information to one more player. Information about a new proprietary hi-tech production process may be rival and exclusive. Not only is it in the interest of the owner to exclude others from it, but it is also easy to exclude others because it is complex. But some new products, perhaps toys based on clever ideas, reveal how they are made on display. The information needed to make them may be rival, but it is also nonexclusive. These problems will be discussed in more detail shortly.

IMPERFECT INFORMATION

A central problem of market theory is that it presumes buyers, sellers and producers have perfect information. There are many types of information needed for proper functioning of markets. Buyers and sellers must know where markets are and what prices are. Buyers and producers require different types of knowledge about goods. Buyers need to know what the good will do for them, but producers need to know how it is made. Production technology must be known to potential producers, and the characteristics or qualities of available goods must be known to potential buyers. This knowledge allows market production and trade to be efficient. In short, everyone knows what their options are.

In fact, these types of information are frequently not equally available, or they are not available at all. There are four fundamental reasons why information is not perfect. Two of the reasons are related to the inherent nature of things: in one of these the sequential nature of production, trade, and consumption, and in the other, the nature of certain goods.

1. The information cannot be known at the time the decision to produce or buy must be made (the *temporal* problem).

2. The information is not revealed by the good or process (the *revelation* problem).

These two reasons enable imperfect information. The last two reasons are caused by competitive behavior; they are endogenous to the competitive process.

3. The information is a private rival good developed and protected as property that is

withheld (the *property* problem).

4. Information can be and is made available to some selected players before others (the *insider* problem).

The Temporal Problem

The information required for competitive markets to work often cannot be obtained because production, trade, and consumption occur at different times.

1. Sellers normally cannot know prices and/or quantities to be sold at the time supply decisions must be made because production occurs before sale.

A central problem of production is that a time lag separates the decision to produce from investment, then production, and finally sale. The price-taking producer normally cannot know what his revenues (price times quantity) and costs will be at the time he must decide whether and how much to produce. Uncertain future prices mean uncertain costs of production, and revenues are also subject to uncertain sales.

Free enterprise has developed market mechanisms to protect producers from the unknown future. Contracts, especially forward contracts; futures markets; and many other trade mechanisms are used to reduce or eliminate the seller's temporal problem, but these relatively modern arrangements have not eliminated this most basic production risk. The risk is especially large for new products, since no prior experience, markets, or other information about price and quantities may be available at all, and the time lag separating investment from sale is usually large.

2. Buyers normally cannot know what they will get at the time they buy because consumption occurs after purchase.

In the free market model, the buyer, by the assumption of perfect knowledge, knows what he is getting. In fact, most goods yield their services after they are purchased. At the time of trade, a buyer knows the price he will pay, but he cannot know exactly what he has bought until the good is completely consumed or worn out. At the time of purchase, the buyer can only predict what the good will provide in the future when it is used.

Therefore, free enterprise has developed market mechanisms to protect the buyer from this uncertainty. Sellers provide guarantees and warranties, and buyers are frequently able to return their purchases. Despite these protections, many goods yield much of their services long after such assurances have ended. Especially, most of the services of machinery come far in the future after the warranty has expired. The buyer of insurance and financial goods cannot be assured that the company will be solvent and able to pay future obligations as claimed.

Even if buyers know exactly what they are getting, they may not know how much value they will get out of it. The amount of use of many types of goods is expected, not known, and the amount of enjoyment or other value from each use is also unknown. Everyone can think of a case where an appliance, a tool, or a sporting good was bought with high expectations for amount and value of use that simply did not happen.

Sellers gain competitive advantage by assuring buyers that their expectations will be met. For products purchased frequently, this can be accomplished by standardization. Fast food and hotel franchises have been successful because purchases are less risky. The buyer, having chosen that franchise before, expects the same qualities in any location at any time, and the perceived risk associated with the buyers' problem is substantially reduced.

In a few cases, buyers consume their purchases before paying. Restaurants are an example, but it is quite hard to avoid payment once the meal is consumed. Still, some consequences of the meal, food poisoning perhaps, will not occur until long after the customer has paid and left.

Of course, sellers are buyers too. The purchase of inputs by producers is based on the expectation of what the inputs will provide, not a known fact. Therefore, production decisions involve uncertainty in the costs of production not only because the future price of inputs is uncertain, but the services of inputs are often unclear when they are bought.

Risk, uncertainty, and expectations, which complicate nearly all production and purchase decisions, have been extensively studied in economics. The economic theory of risk states that, in most circumstances, most economic players are risk-averse. Risk has a cost because, in serious matters, people prefer certainty. The importance of risk and uncertainty is understated in conventional theory, especially market theory, because the theory presumes that knowledge, not expectations, guides most economic transactions. In fact, buyers and sellers almost always act on expectations, not knowledge. Also, it is normally presumed that expectations are on average correct. In fact, expectations are frequently biased because (1) many trade situations create incentive and ability for players to mislead others through withholding, concealment, and distortion of information, (2) the costs of information limit players' incentives to obtain accurate information, and (3) players are not aware of the expectations and plans of other similar players (chapter 5). A general theory of economic behavior would be better to assume that all information is a good, not a given, and information must be acquired at a cost.

Also, interactions between variability, expectations, and survival problems are not considered. Unexpected variation in income is financially difficult to work with. Payment obligations tend to be relatively fixed, and failure is associated with large penalties, but income (price times quantity sold), often needed to make payments, tends to be variable and unpredictable. This problem is also covered in more detail in chapter 5.

The Revelation Problem

To make matters even worse for buyers, many goods by their very nature do not display their pertinent attributes. Commodities such as gases, drugs, food additives, microbes, or other minute quantities cannot be seen or are difficult and expensive to measure. These goods can require a large cost just to determine what they are, much less how much there is. How could buyers have good, much less perfect, information about such commodities?

Products that do not readily reveal their pertinent attributes have frequently been brought into extensive regulation. The Food and Drug Administration (FDA) annually reviews thousands of applications for new products or constituents that cannot even be sensed. The U.S. Department of Agriculture (USDA) and Environmental Protection Agency (EPA) have similar responsibilities. Many products must now be labeled with a list of ingredients, but ingredients can sometimes be protected as proprietary information. Cigarette manufacturers have protected their formulations in this way.

When buyers' information is not readily revealed by the good, the seller is usually the best source of information, but the seller may choose to distort or withhold the information to maximize profit. Sellers have incentive to withhold information to make a sale and get a higher price, and the buyer must overcome this problem by incurring costs to unearth the facts. Sellers can distort information about goods precisely because consumption occurs after purchase, and many goods do not reveal their characteristics to buyers. Therefore, buyers must incur costs to overcome a lack of information or misinformation. At a minimum, there are important costs that must be paid to ensure that quality and quantity is what the seller claims. In contrast to the perfect world of market theory, the whole process of hiding and finding information can be quite inefficient.

The tendency of unimpeded sellers to exaggerate, distort, and hide information is legend. Advertising and other sales strategies are frequently a misrepresentation of the facts; a distortion of information, not the truth required for proper functioning of perfect markets. Consumer products frequently have qualities and effects much different than those advertised—cigarettes and sweepstakes, for example. Consumers are told that one product is different and superior to another, when in fact, they are largely the same. Consider aspirin and other common drugs and many household goods and services. Advertising continues in the long run because it works, and advertising is biased, so we could conclude that consumer information is biased even in the long run.

Therefore, mixed economies create laws to control and limit distortion of information. The Federal Trade Commission and state consumer protection agencies discourage massive inefficiency in production and consumption by regulating deceptive advertising. Advertising would be much less effective, and there would be less of it, if the true information were revealed costlessly by mere inspection.

Consider the recent regulation of labeling of low calorie products. Until regulated, light products were sometimes no more light than the regular brand. One brand, faced with regulation, even had the audacity to replace the word *light* with *right*, apparently hoping that no one would notice. In another recent case, a common cough remedy, which sold for $5.00 a bottle, was repackaged for asthma and emphysema patients and priced at $50.00.

Firms are sometimes successful in influencing the agencies who are responsible for regulation of advertising and invisible products. The influence of the tobacco industry in government is renowned. A similar controversy about monosodium glutamate (MSG) is developing. Since 1986, the FDA has allowed MSG to be identified on food labels as hydrolyzed plant protein or hydrolyzed vegetable protein. In 1988, the terms "natural flavoring," "flavoring" and "seasoning" were allowed.[3] Other products that contain MSG include autolyzed yeast and sodium or calcium caseinate. If MSG was simply a good flavor, this would not create a problem, but numerous studies have found that MSG can act as a neurotoxin, resulting in headaches, nausea, diarrhea, asthma and skin pathologies in sensitive persons. "Government-sponsored research consistently finds far higher rates of adverse reactions to MSG than food industry sponsored research."[4] "Food-industry supported groups go to great lengths to discredit past and current research in this field."[5] In this case, labeling has failed in its most important function, and the disparity in research results suggests an attempt to influence information and public policy.

Much important information about production techniques is not revealed because of the revelation problem; competitors cannot determine how it was done, and the information is exclusive. More often, the mere display and sale of a good can reveal a lot about how it was made. This latter case is consistent with the assumptions of market theory and helps promote static efficiency but is inconsistent with the self-interest of the seller unless there are many sellers. Even when it is costly to exclude others from the information, the private benefits of exclusion may exceed the costs. If other sellers participating in markets can copy the good, and the original seller is otherwise unable to protect the information displayed by the good, the seller may choose to produce and market in secrecy to avoid unnecessary disclosure. The potential for information to be inadvertently provided to competitors provides incentive to withhold it.

The Property Problem

Proprietary information is information that can be protected as private property, and proprietary information is a fact of law. Property rights to information mean the ability to exclude others from the use of it, but a property right is not the only means of exclusion. Contracts may be used. Nondisclosure agreements are often required when information is brought to a third party who could expose and profit from it. Much information is kept from others through formal agreements with employees, loyalty, or merely by lock and key. Real property rights—the right to exclude others from a place of production or sale—allow information to be withheld merely because physical entry can be controlled. Threat of force may also be used.

In the perfect markets of economic theory, each player is small relative to the market, so the provision of information to one more player has no effect on the market. The information is nonrival. Therefore, there is little incentive to withhold information. A corn farmer may provide information about corn prices freely to his neighbor, since corn prices will be unaffected. A widget manufacturer does not care if widget production technology is provided to another widget maker because one more widget maker won't matter to the market. But when there are few players, information becomes increasingly rival. Then, players have incentive to exclude each other from it. Much economic information is rival because it can be used to gain competitive edge in a situation with few players. Important information that may be withheld includes the following:

Sellers' information about buyers. Information about the location and identity of buyers is withheld by sellers to reduce the number of sellers. The incentive to withhold information about buyers increases with a smaller number of sellers.

Buyers' information about sellers. Information about the location and identity of sellers is withheld by buyers to reduce the number of buyers. Buyers' incentive to withhold information about sellers increases with a smaller number of buyers.

Information about prices. Sellers have incentive to withhold information from other sellers about prices they receive. If other sellers knew prices, they might undercut them. Buyers withhold information from other buyers about prices they pay. If other buyers knew prices, they might bid higher. Incentive to withhold information about prices also increases with a smaller number of buyers or sellers.

Information about contents of goods or production processes. This information is withheld by producers to keep other producers from producing the same or a similar product or, at least, to increase competitor's production costs as much as possible.

The Insider Problem

The insider problem occurs when some players are better situated to obtain use and trade information than others. Insider trading does not create an inefficiency problem by itself when it only affects the distribution of wealth and profits, but it raises important equity issues.

Insider trading creates economic problems through indirect means. For example, insider knowledge provides a means to acquire favors from other players such as representatives and bureaucrats. Insiders may use their position as experts to distort information and manipulate prices. Information is power, and that power can be used to pursue other economic goals.

Insider trading in stocks is presumably regulated by the Securities Exchange Commission, but some studies have found that the current regulatory framework provides little help. "After six months, insider's premiums, if not too blatantly a product of specific nonpublic information, are as safe as a key to the executive bathroom . . . much insider trading is carried out through third parties so as to escape detection."[6]

THE PARADOX OF INFORMATION

The most perplexing omission of market theory involves property rights to new ideas, especially information used to create new goods. Conventional economic thought implies that control of entry by withholding information is inefficient. Technical information must be equally available so that many producers can enter the industry and produce the same good. Static efficiency means that no one can be made better off now without making someone else worse off (the Pareto principle) *given existing technology and resources*. Efficiency requires that everyone can find out what the current technology is. Goods either reveal the information or it is available in competitive markets.

In fact, information is also a product or good developed with labor and materials like any other good. An innovator invests in the creation of new information. The innovator requires, at a minimum, that his investment can be recovered in the future. Some innovations do not reveal how they are made or how they work on display, and this is good for innovators. These innovations may be minute, invisible, or so complex that potential imitators cannot determine how to reproduce them, or the costs of extracting the necessary information are prohibitive. Sometimes, an innovator can construct the product so that the necessary information cannot be revealed. In other cases, the innovator has such a head start that no one else can catch up with him. This can occur when the innovation can be upgraded frequently; consider computer software. By the time a competitor can successfully copy the innovation, the original innovator has made the innovation obsolete.

In most cases, however, the information on how it was made is revealed when the innovation is first displayed or sold. If the information is freely available to imitators, then the innovator could not obtain any return for its development because the imitators do not need to pay the costs of innovation. They could sell the innovation at a lower average cost than the innovator. Rational information producers would not even develop the innovation because their investment could not be recovered.

To make it worthwhile for firms to produce information—to ensure that the production of new information is efficient—information creators must be able to exclude others from it. New information must have well-defined property rights like any other good to be produced efficiently in accordance with market signals. But new information is, by definition, unique property. If information is private property, the innovation based on that information will not be produced efficiently because the owners of the pertinent information can exclude others from it. The most profitable way to sell the innovation is by, first, skimming the market and, then, by establishing and maintaining monopoly.

The longer information producers are allowed to exclude others, the more money they can make from it and the more incentive to produce more new information. In the short run, static efficiency is maximized by open access to information, but the speed and quantity of innovation is maximized by closed entry. The fact that open and closed entry cannot exist simultaneously creates the *paradox of information*. The paradox of information creates a trade-off in economic policy. The law cannot, at first, maximize innovation by promising perpetual exclusive property rights and, then later, break that promise and obtain static efficiency by requiring open access and free entry. The incentives for innovation must be based on stable property rights. Producers must know what to expect.

Society has found it necessary to protect information producers through the laws of intellectual property. Western economies provide innovations with exactly the control of entry that is the antithesis of free market theory. Intellectual property—patents, copyrights, trade secrets—and the control that follows demonstrate that not only does society tolerate control of entry, we help enforce it to promote technological progress.

The current policy for patents is seventeen years of complete protection, but real protection is limited by the degree of enforcement possible given the nature of the good. Literature, music, film, and other artistic works are protected by copyright laws, but the economic return to their development is diminished by widespread unauthorized reproduction and sale. If one reads a photocopy of this book, one is a disincentive for my innovation. Protection is also limited by the legal and technical ability of others to create close substitutes. Chapter 7 discusses more of the problems of creation and protection of intellectual property.

Market theory fails even as a model of economic welfare because only static economic efficiency is considered. The market model is merely a description of short run economic welfare enabled by existing goods and resources. Incentives needed to increase the stock and types of valuable technology and information are not considered. In market theory, property rights to existing goods and information are exclusive. Since there are many sellers of the same goods and information, there is no economic problem. The paradox of information only applies because the economy creates new and unique things. In fact, society encourages the creation of unique ideas by grant of exclusive rights, and these rights are a grant of monopoly.

Market theory fails as a descriptive device merely because control of entry through information is a common aspect of free enterprise. Information is certainly not perfect or free as market theory requires. It frequently cannot be revealed by the good or the trade process; it is intentionally and legally withheld as private property; and it is withheld or distorted to increase sales or prices. Nonetheless, society allows information to be private to encourage investment and innovation, and because it is a matter of economic justice that information developed by investment and labor be private property.

Table 3.1 summarizes some distinctions and findings made in this section.

Table 3.1

Characteristics of Information About Goods, Relationships to Static Efficiency and Innovation, and Legal Solutions If Needed

Characteristics of the good	Efficient Purchases?	Efficient Production?	Incentives for Innovation?	Solutions to a problem
Good Reveals:				
What it will do*	yes	—	—	No problem
How it was made	—	yes	no	Intellectual property
Good Does Not Reveal:				
What it will do	no	—	—	Consumer protection
How it was made	—	no	yes	Antitrust or public information

* A dash means that characteristic does not apply.

In summary, the nature of goods in terms of how easily they reveal information on display affects the efficiency of their development, production, and sale. There is little profit incentive to create goods that costlessly and immediately reveal how they are made because the innovation investment cannot be recovered. But once created, such goods will be produced efficiently. Goods that need not reveal how they are made will be created, but they will not be produced efficiently. Goods that do not reveal what they will do for buyers may not be bought efficiently because buyer's expectations may not be met.

TRANSACTIONS COSTS

The open marketplace of many buyers and sellers is an easily visualized example of the perfect market. The marketplace has many advantages for buyers and sellers. Buyers are able to compare price and quality and develop expectations about many sellers' goods. They are able to shop in one place, enabling them to efficiently purchase a portfolio of goods in the desired quantity; markets often serve to aggregate small quantities of similar products. Sellers are able to market their goods to many buyers.

All markets, even the open marketplace, have costs to both buyers and sellers.

For purposes here, transactions costs are costs of trade above and beyond the price of the good measured at the point of production. By this definition, transactions costs include transportation costs and the time and expense required to participate in the market. Goods must be moved to and from the marketplace. It is unlikely that the marketplace is located directly between all buyers and sellers. The combined travel distance of some buyers and sellers may exceed the distance traveled if one went directly to the other. These players will use the market only if the advantages of the physical marketplace outweigh the additional transportation costs that must be paid to use it.

Other transaction costs are paid displaying and pricing goods, in the sales time and effort required, and in ensuring that the goods appear competitive with other sellers. The operator of the market may collect a fee to cover his own costs. The fee might include profits inversely related to the availability and quality of alternative markets.

The transactions costs associated with some types of goods are inherently large. The marketplace requires transportation, but some goods are just not mobile. Some bulky goods such as hay, mineral ore, and untreated water are not generally brought to a marketplace to be exchanged like food, clothes, or other finished goods. Bulky goods have a low price per unit weight or volume, so the incremental costs of transporting them from seller to market and again to the buyer can outweigh any potential benefits. Other commodities, such as real estate, cannot be moved at all. For these bulky and immobile goods, buyers must travel to numerous locations to see the product. Real estate is an enormous business partially because potential buyers require a lot of assistance to overcome the immobility problem. Real estate agents travel a good deal. There is still a market for bulky and immobile goods, but it does not occur at one, central place.

Some commodities, such as gases, fish, or livestock, have important costs associated with just holding them in place. They are fugitive goods. Perishable goods also require special storage. Often, suitable storage must be moved with the good. The need for storage may require another transportation cost and expense at the market which makes fugitive and perishable goods more expensive to trade through a marketplace.

Sellers at the open market typically face the seller's temporal problem of information; they do not know how much they will sell. Therefore, they may bring too much or not enough product to the market. If the good is perishable, any unsold excess may be lost. If it is not perishable, transportation back home or to the next market will be required. The entire variable transportation cost associated with any unsold excess is lost. If all of these transactions costs are large enough, sellers and buyers will consider different ways of trading which involve different transactions costs patterns.

Many transactions costs can be avoided when goods move directly from seller to buyer. By avoiding the open market, price at the destination may be decreased. No goods are moved unless they are sold, and there is no intermediate point where storage or market fees may be required.

But then, many of the advantages of the open marketplace are lost. In particular, the quality of information in decreased. Buyers are not able to shop and compare as effectively because all goods are not being compared under the same (market) condition. When trade is removed from the marketplace, the potential for inefficient behavior, such as withholding or distorting information, is increased. For example, some catalog or TV shopping is less expensive than driving store to store, but catalog or TV pictures may not reveal the good's qualities as well as the store or marketplace. The revelation problem is a function of the marketing channel. Catalog goods can only be seen as shown by the catalog; they may not be touched, heard, or smelled. Many catalog sellers overcome this deficiency with a reputation for quality.

In summary, there are costs associated with establishing and using well-behaved markets. Some transactions costs are created by the attributes of the good; it may be immobile or hard to store or transport. For some types of goods, especially bulky and invisible ones, transactions costs can be large relative to the good's price. Players can avoid these costs, but this may result in a loss of information or other free market attributes.

SUMMARY

The nature of many goods runs contrary to the premises of market theory. Modern goods and modern information are complex. Information is not perfect—it is a good that requires a cost to improve. The information needed to produce goods or to know if they should be purchased can only be obtained at a cost. Enforcement of property rights requires a cost. Transactions costs created by immobile goods and other uncontrollable factors can make it expensive to establish well-behaved markets. In general, free enterprise works to minimize the sum of transactions, information, and property rights costs, but this optimum results in some combined loss of perfect market conditions as defined by the theory.

Economic competition creates endogenous incentives to withhold information, control entry, and influence property rights. Information is often rival and exclusive, so players keep it from others. Much important economic and technical information is private and rival, and it can be used to restrict entry. The information presumed by market theory to be freely available is often not available at all. Information is withheld with property rights, contracts, and physical control, and distortion of information is a legend of free enterprise. The cost of acquiring more information and overcoming misinformation is a major economic problem for buyers and sellers. Sellers' costs of withholding information from other sellers or distorting buyer's perceptions must be overcome by costs incurred to reveal it. Clearly, this is a loss of perfect competition and static efficiency in the most practical meaning of the terms.

The prevalence of transactions costs, imperfect property rights, and imperfect information support a theory of trade more general than market theory. Exchange and markets are voluntary. Production and trade occur how, when, and where they are expected to be in the best interests of buyers and sellers. The assumptions of market competition involve the nature of things, but they must also involve the institutions, customs, and conventions of information, property, and trade. Economic players create, change, and influence these human artifacts.

Property rights to innovations must be protected to encourage research, development, and dynamic progress, and this need results in a trade-off between static economic efficiency and future economic welfare through the laws of intellectual property. Patents, copyrights, trademarks, trade secrets, and many other mechanisms are used to keep competitors from entering markets for innovations and other unique goods.

NOTES

1. Nicholas Kaldor, *Economics without Equilibrium*, The Arthur M. Okun Memorial Lecture Series, Yale University (Armonk, NY: M. E. Sharpe, 1985), p. 14.

2. The terminology here is from Alan Randall, "The Problem of Market Failure," *Natural Resources Journal* 23 (1983): 131–148.

3. Alfred L. Scoop, "MSG and Hydrolyzed Vegetable Protein Induced Headache: Review and Case Studies." *Headache* 31 (February 1991): 107–110.

4. M. Barinaga, "Amino Acids: How Much Excitement Is Too Much?" *Science* 247 (1990): 20–22.

5. From material provided by the National Organization Mobilized to Stop Glutamate, "MSG: Questions and Answers," Santa Fe, NM, undated.

6. J. C. Boland, *Wall Street's Insiders: How You Can Profit with the Smart Money* (New York: William Morrow, 1985), p. 59.

4

Problems of Scope and Diversity in Production and Trade

This chapter identifies and discusses some neglected problems in production and trade for three purposes: (1) to show that the conventional theory is too limited in scope to be generally useful, (2) to highlight some neglected problems of producers and sellers, and (3) to introduce some business problems related to contracts, timing, and costs that affect antimarket behavior.

The theory of production fails as a useful descriptive device merely because many types of economic phenomena that affect production and business are not covered. Five types of phenomena are discussed here. First, the theory of production considers only fixed costs and variable costs. Many other types of costs create incentives not considered by the theory, and the results of the theory are often wrong because of this omission. In particular, private contracts and public laws affect cost structure in ways not considered by the theory. Furthermore, the nature of many costs, especially the extent to which costs can become sunk, is affected or determined by economic players. The mix of costs is often endogenous.

Second, the theory of production does not address many problems of timing in business. Production is normally a sequential process that takes time. The related temporal problem of information has been discussed. Contracts are often used to overcome timing problems such as uncertain future prices or availability, but contracts create their own problems in the form of short-run commitments and fixed prices. Many conventional costs of production, especially capital and storage, are paid to overcome timing problems.

Third, the theory has a limited perspective with respect to options for trade. Usually there is not one market for a good. Instead, there are many trade options. Players affect trade options and create more options in their self-interest, and these options may not be similar to the markets of perfect competition.

Fourth, the theory has a limited perspective on the interactions between the economy and society as a whole. Social values are the beliefs of a society that influence and impose on economic behavior. Government, affected by social values, intervenes in the economy for many reasons, most unrelated to efficiency. This intervention imposes costs and benefits on players and creates economic incentives in ways not considered by the theory.

Fifth, the conventional theory of production only covers the production and sale of existing things. Many firms are in business for the purpose of creating new things and resources. Many special problems apply to firms in the innovation business. Innovation is discussed as the sole topic of chapter 7.

THE DIVERSITY OF COSTS

As a technical matter, neoclassical theory fails as a useful descriptive device because only two types of costs are considered. There is enormous variety in the technical and contractual aspects of production and, therefore, in the structure of costs. Cost structure profoundly affects production and sales decisions in ways not considered by the theory, and the selection and management of cost structure is an important business problem.

The Omission of Escapable Fixed and Sunk Variable Costs

The theory of production properly considers the degree to which costs can be avoided in a given time frame. In the short run, *fixed costs* are sunk; in the long run, all costs can be avoided—they are escapable. Production theory normally presumes that fixed costs do not vary with output, *and* they can only be avoided in the long run. They cannot be reduced, unfixed, or mitigated in the short run, so they have no effect on short-run decisions. Also, the theory considers whether or not a cost varies with the level of production. In the theory, *variable costs* change with production levels, but fixed costs do not.

There are four possible types of costs involving how sunk the cost is and whether it varies with production. For purposes here, the following terms are defined:

Sunk fixed costs cannot be avoided in the short run and do not vary with the level of production;

Sunk variable costs cannot be avoided in the short run, but they do vary with the level of production in the long run.

Escapable fixed costs can be avoided in the short run, but they do not vary with the level of production.

Escapable variable costs can be avoided in the short run, and they vary with the level of production.

The standard theory of production only uses two of these: sunk fixed and escapable variable. In the theory, variable costs never become sunk costs, and fixed costs cannot be avoided in the short run.

Escapable Fixed Costs. Many escapable fixed costs can be avoided as quickly or more quickly than variable costs. Consider the category of costs commonly known as overhead. A firm can avoid its utility costs by stopping today, but it may have contracts to buy materials, a variable input, for months or longer. Building rent is often charged on a monthly basis. Even if a building is leased, the contract may be escapable for a small cost. Insurance can be canceled with a telephone call. Management labor overhead can be eliminated immediately by laying off employees. It is frequently not possible to change the amount paid for overhead by changing production levels, but overhead is also not sunk because it can be reduced in the short run. Consider retailers, distributors, and other firms who sell products produced by others. The only cost that varies directly with production is the cost of wholesale goods that may need to be ordered months in advance. Most other costs can be avoided or reduced on a much shorter basis.

At first glance, many producers appear to have substantial fixed costs in the form of plant and equipment. "Since the firm's plant and equipment are among the most difficult inputs to change quickly, the short run is generally understood to mean the length of time during which the firm's plant and equipment are fixed."[1] Once purchased, how can these costs be avoided? Arguably, most of the fixed costs of the theory of production can be escaped quite quickly. Very few material and equipment costs are truly sunk for the firm because much of the cost can be recovered at any time by selling the asset. Most types of machinery can be sold or rented for use somewhere else; they are mobile. Entire factories can be and are moved and sold according to changing costs and comparative advantage. There is a transactions cost associated with moving or selling the asset, but it need not be especially large.

Even if an asset is immobile, it can still be sold. Consider a well, the epitome of a sunk cost. If the cost is truly sunk, there is no way to reduce the amount of cost associated with the well once it is drilled. But in fact, the owner can sell it at any time. The asset is immobile, but owners are quite mobile. A cost becomes truly sunk when the expense is for something that cannot be resold within a given time frame.

Not only can most costs be immediately avoided by selling the associated asset, but most purchases of equipment can be put off or avoided in the short-run by substitution. The economic life of a mine can be extended with better extraction technology. More maintenance and repair of machinery will reduce breakdowns and sustain its productivity. Many productive assets are available for rent or lease, and this arrangement can substitute for the more inescapable cost of ownership. In the long run, the firm can often select between ownership, a long-run commitment such as a long-term lease, or a cost that is even more escapable such as month-to-month rental. In general, renting has a higher cost per unit time, but there is less financial commitment, less risk, and, perhaps, less transactions cost. Firms who chose escapable arrangements such as renting over purchase may be more willing and able to close temporarily because they can avoid larger start-up and closure costs in the short term. Laborers who do not buy homes avoid more transactions costs if they must move. Renting allows the option of reducing costs faster if conditions dictate, but there may be more short-run price risk. Monthly rent can be increased monthly. On the other hand, renting has other advantages. Players who rent computers avoid depreciation caused by technological obsolescence.

The decision on how to acquire productive assets entails much more than its average cost and the profit from production as suggested by market theory. The firm contemplating options for acquiring the services of machinery can often select from many options, which vary in terms of duration and amount of commitment. The decision involves transactions costs, price risk in the price of the asset, expectations about substitutes and future technology, as well as the value of what the asset produces. The mobility of the asset is important, and mobility may involve transportation costs. Financial feasibility is also important. Many players may be simply unable to finance the purchase price of the productive asset.

While one player can readily sell an asset to others, an industry may not be able to sell its assets outside of the industry. This is especially true when the assets cannot be efficiently converted to any use other than their original purpose. Oil wells are only good for pumping oil, so the price of oil wells is largely a function of the price of oil. If oil prices decline unexpectedly, the price of oil wells declines unexpectedly as well. If oil wells had alternative uses, then their value would be related to the markets in these other sectors as well, but this simply cannot be.

Therefore, sunk costs associated with productive assets are often a market problem, not a firm problem, created by the fact that assets such as machinery often have limited use outside of their original intended use. If the industry as a whole had perfect information about future prices, the specificity of machinery would not create a problem because the right amount of inconvertible machinery would be made given the known future market. In fact, the temporal problem of information (chapter 3) means that future prices cannot be known, expectations can be biased industrywide, and the wrong amount of capacity is often produced. This latter theory is developed in more detail in chapter 5.

Many of these principles can be shown by the example of farm machinery. Tractors and farm implements are easily moved and sold. The cost of farm machinery is not truly sunk in the short run because some of it can be recovered by renting or selling it. Farmers frequently double as custom operators, renting their services to other farmers who do not have the appropriate machinery. Many farmers are too small to justify ownership of a specialized piece of equipment. If the price of one crop collapses, some equipment, such as tractors, can easily be used or converted for production of other crops. But if agricultural prices decline generally, it is difficult to move farm machinery out of agriculture entirely.

How quickly can a cost be avoided? The problem of what costs are sunk in a given time frame depends on a variety of contractual and physical constraints and transactions costs, not whether the cost is variable or fixed. Conventional theory introduces the concept of short run constraints but incorrectly assigns the constraint to costs that do not vary with production. When a firm's costs are unavoidable in the short run, it is usually because of contractual constraints or because of an irreversible process, not because of plant and equipment.

When a cost is sunk, all short-run economic incentives do not go away. Sunk costs affect current economic decisions through the pattern of services and costs provided by the investment, through depreciation and property taxation, through effects of past expenditures on current wealth, through the asset's value as collateral, and through other considerations of financial requirements and financial feasibility. The conventional theory of production is far too general to consider these facts.

Sunk Variable Costs. A sunk variable cost involves an input that normally varies with production, but somehow, the cost cannot be escaped or avoided in the short run. Many types of variable costs cannot be avoided in the short run because (1) they are already purchased, or there is a commitment to purchase them; *and* (2) they cannot be resold, or they become committed to an irreversible process. That is, ownership is already established, and the cost cannot be unsunk because the associated asset cannot be sold, stored or recovered.

Short-run ownership is established by contract or previous ownership, but sunk costs occur when the resource cannot be economically sold or stored in its current form. Perishable variable inputs, such as some agricultural products, often become true sunk costs. The variable input must be used this period or its entire value will be lost. In some cases, the variable cost can be avoided by ceasing production because the variable input can be stored for later use or sale. Then, the short-run decision must consider the cost of storage required if production ceases. In another case, the cost might be avoided by selling the variable input to someone else. Again, there are transactions costs, so these costs must be considered in the short-run decision.

Often, the input that required a cost is tied up in an irreversible process. Goods are made up of the variable materials and energy required to make them. The sunk variable costs were paid on a per-unit basis, and the goods have been completely or partly made but not sold. The energy and materials embodied in the good are sunk to the extent that they cannot be recovered, or the partly completed goods cannot be sold. Energy expenses normally become sunk in this way. The variable farming inputs of energy, seed, and fertilizer cannot be recovered once they are in the ground. The costs of wheat production cannot be recovered by disassembling the wheat, so the production of wheat must be finished and the wheat sold to recover the variable costs.

Many of the problems of sunk costs apply equally to sunk variable and sunk fixed costs. The extent to which the costs are sunk depends on the nature of the input (can it be moved or is it perishable?) as well as the markets for things the inputs may be used for. If the market for the good collapses, and the goods have no alternative use, then irreversible costs are truly sunk. Again, contracts and other irreversible commitments often affect what costs and decisions are fixed in the short run. The sellers' temporal problem of information often requires that goods be produced prior to sale, and imperfect information often means that variable costs can be paid that end up being larger than the value of the item available for sale.

One-Time Costs, Start-up Costs, and Discretionary Fixed Costs

There are several types of costs that affect business decisions in ways not considered by the standard theory of production. The fixed costs of economic theory do not change with the amount of production each period, and they can be avoided once per period. The fixed cost is implicitly the same fixed amount each period so the average fixed cost (fixed cost per unit produced) declines only with the amount of production in each period. Within each short-run period, it is sunk and ignored. A long-term property lease that does not allow for a sublet is a good example of the conventional fixed cost. The lease term is long relative to the time frame in which most costs are avoidable, and the cost cannot be avoided by selling the lease, since no sublet is allowed. The lessee can only decide to continue or cancel the lease once per year. In the logic of simple production theory, all such costs can be continued or canceled only at the same point in time.

Discretionary costs are not necessary for production, at least within a given time period. There is substantial leeway in how often and when they are paid. The short-run average cost per unit depends not only on how many units are produced, but also on how often the discretionary cost is incurred. The other significance of discretionary costs is that they may be avoidable in the short term if business conditions are poor. It may be optimal to pay them in the long run, but the fact that they are discretionary in the short run provides flexibility in a variable and uncertain business climate.

In some cases, a cost buys a stream of future benefits, but the benefits decrease in a regular way over time. For example, damage from pests is momentarily eliminated following investment in pesticide application, but then grows slowly as the pest population recovers. The investment at first provides major cost savings from reduced pest damage, but these benefits decline over time. The benefits of some assets decline over time with new technology, for example, personal computers. The benefits decline as other competitors acquire better computers, putting them in an improved competitive position.

An important business problem that is not considered by the conventional theory of production involves how frequently these costs should be incurred. If machinery experiences more frequent breakdowns, then, at some point, it is replaced. When a computer is so outdated that it cannot compete, it is time for another. But exactly when is it time to buy another? In all of these cases, there is a trade-off. The less frequently the cost is paid, the less average cost per unit time is. Fixed cost per unit time declines as equipment is replaced and its cost paid less frequently.* On the other hand, the machinery provides less average benefit over time because it is, on average, older and not as productive, or it requires more repair.

Firms that normally stop and start operations from time to time incur short-run *closing and start-up* costs. A start-up cost occurs whenever a business starts operating. The average cost per unit then declines for as long as the firm continues producing. Similarly, closure costs are paid whenever the business stops operating, so closure costs are avoided by staying in business. Closure decisions are discretionary once the firm is in business, and start-up costs are discretionary when the firm is not producing. Start-up and closure costs provide a large incentive for operating firms to absorb short-run losses. The typical short-run stoppage decision would require consideration of both because the firm hopes to restart again.

The short-run operations decision may affect a variety of operating costs. Some costs are permanently increased if a firm stops producing temporarily. For example, if a firm lays off its employees, its unemployment insurance costs can be increased when it starts again. Since these costs are a function of the decision to operate or not, they must be actively considered in the short-run decision.

A *one-time* start-up cost is paid to produce any output and must never be paid again. Initial research and development costs are a good example. The average cost per unit depends on how much is produced forever, not just this period. Like any fixed cost, the one-time cost buys something, and that something might eventually be resold. One-time costs differ from conventional fixed costs because to calculate an average cost, the total duration of production must be known. Usually, this duration cannot be known.

Research and development costs are the one-time cost of innovation, and one-time costs are especially important in the production of innovations. One-time costs are also important in relation to the demand for capital. These relationships are discussed in chapter 7 and later in this chapter.

Some types of operations eventually require one-time closure costs. When an industry closes forever, for example, society may require its plant and equipment to be removed and disposed of properly. Nuclear power plants and dams are examples. Operations may continue at a loss because the net present value of expected annual losses are smaller than the costs of closing.

---

* This type of trade-off is considered in a branch of operations research called inventory control theory.

Toward a Taxonomy of Costs

Table 4.1 provides a simple cost taxonomy based on the descriptions previously provided. The taxonomy starts with four mutually exclusive categories. Given that a fixed cost is defined as a cost that can be avoided more than once, one-time costs are also another distinct category because they are only paid once.

Table 4.1
A Simple Taxonomy of Production Costs and Their Implications for Incentives

Name	Varies with output?	Avoidable in the short run?	Incentives affect:	Example
Escapable variable	Yes	Yes	Short- and long-run output and production decision	Materials and energy bought on spot market
Sunk fixed	No	No	Long-run production decision	Annual lease with no sublet, annual tax preparation
Escapable fixed	No	Yes	Short-run production decision; buy, sell or rent	Most equipment expenses, overhead, insurance
Sunk variable	Yes	No	Long-run output and production decision	Materials bought under long-term contracts
Discretionary Fixed Costs	No	Yes, or at least can be delayed	Decision on when to invest or reinvest	Pest control, some depreciable equipment
One-time costs	No	No, avoidable one time	Decision of whether to ever produce or quit producing	Research and development, planning, environmental assessment
Start-up and Closure Costs	No	Yes, avoided by not starting or closing	Short- and long-run stop and start decisions	Contracting, initial fees, moving and relocation

Given that the conventional fixed cost must be paid at some known interval, the discretionary fixed cost is different in that it can be put off. Start-up and closure costs are discretionary costs tied to the decision of short-run operation or closure, and one-time costs are discretionary and tied to the similar long-run operation decision.

IMPLICATIONS FOR SHORT-RUN PRODUCTION DECISIONS AND MARGINAL COST PRICING

What are the implications of these many cost categories for the theory of production? In the conventional theory, firms enter the industry in the long run if price is greater than average costs. In the short run, only variable costs are considered. The conventional short-run theory of the firm finds that the firm will cease production when average variable cost is more than price.

Once it is admitted that some fixed costs can be avoided in the short run, and some variable costs avoided only in the long run, some of the major findings of the logic of the theory of production are no longer true. The important short-run consideration to the business is not whether the cost is variable, it is whether or not it is sunk.

First, ignore short-run closure and start-up costs. Since many fixed costs can actually be avoided in the short run, firms will exit and enter even in the short run based on their ability to cover average costs, variable or not, that can be avoided in that time frame. The cost that determines the short-run decision to continue production is the average escapable variable cost plus the average escapable fixed cost per unit. If price is less than this sum at any possible level of production, then the firm will cease production unless and until price increases to a level above the sum. *A priori*, it cannot be known whether this sum will be more or less than the average variable cost of the conventional theory because sunk variable costs subtract from the average variable cost and escapable fixed costs add to it. That is, sunk variable costs provide no incentive to stop operations, but escapable fixed costs provide incentive to leave business in the short run.

The conventional theory also finds that the firm sets its output level where marginal cost equals price. Marginal costs and market prices guide the output decisions of firms. The market sets the price, and the firm's profit maximizing quantity occurs where its marginal cost equals price. Marginal costs are a function of variable costs only, and these costs are the only costs included in the short-run decision.

If some variable costs are actually sunk in the short run, then their marginal costs do not figure into the optimal short-run production decision. Firms should produce the quantity of output where marginal cost equals price, but these marginal costs can only involve the variable inputs that can be varied in the given time frame. Variable costs that are sunk in the short run will not figure into the short-run decision. However, things can get much more complicated because production is a function of the quantities of the sunk variable inputs. If some variable inputs are sunk, the producer cannot use less, but can it use more? Can more even be acquired in the short run? If not, are there substitutes available? Once it is admitted that all variable inputs cannot be bought or sold in any quantity in the short run, the short-run decision becomes much more complex. Very generally, it is often costly to change production levels in the short run because variable input levels cannot be easily changed.

Start-up and closure costs will also enter into the short-run decision. These costs can be avoided by staying in business. If the firm expects to be in business in the long run, then the firm may take a short-run loss from production to avoid larger expected costs associated with stopping and starting again. Similarly, one-time costs must be considered in the long-run production decision, but the long-run decision will also involve uncertain future costs and markets.

The marginal cost pricing principle is not an especially tenable theory of behavior for several other reasons, especially the following: (1) marginal costs are often indeterminate, (2) the relevant costs are often unknowable when business decisions must be made, and (3) financial problems are not considered.

Marginal cost pricing is frequently not used because the firm cannot determine the relevant marginal cost of a unit of production. Some variable costs are easy to calculate, but some are not. For example, some machinery depreciates as a function of use, so its use creates a variable cost, but it also depreciates over time as it ages or is made obsolete by new technology. To practice marginal cost pricing, the firm would need to know the share of the machineries' depreciation caused by its use. In practice, this is a difficult calculation.

In fact, there is little empirical support for marginal cost pricing. One study, based on interviews with top managers of large firms, could find no single principle, such as marginal cost pricing, to explain the determinants of price. "Pricing decisions were usually considered part of the general strategy for achieving a broadly defined goal."[2] Some alternative pricing strategies included (1) pricing to achieve a return on investment, (2) stabilization of price and margin, (3) pricing to maintain or improve market position, (4) pricing related to product differentiation, and (5) pricing to meet or follow competition. Strategy (1) implies pricing to cover average costs, which include one-time costs, (2) implies pricing to reduce risk, and (3) and (4) imply strategic pricing to improve market position. Only (3) and (5) are similar to pricing in market theory. More importantly, "pricing structures could not be explored as manifestations of market structures since the market structures, conventionally defined, were by no means recognized as such by the firms interviewed."[3]

One possible response to this criticism is that the firm does not need to understand the marginal criteria to attain it. Profit maximization or cost minimization must incidentally result in the marginal criteria of the theory. This would be true if the firm could know it was maximizing profit or minimizing costs. In truth, prices, costs, or other important factors often cannot be known when decisions must be made. The optimal production decision is a continuously moving target. The production function and production costs are risky and uncertain. The duration of production is uncertain. It is difficult for firms to determine their long-run profit, much less their marginal or average costs, as a function of output.

On the other side of the optimality equation of price equal to marginal cost, the firm does not face a market price because most goods are sold with some degree of market control. Most commonly, there are not many sellers of the same product as the theory requires; there are a few sellers of similar but differentiated products. In this case, sellers can set their price within a competitive range. Then, pricing is a strategic problem that considers costs, competition, and the expectations of buyers and sellers. Current market conditions and costs are important, but so are long-term competitive position, immediate survival, investment goals, and buyer expectations. In another common case, there are few buyers, and when there are also few sellers, prices are often negotiated.

This discussion demonstrates the limitations of imposing the narrow logic of market theory on real production and business operations. For firms to achieve static economic efficiency, they must set their output at the quantity where marginal cost equals price. For the decreasing marginal cost firm, marginal cost pricing means immediate losses because short-run average costs are not covered. There may be other types of costs to consider. To obtain efficiency, it has been argued that society should regulate price at the lower marginal cost and subsidize the firm to ensure that average costs are covered.[4] This approach makes sense from the perspective of economic logic but fails the common sense test. The subsidy solution ignores the transactions costs that may be involved in implementing such a scheme, and it ignores perverse incentives and capabilities created by the intervention (chapter 8).

THE DIVERSITY OF TIMING PROBLEMS

The conventional theory of production ascribes limited importance to timing problems in production. In the conventional theory, the short and long run are important only in terms of (1) what costs are sunk and (2) the elasticity of demand and supply.

All processes require some time, and the amount of time required and the sequence of the process over time affects costs. Production, selling, and buying are characterized by diverse timing problems that affect behavior in ways not considered by conventional theory. Especially, timing problems can create incentives or capabilities to control markets. Some common timing problems are as follows:

1. Production must occur in advance of sales, so information about prices and quantities can be imperfect. The sellers' temporal problem of information creates a demand for

contracts.

2. Expenses for inputs of production normally occur in advance of sales. This fact creates a demand for capital used to finance production.

3. Contracts are used to borrow capital and to reduce future price and quantity risk, but these contracts may fix prices and create specific timing requirements that are unavoidable.

4. Circumstances beyond control of the producer cause the timing of some events to be uncontrollable.

Some parts of the production process are sequential. The sum of time needed to accomplish sequential production steps determines the amount of time separating the commitment to produce from sales. The minimum time to accomplish something in consideration of sequential steps is often called the critical path.

Production is also an iterative process. The results of each production step feed back to earlier steps through experience and learning, and sales income is used to finance the purchase of more inputs of production and information. Once sales have begun, the steps in this process often go on simultaneously because different batches of production are being planned, sold, and produced. The firm can be learning, producing, and selling all at the same time.

Contract Problems

Contracts are often used to set prices, quantities, and other terms in advance of production. Contracts can reduce or eliminate sellers' risk, and they coordinate buyers' and sellers' expectations about future prices. However, contracts then fix short-run prices and quantities. Unforeseen economic change can create an economic disequilibrium because terms are fixed until they can be renegotiated. If spot prices change, one party would prefer to not perform on its obligation, so the trade differs from the mutually desirable trade of market competition.

A firm usually has a number of contracts that will cause some commitments to be unavoidable in the short run. The firm is able to escape the commitment only when contractual terms are completed. It is unlikely that all contracts can be executed at the same time. Therefore, at any given point in time, there are likely to be outstanding commitments. In practice, there is no long run where all contracts are escapable because there is no point in time when all contracts can be avoided at the same time. At least, the decision to stop business may entail closure costs associated with outstanding contracts.

Economic decisions often require commitments for future actions that affect timing. Deliveries or purchases must be made by a certain date. These commitments must be made in the context of an uncertain future. Despite best efforts, it sometimes becomes difficult to meet commitments. Then, the firm must consider the penalty involved if the commitment is not met. Penalties such as forfeiture of collateral can be quite large, and the process of exchange by force of contract bears little resemblance to the market model.

The Problem of Uncontrollable Timing

Another timing problem occurs because the timing of certain events are beyond the control of the producer. These events may involve parts of the production process or the timing of demand. In agriculture, the timing of the seasons is uncontrollable. Most demands occur all year, but production can only occur in summer. Uncontrollable timing creates more business problems when it is also uncertain. Annual variations in weather are the single largest factor affecting annual variations in agricultural supply. Rain and temperature are not only uncontrollable, they are also uncertain so the timing of harvest is also uncertain. Most production outdoors must be planned with the unknown vagarities of weather in mind. This creates problems in planning and timing of contracts.

To make matters worse, some types of demands occur only at certain times—holidays, for example. In general, it is expensive to conduct production in line with the timing of demands, so storage is used to conduct continuous production for uneven demands, and storage is used to ensure supplies for unpredictable or seasonal markets. In addition, storage is used to coordinate timing of production and sales, but storage also creates a physical ability to control sales. Storage can be a cost-effective means to allow production to occur when it is most cost-efficient, but it creates an ability to control marketings.

The Capital Problem

The term "capital" has been used by different economists to mean different things: machinery, the value of machinery, or money invested in a business, for example. Financial capital is money or, at least, a stock of liquid wealth, and the cost of holding capital is the interest rate. Conventional economics has often assigned an important role to capital in production; capital has been considered an input of production on par with labor or land.

The normal demand for capital for production is a reflection of the normal ordering of production and trade. The cost of capital is created by a need to buy production inputs in advance of sales. Plant, equipment, and other inputs are needed to produce, but the resulting sales income can only be obtained over a long time horizon in the future. Production does not necessarily require a capital cost. If a producer can sell output at the same time his costs are incurred, capital is not needed at all. If product can be sold in advance of production, the producer can actually earn interest by lending his sales income to others before it is needed to finance production. Initial stock offerings sometimes yield more capital than needed to finance production.

When capital must be raised from outside sources, it requires a contract. Like other contracts, the financial contract can affect what costs are unavoidable in the short run. This problem is discussed in the next chapter in detail under financial feasibility. Firms try to design production to avoid unnecessary costs and risks of capital. For example, a prototype may be developed to convince buyers to provide some payment in advance, and contract terms are negotiated when possible to accommodate expected sales and to provide flexibility when possible. Lenders, however, normally prefer less flexibility.

Timing problems create incentives to control markets. Prices and quantities are often fixed in the short run by contracts designed to eliminate risk at the expense of flexibility. Contracts, however, are not the only method available to eliminate risk.

THE DIVERSITY OF TRADE OPTIONS

In perfect competition, trade occurs only through markets, and all markets are homogenous (the same) in that they all meet the same assumptions of the theory.* Even when multiple markets for a good are allowed, as in international trade theory, they all typically operate under the same competitive assumptions. The multiple markets vary only in terms of transportation costs and the position of demand and supply functions. As a matter of convention, trade of a good is analyzed by looking at only one trade structure at a time.

In fact, there are often many options for trade of a good. At any point in time, many goods can be sold through many channels that differ in terms of how well they meet the conditions required for perfect competition. Consider the case of agriculture. There are many mechanisms a farmer can use to sell his crops. He may be able to eat them, barter with other farmers, feed them to livestock, sell them locally through farm markets or roadside stands, transport to more distant markets, store for later sale, participate in futures markets or forward contracts, or participate in farm programs. Marketing cooperatives allow farmers to work together to sell their crops. Production and marketing decisions depend on the costs and benefits of all these options, and these costs and benefits depend on the degree to which each is a perfect market.

In the arts and crafts business, artists can also select from many trade options. Some artists sell only to wholesale buyers. Wholesale sales can be by consignment or purchase. Marketing for wholesale sales can use sales representatives, trade shows, or direct marketing. In some cases, artists sell directly to retail sellers or pay a rental fee or a share of sales to the retail agent. Other artists conduct retail trade through crafts and art shows, catalogs, or home sales. The decision on which marketing arrangements to use is a major business problem,

---

* *Homogenous* means all the same or identical as within a group.

and each option can vary considerably in terms of how well it meets the assumptions of perfect markets. Many buyers and sales representatives demand regional exclusives—they ask that the artist use no other buyer or representative in the region—and some will not represent other artists' similar products.

Multiple trade options are commonly used for a single type of good, and they can differ in many regards. Important differences involve risk, information, transactions costs, protection of property rights, services provided to buyers and sellers, rules for participation, quality requirements, regulations, and potential for future expansion. Different options may provide different levels of comparison to the same or similar products. Different options determine price in different ways: prices may be fixed, negotiable, set by auction, private bids, or other means. The strategy of players with respect to trade options depends on a complex array of risks, costs, and benefits. For a player, the choice of trade options may depend not just on the simple efficiencies of market theory, but also on the degree to which each option varies from the assumptions of market theory.

Trade has a short- and long-run perspective similar to the short- and long-run of economic theory. In the short run, trade options may be limited. In the long run, not only are fewer costs sunk, and contracts committed, but more trade options are possible. In the long run, rather than produce and sell a good in an existing trade option, it may be better to direct limited goods or resources to the creation of completely new trade mechanisms.

Economic theory ignores the significance of the fact that trade is created by the players who use it. Economic players change trade conditions and create new trade mechanisms that are not at all like the idealized markets of economic theory. Economic players can create new trade mechanisms when the assumptions of perfect competition are not strictly true to begin with. Trade options are most often created by sellers. When sellers create a market, they can control rules of entry, requirements for disclosure of information, number of sellers, and similarity with other sellers' goods. Sometimes, buyers create trade options such as cooperatives. Imperfect rights, information problems, and transactions costs can provide incentive for buyers and sellers to create trade mechanisms unlike perfect markets, but the incentive can also arise precisely because the assumptions are true to begin with. New trade options may allow sellers to control entry and information. The control is temporary until and if the conventional forces of economic competition do their work.

THE PROCESS OF TRADE

In economic theory, trade is viewed as one simple activity. Buyers and sellers do not negotiate because the prices of homogenous goods are set by markets. The significance of contracts, finance, and contractual terms to provide goods or payment when, where, and how specified are not explicitly recognized. In fact, trade is usually a process consisting of several distinct activities, or components, which are frequently spread out over time. Trade options can differ in the order and setting of these components, and these differences can affect how well the options meet the assumptions of market theory.

The components are negotiation, where terms are discussed and debated; a contractual component where buyers and sellers formally agree to all terms; a sellers' obligation where the good is provided to the buyer; and a buyers' obligation where money (usually) is provided to the seller.

When trade occurs frequently and the cost of items traded is relatively low, the contractual part of the exchange occurs almost simultaneously with the sellers' and buyers' obligations. In retail sales, money and goods are exchanged over the counter, but there is still an unspoken contract. As the size and dollar amount of trade increase, certain risks and transactions costs also increase. The buyer becomes more concerned with warranties, repair costs, and return policies. The buyer is more likely to require financing, and the seller becomes more concerned with the buyer's ability to finance the purchase; there is more at stake.

Negotiation occurs when terms are not set in advance by markets or convention. Often, there are not many sellers and buyers. Typically, both buyer and seller have some leeway in the price they will accept, and both believe that negotiation will be to their advantage. The buyer seeks to determine and obtain the lowest price the seller will accept; the seller seeks to determine and obtain the maximum price the buyer will accept. The negotiations may involve trade-offs between price and the other terms of trade. Both sides may withhold some information from the other in negotiations.

The forum for negotiations has a large influence on contractual terms, so players seek to affect the forum for negotiations. Negotiation occurs anywhere people meet: over the telephone; in company boardrooms and offices; at the golf course; in bars, restaurants, and hotel rooms; on the street; and in homes. Negotiation occurs in local, state, and federal executive, legislative, and judiciary branches; in courtrooms; government bureaucracies; and in the proceedings of commissions. Players invest in measures to improve their bargaining position during negotiations and strive to conduct their bargaining in a strategically favorable environment. The environment may be set up to enhance differentiation, withhold or enhance information, limit entry, or otherwise affect terms.

The contractual component defines the mutual obligations. The seller's obligation defines what, where, and when the seller is to provide the good. The limits of liability, warranties, conditions for returns, refunds, and repairs, and quality requirements are clarified. The buyer's obligation specifies the price and when and how the buyer must pay the seller. Contracts may specify terms for market control, such as exclusive rights and rights to use, disclose, or sell information. The buyer's obligation may allow the buyer to pay at a different time than the seller's delivery of the good. With seller financing, contracting and the seller's obligation occur now, but part of the buyer's obligation occurs in the future.

Contracts are especially important when the seller's and buyer's obligations occur at different times. The party who delivers first on his obligation is vulnerable to failure on the part of the other, so contracts often define the penalties that must be paid if one party fails to deliver. The risk and cost of penalties have an important effect on future economic behavior.

Trade options are often developed to deal with complex business problems, and the process of contracting and trade becomes similarly complex. For example, buyers and sellers use contracts to reduce temporal information problems. Futures and options markets and forward contracts are examples of trade mechanisms created in order to overcome one economic problem: risk and uncertainty associated with future economic conditions. The contract occurs now but much of the obligations of buyers and sellers occur in the future. In another complex case, a third party, the financier, is involved through inter-related contracts.

In summary, trade in the complex modern economy is often quite different from the trade of market economics. Goods are not homogenous, and there are many trade options available and prices are not set by markets. Therefore, we shop. Goods and trade are complex, the economy is constantly changing, information is never perfect, there are many potential options and strategies for selling and buying goods. Trade is a human creation, and people try to create new forms of trade in their self-interest.

THE SIGNIFICANCE OF SOCIAL VALUES

Conventional economic theory assigns a limited significance to the complex roles of social values, or commonly held value judgments, in affecting or controlling economic behavior. Many economic values of great personal and social concern are associated with free enterprise. Social values are important because (1) free enterprise is justified by many social values besides efficiency, and many values other than efficiency are used to justify private and public actions; (2) many social values come into conflict with the assumptions and results of economic theory; and (3) economic players use social values to further their self-interests through the influence of public opinion.

For our purposes, we need not define what the values really mean. Regardless of what they are, society considers them to be important, and we can observe their effect on the economy. Some of these values include technological progress, private property rights, survival and avoidance of pain, equity, rights to self-determination, opportunity, and personal responsibility.

Very generally, I propose that most members of Western societies believe these are good, that free enterprise enhances all of these values, that they are consistent in that they usually don't conflict with each other, and that they are all consistent with free trade and economic efficiency. At times, however, society finds that free enterprise or free markets do not promote important social values, at least for some elements of society. Society is then willing to give up free markets and static efficiency to correct a perceived problem, and government is called on to codify and administer laws to influence production and trade.

One of the major economic roles of government in mixed economies is to influence economic behavior in response to social values, and this influence often conflicts with efficiency. Private property rights are a social value associated with free enterprise. At times, values of privacy and protection of property rights conflict with the freedom of entry needed for economic efficiency. Private property rights conflict with efficiency when the private property rights are for unique information or resources that enable market control. Sometimes the social value of private property takes precedence over immediate efficiency. We allow intellectual property rights partially because, when information is the product of one's labor, it is only fair that this information should be private property.

Most people would probably agree that free enterprise is conducive to human survival and material comfort, yet free enterprise provides no opportunities for survival for those who are unable to produce. Therefore, we pay for the survival of others through the welfare system and other services for the poor. Perhaps we just don't want to see the inevitable product of pure competition. But clearly, the support of the poor can conflict with static economic efficiency and economic freedom. Taxation is often used to acquire resources to promote social values, and taxation is essentially involuntary. In the eyes of many, economic freedom and justice are perpetually in conflict with taxation.

We have environmental laws not only because of the efficiency problems identified by environmental economics, but also because of some strong value judgments associated with environmental issues. These values may involve a sense of justice or equity. At any rate, environmental issues are often emotional and value-laden, and they often conflict with immediate economic efficiency.

International market control is used to promote social values. International trade restrictions are used to prod offensive nations to comply with international human rights standards. Recently, public and private trade sanctions were instrumental in securing more democracy for South Africa.

Unlike the win-win results of market theory, there are often winners and losers when governments intervene. Society trades off the social and economic values and aspirations of one group to favor another. Somehow, these decisions are made, but how they are made is not a concern of neoclassical theory.

Selfish economic interests and social values interact at many levels. Selfish interests support government and social values that help them and work against any that hurt. The influence of public administration, legislation, elections, and social values is an important part of the economic story. Rational economic players try to influence government whenever and however it is expected to work out best. Sometimes, public appeal to commonly held value judgments is used to obtain favorable trade, property laws, or direct market control. If successful, government may provide the rights or resources needed to develop, administer, and enforce the control. This problem is developed in more detail in chapter 8.

SUMMARY

This chapter has argued that conventional economics does not consider the diversity of economic experience in terms of costs, timing problems, trade options, and social values. The realm of costs and production decisions is much more complex than treated by the theory of production. The disparity between the simplicity of theory and the complexity of reality was shown by analysis of types of costs and their incentives. Fixed expenses are frequently not sunk costs, even in the short run. The average cost per unit production associated with one-time costs may be incalculable at the time the cost is paid. Variable costs are avoided by producing less, fixed costs are avoided in the long run by quitting business, but start-up and closure costs can be avoided by doing nothing, even if that means staying in business. *A priori*, there is no reason to believe that all costs are merely fixed or variable or that fixed or variable is the only thing that matters.

The nature of many costs is an entirely human creation. Complex contractual arrangements can be used to achieve a more desirable cost structure, and society imposes costs on business without considering the artifices of theoretical economics. Firms can affect whether a cost will be sunk or escapable, and they have discretion in when costs are paid. A business can frequently substitute a stream of very escapable costs for a long-run cost commitment. Part of the business problem is to change the nature of costs to achieve a desired mix of cost, flexibility, and certainty.

Timing problems can create incentives to control markets through contracts or other means. Markets and other arrangements for trade are human creations. Therefore, they respond to economic incentives, and selfish motives may result in trade quite unlike the competitive trade of market competition. Trade diversifies as selfish interests search for better ways of trading, and modern contracts reflect this complexity. Contracts may fix prices in the short run, they affect timing constraints, and they are used to implement trade options and market control.

Conventional economic theory finds it convenient to make many implicit assumptions about the exogenous nature of costs, market structures, and intervention. In truth, economic players influence cost structure, trade options, social values, and government. Government is also a human creation, and government evolves under the influence of selfish interests and social values. In past chapters, it has been argued that economic players also affect information, rules of entry, property rights, and the other explicit assumptions of perfect competition. In this light, economic systems must be viewed more openly. Everything has the potential to affect everything else. Human behavior responds to every constraint, and nothing can be taken as given. Therefore, no static model should be taken at face value as an accurate depiction of economic behavior. There is simply too much variety in the structure of production, costs, and trade to say anything uniquely useful. The diversity and complexity of production and trade argues for more concern with the facts of unique economic circumstances, that is, an empirically based economics. Observation, not theory, should guide economic analysis.

NOTES

1. Edwin Mansfield, *Microeconomics Theory and Applications,* Third Edition (New York: W. W. Norton, 1979), p. 145.

2. A.D.H. Kaplan, Joel B. Dirlam, and Robert F. Lanzillotti, *Pricing in Big Business: A Case Approach* (Washington, D.C.: The Brookings Institution, 1958), p. 3.

3. Ibid., p. 7.

4. Harold Hotelling, "The General Welfare in Relation to Problems of Taxation and of Railway and Utility Rates," *Econometrica* (July 1938): 242–269.

5

Problems Related to Survival, Expectations, and Market Structure

This chapter extends the analysis of the prior chapter related to problems of information costs and contracts in free enterprise with emphasis on problems of survival and market control. First, several types of economic motives and constraints are not fully considered by economic theory. In particular, the short-run behavior of economic players is often driven by human and economic survival. When desperate players have few options, they may behave quite differently from the results of market theory.

Financial feasibility, as the term is used here, involves an immediate need for funds to avoid unacceptable consequences, and these consequences usually involve the terms of a contract. The short-run problem of financial feasibility can occur because all sunk costs are not the same. Some costs cannot be escaped because they are already paid for, and some cannot be escaped because they must be paid for now.

Chapter 3 introduced the seller's temporal problem of information. Simply put, producers normally cannot know the outcome of production and trade decisions when the decisions must be made. Therefore, much investment is based on expectations, and this creates some special problems for production. The previous chapter argued that assets with minimal alternative uses can become sunk costs at an industry level. This chapter describes a supply problem involving price expectations, investment, and capacity. A combination of circumstances—many similar firms, sunk costs involving assets with minimal uses outside of the industry, and the temporal problem of information—results in an efficiency problem that is common to free enterprise.

Expectations create other efficiency problems. In pure speculation, markets and prices are driven completely by expectations, not supply and demand. The prices of goods and resources can become completely detached from their economic values as described by economic theory. Expectations can create efficiency problems because they are commonly biased, and much economic behavior is based on expectations.

Government regulates both market conduct and market control. The most extreme form of market control is monopoly. The conventional economic approach to imperfect competition uses comparative statics to analyze the implications of a few or one firm.* The conventional explanation for monopoly is natural monopoly caused by declining costs, but increasing production costs do nothing to discourage a monopoly in selling. A downward sloping demand function is all the incentive needed for monopoly, and control of entry makes it possible. Many laws and property rights are the means to control entry and limit competition, and economic rents created by monopoly help to sustain the control. In many cases, market control is enabled by control of entry allowed or even enforced by government.

It is useful to review the extent of influence of government in the economy to show that the market model frequently fails merely because many industries are heavily regulated. Government, not the market, controls profit, and consequently, government becomes the focus of economic competition.

ECONOMIC MAXIMIZATION AND THE PRIORITY OF SURVIVAL

In neoclassical theory, firms and consumers seek to maximize profits and utility in a setting of options. In fact, economic players must first survive to maximize anything. The survival problem has two attributes: (1) catastrophic failure is at stake, and (2) there are limited options, usually just one, for avoiding the failure. Economic theory includes substitution between goods and inputs and alternative opportunities for use of resources. The nature of an immediate survival problem is that there are no economic alternatives or substitutes available. Survival is no analogy for the poor who have immediate survival needs. Firms often require cash or goods to meet contractual obligations, and the consequences of breaking a contract can be severe.

A short-term or immediate need for money or resources can cause players to behave very differently than suggested by market theory. Immediate needs can dominate decisions. The survival priority means that profit or happiness may need to take a back seat in the short run.

Survival problems can cause supply response to work that is opposite from the conclusion of economic theory. The theory of labor supply suggests that people work less when wage rates fall. In fact, lower wage rates sometimes force people to work more to maintain the same level of income to meet their subsistence needs. Economic theory suggests that firms should produce less

---

* Comparative statics is the comparison of two or more equilibrium states where the states differ because of some exogenous change to one of the states.

when prices fall. In fact, if there are payments that must be made at the risk of a large cost, the firm may need to sell its inventory or assets at less than cost to pay the bills.

Survival problems have several implications for antimarket behavior. First, market competition can force prices to a point where survival is threatened, and economic players may appeal to society to control or remove the competition. Second, antimarket behavior is sometimes directed to eliminate marginal competitors. Finally, survival sometimes results in innovation as in "necessity is the mother of invention."

FINANCIAL FEASIBILITY

The theory of production in the short run essentially presumes that current variable costs are paid with current revenues and sunk costs are already paid for or can be paid for out of wealth. If costs cannot be paid with revenues in the long run, the firm quits. In the short run, it doesn't matter how sunk costs were paid; sunk costs are ignored. In the real world, there is no rule involving the timing of revenues and expenses. Rather, the rules are the unique rules of contracts. Contracts determine when payments must be paid and when sales income will arrive. The timing of cash income and expenses does not necessarily correspond to the timing of sales or production.

Financial feasibility refers to the ability of the firm or other player to meet its contractual payment obligations. Financial feasibility causes economic behavior different from that of market theory in four ways:

1. The theory of production in the short run finds that the firm will stop production if revenues are less than avoidable costs and all sunk costs are not avoidable so they do not affect the short-run decision. In fact, some costs are unavoidable because they must be paid for now. Therefore, they must be paid in the short run regardless of how much is produced or whether production occurs or not.

The financial requirements created by inescapable commitments can dominate short-run output and sales decisions. Market theory states that sunk costs do not affect short-run decisions, but this is clearly not the case if a payment on the sunk cost must be made now. With financial considerations, sunk costs can affect and even control short-run business decisions.

2. The costs of noncompliance, a contractual term, can be extreme or open-ended. Therefore, a real risk of noncompliance creates a survival problem.

A financial problem occurs when wealth carried into a period, plus revenue obtained in the period, are not enough to pay current financial obligations. The contractual rules of compliance often create a survival problem for players because the penalties of noncompliance are large relative to the cost of the transactions covered in the contract. For example, foreclosure allows for the financier to assume title to the collateral covered by the loan regardless of its value in relation to the amount of debt. Contracts often contain terms that allow parties to make open-ended claims of damages. In any case, the transactions costs, such as legal fees, associated with a broken contract may be large.

3. The pattern of payment for inputs under a contract can be different from their real economic cost, so the incentive for efficient behavior is distorted.

Contracts can create incentives and behavior independent of the real economic costs of resources because the payment required by the contract is not necessarily related to the real economic cost of the resource. Often, a loan requires a fixed payment per unit time. When the true economic cost of the resource is actually related to its use, then the resource is not charged its real economic cost each time period. For example, consider a piece of machinery that depreciates as a function of its use. Depreciation is then an escapable and variable cost, but the payment for the equipment cannot be reduced by producing less, so the real cost of the equipment is not internalized. The owner may continue to produce in the short run as if the equipment were a sunk, nonvariable cost because, from the owner's financial perspective, it is.

It is worthwhile to consider why financial contracts have terms that do not align with the real economic costs of resources. First, the major consideration for the financier is the opportunity cost of money, not the opportunity costs of the resources acquired with that money. Financial contracts could be better tailored to real economic costs and values, but then the financier would be assuming a variable and uncertain pattern of income. Second, firms sign contracts on the basis of expectations. Expectations need not be correct, and the chance of infrequent or extreme events, such as very low prices, may be discounted.

4. The source of money used to finance business can affect behavior, competitiveness, and survival.

Financial obligations can be met with current income, by borrowing, by selling interest in the firm, or with wealth. The availability of these sources of money in combination with variability in revenue and cost patterns often affects business decisions in ways not considered by market economics.

Firms facing exactly the same technology, market, and prices may behave in very different ways depending on whether they were financed internally or externally. Consider a firm that financed its equipment internally with wealth. This firm is more able to act like the firm of market theory; it has more latitude in its production and pricing decisions. If prices fall, it can stop producing and reduce depreciation in the hope that prices will be high enough later to justify production. The internally financed firm may be unable to cover the depreciation or make a return on its investment this year, but at least it does not have to worry about foreclosure. At the same time, the indebted firm may need to expand production to increase revenues to make its payments, perhaps taking a real economic loss in the process.

For the firm who has the luxury of paying for investments or other costs with wealth, real economic costs and prices can be recognized and internalized in the way contemplated by economic theory. Economic wealth provides a firm with competitive advantage in that financial feasibility is less of a constraint to short-run business decisions; the firm can behave more efficiently or strategically. In a condition of falling prices, the wealthy firm might be able to expand production, lower prices a bit more, and force its indebted competitor out of business permanently.

Some economists argue that financial feasibility is a separate issue from economics. This may be an issue of semantics, but still, the worth of economic theory is reduced to the extent that financial considerations and not economic criteria control economic behavior. Clearly, survival problems are more relevant for the more marginal elements of the economy. They have few alternative opportunities in the short run. They accumulate little of the wealth needed to find or purchase other opportunities. Survival problems also become more important when economic conditions are not meeting expectations.

EXPECTATIONS, SUNK COSTS, AND SUPPLY INSTABILITY

The problem of inefficient capacity in supply caused by biased price expectations has been discussed in relation to numerous industries, including agriculture, railroads, and oil. This capacity problem arises in industries having several features. First, each firm cannot know the price of goods it will sell at the time investment decisions must be made. Firms face the seller's temporal information problem. This feature becomes more important as the time separating production decisions from sale exceeds the time within which prices can be predicted. The decision to invest, produce, and supply must be based on expected prices, but expectations may be based on limited price information.

Second, each firm, as required by market theory, responds only to price signals. Each firm then makes the same investment decision based on the same price expectations, but without knowing the plans of other similar sellers. Each firm is the same in that each is similarly ignorant of the other's plans.

The third feature of the capacity problem is that some of the investments become true sunk costs at the industry level. The investments cannot be easily converted to make anything else outside of the industry. Oil wells, fruit trees, passenger jets, and trucking fleets are examples of assets that for all practical purposes have just one use.

When the combined supplies of the similarly optimistic and oblivious firms finally reach the market, prices are forced down along the demand function and become lower than originally expected. The firms cannot sell their assets to recover their costs because the price of the sunk assets becomes less than their original cost, and the assets cannot be converted to other uses.

As Andrew Carnegie explained, "Unusual profits lead to new firms and expanded productive capacity. Supply soon becomes greater than demand, and prices fall to below cost. In industries with large capital investments and a large work force it costs the manufacturer less to run at a loss than to stop production altogether."[1] Firms continue to operate as long as they cover their short-run costs, even though they do not make enough to cover their sunk costs. When supply decisions must be made in advance of trade, and when firms do not share planning information, free enterprise can result in inefficient output levels in that prices do not adjust to average costs.

A market theorist might argue that this problem is not a malfunction from the perspective of economic theory. Rather, it is only a short-run problem. Market theory argues that things will work out in the long run as unprofitable prices cause firms to quit, prices rise, and firms eventually attain the right level of capacity. Given that the past sunk costs cannot be unsunk by anyone, the theorist would say, temporary oversupply is not a problem. Even if firms are foreclosed, the new operator will see that the best option for the inconvertible asset is to continue with production, so output will continue to be optimal given that the asset cannot be converted to other uses.

The first fact ignored by the market theorist is that the capacity problem was created by a market malfunction in the form of misinformation. The problem is caused because firms respond only to prices, exactly as required by market theory, but current prices are not the prices that will eventually be obtained because each firm is unaware of other firm's plans to increase production. The very conditions deemed necessary for efficient markets—freedom of entry and numerous firms independently responding to market prices—can also lead to biased expectations and inefficiency in supply capacity.

Second, the conventional economic argument that equilibrium can be attained in the long run may not be true. The disparity between the timing of investment decisions, the subsequent supply of goods, and the dynamics of price expectations may lead to a permanently unstable market. Misinformation can continue in the long run because people forget, or fail to learn, or because new entrants do not have the benefit of prior experience.

If supply decisions were made by coordinated decisionmaking, then firms would be able to align planning of capacity with demand. In fact, free enterprise has developed market and information systems that provide some capability for coordinated decision making. Modern technology makes more information about production intentions readily available, and futures markets provide some price information and protection. However, the economic life of many productive assets extends beyond the protection provided by futures markets, and firms often choose not to publicize their intentions.

Such economic circumstances can lead economic players to seek market control. When most costs are sunk, then the potential to earn a profit occurs only through revenues, and this requires control of prices and/or quantities sold.

The obvious solution, from the perspective of the industry, is to work together to plan capacity, control production, and increase prices. Market failure provides incentive for market control.

EXPECTATIONS AND SPECULATION

Many economic problems of demand are related to the buyers' problem; buyers typically cannot know exactly what they will be getting at the time they buy. Therefore, buyers' information is not perfect, demand is guided by expectations as opposed to knowledge, and expectations can be wrong. Sometimes, economic players act as buyer/sellers, buying now in the hope of selling at a profit later.

Speculation is an economic problem associated with price expectations. When prices rise, expectations of continued price increases develop. Buyer/sellers then buy based on the expectation of even higher prices later, which further increases prices, which then encourages further speculation. Speculation, like most economic behavior, is driven by self-interest, but expectations and prices become detached from the marginal and average criteria of economic theory. The speculation takes on a life of its own, independent of the forces of market supply and demand. When investors finally decide that prices will rise no more, speculation often ends with chaotic price declines, massive business failures, and economic hardship.

Speculative pressures have often driven real estate markets. In California, the promise of perpetually rising prices was finally broken in the early 1990s. Some southern California homes lost up to one-half of their late-1980s value. Speculation in the 1990s shifted to the intermountain region, where home prices in some areas had fallen in real dollars from the late 1970s to about 1991. As recently as 1990, the price to rent homes often exceeded their mortgage payment because people would not buy homes on the expectation that home prices would continue to decline. But then, the region began to attract new immigrants and business based on relative cost advantages. From 1991 to 1995, home prices in some areas doubled, and people began buying real estate based on the expectation of further price increases.

A most bizarre case of speculation involves Dutch tulips in the seventeenth century. At the height of the speculation, a single rare tulip bulb bought thousands of dollars worth of other goods. The entire Dutch economy became geared toward tulips.[2]

THE THEORY OF THE FIRM, MONOPOLY, AND ENTRY

The problem of natural monopoly was introduced in chapter 2. The conventional natural monopoly occurs because of increasing returns to scale. There is, however, no technical reason why monopoly should not occur with decreasing returns because decreasing returns can be avoided by producing with identical autonomous units of production, each producing at lowest average cost. Free enterprise only results in numerous sellers if there are diseconomies in selling; diseconomies in production do not matter at all.

Natural monopoly has led to regulation of many industries, but decreasing costs alone do not necessarily lead to a monopoly problem that justifies a regulated natural monopoly. First, competitive behavior is ensured by a large number of sellers, not a large number of producers. The natural monopoly problem may be solved by allowing numerous sellers to use the services of one producing unit jointly owned by all the sellers. Second, if the demand function is flat, the monopolist cannot affect price anyway. Third, if the natural monopolist tries to charge a profitable price much higher than average cost, other firms may try to compete. The natural monopolist's prices must still be kept low enough to discourage competitors.

The existence of downward sloping demand, not declining average costs, is often the incentive for monopoly. The steepness of the demand function, not costs, is often the factor that makes monopoly profitable. The steeper the demand function, the more price can be increased by restricting quantity and the more potential for monopoly profits and static economic inefficiency. Therefore, monopolists have incentive to make demand steeper. This can be done with product differentiation, by eliminating substitutes, or by creating complements.

Inefficient monopoly is often obtained, maintained, and enforced by limiting entry. Barriers to the entry of competitors, not cost relationships, are often the cause of successful monopoly. With the exception of strong natural monopolies, the firm must establish and maintain control over entry to sustain substantial monopoly profits.

Mechanisms to limit entry and exploit downward sloping demand are a fundamental attribute of free enterprise. Intellectual property laws, proprietary information, and other property rights limit entrants and establish and maintain monopoly. These rights are discussed extensively later. Sole ownership of critical resources is often used to maintain monopoly. For example, "for many years Alcoa owned almost every source of Bauxite in the United States. This control of resource supply, coupled with certain patent rights, provided Alcoa with an absolute monopoly in aluminum."[3]

When a monopolist makes monopoly profits, these profits can be used to block entry. Control of entry may be bought, as in purchase of critical resources or competitors, or by price cutting below cost in selected markets, or, perhaps, by contributions to the right elected officials who can pass new laws or prod administrators in the right direction. Monopoly is self-sustaining through its profits.

Monopolies are tolerated or granted by government under a variety of rationales, including efficient pricing and investment in natural monopolies, control of production in unstable industries, and national security. Government "establishes the firm as a monopoly in return for various types of control over the price and output policies of the business."[4]

In summary, a declining average cost function can provide incentive for monopoly, but neoclassical economics places far too much emphasis on this factor. The incentives for monopoly are inelastic demand and the potential for control of entry.* The more unique the good, the more inelastic the demand function, the more profits can be increased by control of entry, and, therefore, the larger the incentive to secure the rights to enable that control. Entry is controlled by application of wealth, by law, or both.

A REVIEW OF REGULATED INDUSTRIES

Many industries do not have the freedom to behave like market theory requires. A large segment of the U.S. economy is controlled or substantially affected by government, and market theory has little descriptive merit for these regulated industries. The market model fails as a descriptive device when (1) firms that would otherwise act freely are dominated by regulation, subsidies, or taxation, (2) regulation to make an industry behave more like the firms of free market theory fails to accomplish this purpose, or the regulation is inefficient or ineffective in accomplishing the purpose, or (3) the firm and government develop an exchange relationship (chapter 8).

Some forms of regulation are initiated to force firms to behave more like the stylized firms of market theory. The Antitrust Division of the Department of Justice and the Federal Trade Commission both enforce antitrust and trade laws. The Sherman Antitrust Act was passed in 1890, "declaring it illegal to (a) enter into a contract, combination, or conspiracy in restraint of trade; and to monopolize, attempt to monopolize, or combine or conspire to monopolize trade."[5] The Clayton Act was directed at four restrictive practices: price discrimination, exclusive dealing and tying contracts, acquisition of rivals, and interlocking directorates. The Federal Trade Commission "is an independent administrative agency responsible for the administration of a variety of statutes which, in general, are designed to promote competition and to protect the public from unfair and deceptive acts and practices in the advertising and marketing of goods and services."[6]

Some industries are entirely or partly exempt from some provisions of antitrust laws. Monopoly or partial monopoly has recently been allowed in labor, public utilities, professional baseball, certain activities of exporters, schools and hospitals, public transit and water, military equipment suppliers, and joint newspaper publications.

The Food and Drug Administration concentrates on fair trade where public health and safety are important. Health and safety are concerns of the Consumer

---

* Inelastic means that quantity of the good bought is not very responsive to its price specifically, the percent reduction in quantity demanded is less than the percent increase in price.

Product Safety Commission, the Federal Aviation Administration, the Occupational Safety and Health Administration, the National Safety Council, and the National Highway Traffic Safety Administration. Important environmental regulation falls under the purview of the Environmental Protection Agency, the Nuclear Regulatory Commission, the Army Corps of Engineers, and the Department of Energy.

Financial markets are heavily regulated. Banks are organized either under state and federal laws and are regulated by the state, or by the federal Comptroller of the Currency. The Federal Depositors Insurance Corporation provides free insurance for depositors in exchange for substantial regulation. The Federal Reserve Bank has broad control over interest rates and money supply. Federal credit agencies are supervised by the National Credit Union Administration, and state credit unions are similarly regulated. The price at which banks can offer their deposit services and the types of services that may be offered were recently regulated.[7]

The Securities and Exchange Commission was established in 1934 to protect the public against malpractice and insider trading in stocks, bonds, and financial instruments. The Commodity Futures Trading Commission has similar functions in commodity markets. The Federal Communications Commission, established in 1934, regulates interstate wire and radio communications; perhaps 90 percent of revenues are covered. The Interstate Commerce Commission regulates interstate transportation, and the Federal Energy Regulatory Commission has set rates and charges for transportation and sale of natural gas.

Labor is one of the finest and oldest examples of group control and market intervention through government. The ability of labor to affect its price through labor unions and minimum wages is law. The Equal Employment Opportunity Commission and the National Labor Relations Board have important responsibilities in labor markets.

Insurance is highly regulated, primarily at the state level. States operate unemployment insurance funds, most states set prices for property and casualty insurance, and life insurance reserves are specified by law. Even at the local level, local zoning and other land use planning can be very important, especially to the real estate and construction industries.

There are many more important laws and activities of government that affect business. An industry otherwise able to operate freely can still be substantially influenced by regulation if it requires inputs from, or sells products to, regulated industries. Many industries are strongly affected by a variety of nonregulatory functions of government. Many industries, weapons manufacturers, for example, do most of their business with government. Many industries are strongly affected by taxation or subsidies. Small industries have been created around tax shelters.

These examples suggest a variety of institutional constraints and opportunities facing economic players that are largely ignored by conventional theory. Firms do not passively accept the role of government in their affairs; they make the best of it. For many firms, an important part of the activity of business is dealing with the government. First, they work internally to minimize the costs or maximize the benefits associated with regulation or intervention. Second, they work externally to influence the administration of government's role and, at a higher level, to change the law if possible. Such activities have been termed "creative response." In government-dominated industries, a major economic activity is the influence of government. Government is often a regulator, but it is also a buyer, seller, partner, competitor, the source of innumerable laws and their enforcement, a creator, and a source of subsidies and economic rents.

SUMMARY

This chapter has discussed more problems of conventional production and market theory as a descriptive device. In short, the scope of neoclassical economics is incompatible with many observable economic phenomena in modern mixed economies. Financial feasibility, government, and other institutional factors often influence or control economic decisions. These facts reduce the worth of market theory as an explanatory device. Market theory purports to explain prices, but when prices are controlled by government, speculation, finance, or other factors, the descriptive value of the theory is lost.

Free enterprise create incentives to control economic competition. Downward sloping demand, decreasing average costs, planning and survival problems, and other common incentives lead to market control. Problems of investment and price expectations have frequently resulted in excess supply capacity. Economic efficiency requires that marginal firms will leave the industry when prices fall, but they may not want to leave. Not only does market failure mean that public intervention may be desirable, it also means that private market control may be desirable from the private perspective.

These problems have frequently been recognized by economists, but they have not become part of mainstream economic thought. Usually, market control is believed to be an aberration, perhaps only occasional, temporary, and specific to relatively unimportant goods or industries. In truth, almost every industry exhibits some form of market control. As a result, the market model rarely provides a complete description of the production and trade process. Market imperfections and some degree of market control are the norm, not the exception, and the diversity of exceptions is part of the normal variety of a complex, dynamic economy.

The last four chapters have provided a different perspective on the process and problems of production and exchange. The picture that emerges is one of diversity, but there are still some useful generalizations. There are the conventional problems of minimizing costs and maximizing profit, but these optimization problems are conducted in an enormously diverse environment where almost all factors are potentially subject to influence or control. Particularly, there are problems of information, contracts, and government. Part of the economic problem of players is to improve this environment, and players may not care about the constraints imposed by the conventional theories of production and neoclassical economics.

NOTES

1. Dudley H. Chapman, *Molting Time for Anti-Trust: Market Realities, Economic Fallacies and European Innovations* (New York: Praeger Publishers, 1991), p. 44.

2. Don Paarlberg, "Economic Pathology, Six Cases." *Choices: The Magazine of Food Farm and Resource Issues* (Third Quarter, 1994), p. 17.

3. C. E. Ferguson, and J. P. Gould, *Microeconomic Theory,* Fourth Edition (Homewood, IL: Richard D. Irvin, 1975), p. 261.

4. Ibid., p. 263.

5. Ibid., p. 220.

6. Code of Federal Regulations. 16 Chapter 1 (January 1, 1992 Edition). Federal Trade Commission. Subchapter A, Organization, Procedures and Rules of Practice. Part 0, Organization. p. 4.

7. Carol S. Greenwald, *Banks Are Dangerous to Your Wealth* (Englewood Cliffs, NJ: Prentice-Hall, 1980).

6

Some Definitions and Premises of Antimarket Economics

The theory of antimarket economics proposes that behaviors to escape or control market competition are a normal and important part of free enterprise. The conventional assumptions of market theory are actually endogenous variables that are influenced by players in their self-interest or, indirectly, in response to many diverse problems and opportunities of economic competition. Antimarket theory expands on conventional market theory by increasing the scope and variety of options for exchange and resource allocation, the diversity and functions of economic institutions, and the range of economic behavior that occurs in free enterprise. In contrast to conventional economics:

1. Normal production and trade conditions for a good reflect rent-seeking (antimarket) and rent-dissipating (market) behaviors.

2. Most economic exchange does not occur through competitive markets as defined by market theory.

3. The assumptions of perfect competition—information, property rights, entry, sameness of product, and number of players, as well as cost and market structure—are endogenous variables.

4. Much economic behavior works against markets through these endogenous variables and is destabilizing in relation to market equilibrium.

5. There are usually multiple trade options available for any given good or resource that vary in terms of how well they meet the conditions for market competition.

6. Society has many economic goals other than economic efficiency that result in market

control. Especially, market control for new products is allowed to protect incentives for innovation and to promote technological progress, and property rights to internally developed resources are allowed as a matter of justice even if they result in market control.

Antimarket economics seeks to augment market theory as a overall description of economic behavior. Market theory explains what happens under perfect competition for existing goods and resources. Market theory tells us that market competition is tough and often unprofitable. Antimarket economics reinterprets and extends market theory to explain why new goods and resources are created in free enterprise and why economic behavior is frequently directed to limit market competition. Players create and evaluate new options to alter or expand on existing market opportunities because these new options are expected to be more profitable than competition in existing markets.

Antimarket behavior is either market control or market escape. Control involves existing trade mechanisms, resources, and goods. Market control is the systematic manipulation of some factors assumed by market theory to be uncontrollable: information, prices, quantities, entry, or property. Market escape, on the other hand, is the development of new exchange or goods. Antimarket behavior can also be differentiated according to the variables of economic competition affected. Antimarket behavior includes control of entry, direct control of prices or quantities, or influence of property rights, information or perceptions.

The principle that economic players compare benefits and costs of options is a fundamental precept of economics. Antimarket economics can be viewed as another extension of this principle. While economic theory clearly requires players to compare benefits and costs, market theory does not allow consideration of antimarket options because the market exchange of existing goods is the only option. In antimarket economics, there are many options. Commonly used options, often used in combinations, include the following: product differentiation and protection of entry; creation of new types of trade, goods, technology, or resources; control of information or influence of perceptions; investment in property rights or activities that can help control entry; and influence of government to control entry, production, prices, sales, or the rules of property or exchange.

Most goods are differentiated and some goods are unique, the demand functions for most seller's goods are downward sloping, and most sellers can obtain some degree of market control through property rights or government. Minimal market control is a persistent state of modern free enterprise.

Free enterprise results in a perpetual conflict between antimarket and market forces. Antimarket behavior seeks and creates economic rents by creating trade situations that differ from market competition. Other economic players look for such situations and try to obtain a share of these rents by the mechanics of traditional market competition, usually entry or information. But then, this market competition decreases the economic rent, and the potential returns to new antimarket behaviors becomes relatively more attractive. The conventional equilibrium of market theory is not a likely result in this dynamic environment, but it does happen. Sometimes, a combination of circumstances enables sustained market competition. In other cases, a combination of factors enables sustained antimarket behavior.

The conventional forces of market competition have an antimarket counterpart. Often, the market force and its antimarket counterpart create economic conflict. Table 6.1 provides a summary of the some factors that are important to economic competition, the related market force, and its antimarket counterpart.

Antimarket economics takes a different perspective on the significance of the short run and long run. In the short run, there are only existing goods, technology, and resources as defined by market theory. However, prices and quantities are often controlled by contracts and other commitments. Options for trade and production are limited. In the long run, there is the potential to develop new products, new trade options, and new ways of limiting competition.

Antimarket behaviors can be beneficial for society when they result in creation of new and better products and trade options. Innovation can create temporary economic rents that direct resources to new uses. Economic players, however, would rather make the same economic rents permanently. Often, market control can only be sustained with the help of government, and this intervention can disrupt the market/antimarket mechanics of competition, efficiency, and creation. Sustained market control is often enabled by government, and this form of control is one of the major issues of modern economies.

The remainder of this chapter describes the scope and meaning of antimarket economics in detail. First, to narrow the scope of the discussion, it is useful to overview and categorize all possible types of exchange. This allows a more clear definition of what is meant by antimarket behavior. Then, the logical argument for antimarket economics is summarized and a distinction is drawn between minimal and substantial antimarket behaviors. Substantial behaviors are taken up in detail in later chapters. Finally, antimarket economics is compared to some related economic paradigms.

THE RANGE OF EXCHANGE

Market theory defines one very specific form of exchange. Selfish behavior and other motives interact with a profusion of institutions to create many other forms of exchange. Exchange can be involuntary or voluntary. *Involuntary* exchange occurs when one or more of the persons affected by the exchange did not agree to it. Frequently, a physical taking occurs without the advance intention or consent of either party. Automobile accidents are an example. *Unintentional* and involuntary exchange often ends up in court. The laws of liability and/or a jury define what must be paid and by whom. The court must

Table 6.1
Some Factors of Economic Competition, Conventional Market Force, and
Corresponding Antimarket Force

Factor Important to Economic Competition	Conventional Market Force	Antimarket Counterpart
Buyers' information	Buyers seek information about what they will get and location of sellers	Sellers or other buyers withhold or distort information
Sellers' information	Sellers seek information on prices and location of buyers	Other sellers or buyers withhold information
Producers' information	Producers seek information about production technology	Other producers withhold information
Homogeneity of product	Other producers imitate and sell profitable products	Sellers differentiate product and seek to limit imitators
Number of sellers/buyers	More sellers and buyers enter profitable markets	Existing participants seek to limit entry
Property rights	Owners seek perfect property rights enforced at minimum cost	Nonowners seek to change property rights
Types of goods available in the economy	Markets allocate existing goods efficiently	Innovators develop new goods to profit from control of entry
Role of government in markets	Antitrust, regulate natural monopoly, correct market failure	Supports antimarket behavior to share in profits
Role of government in property rights	Protects and enforces stable property rights and ability to trade property	Takes and/or allocates property for selfish reasons

decide on the appropriate contract to complete the exchange. In another case of unintentional exchange, a trade has inadvertent or incidental effects on a third party other than the buyer or seller. Again, laws frequently define the extent of the third person's right to make a claim against the buyer and/or seller.

Intentional involuntary exchange means that either the buyer or the seller forces exchange on the other. Theft and many economic crimes can be viewed as involuntary exchange with no immediate compensation to the seller, although the victim may be able to make claims later in court. Economic warfare and slavery are also examples. Involuntary exchange can also be perfectly legal.

Under eminent domain, government can take property and reimburse the owner according to specific rules whether or not the owner wants to participate. Taxation is an involuntary exchange, since every citizen must participate regardless of whether or not they are willing.

Sometimes, property rights are uncertain and variable because the law makes them that way. The certainty, limits, and enforcement of property rights define potential for involuntary exchange. When property rights are uncertain or hard to enforce, players direct resources to influence the assignment and enforcement of rights. Divorce and inheritances are often contested because of ambiguities in the law. Some property, such as water rights, comes with conditions for forfeiture, condemnation, abandonment, or adverse possession.

Society creates the rules of property. These rules are subject to influence and interpretation, and the rules may allow for the assignment of property rights to be reconsidered. Civil law allows players to try to claim others' property under a claim of damages. But the jury decides the award, and this amount may or may not be commensurate with the damages. Was the pain caused by a cup of spilled hot coffee worth a million dollars from McDonalds? A jury thought so.

Voluntary exchange, or trade, occurs with the mutual consent of buyer and seller. Market trade is a relative concept judged according to how well it fits the model of perfect markets as defined by market theory. In market trade, each player controls his own internal affairs and interacts with the economy only through trade and prices set by markets. In *extramarket* trade, voluntary exchange occurs completely outside of any market structures or market competition. If there are exchange rates, they may not reflect economic value at all. Self-interest as narrowly defined by market theory is usually not the driving motive. Exchange within the household and charitable donations are examples.

Antimarket trade falls somewhere between market trade and involuntary exchange. When players do not passively accept the assumptions or results of market theory, there is antimarket behavior. Antimarket behavior is intentional divergence from the assumptions of market theory. In general, buyers and sellers are both willing, there are competition and exchange rates, but exchange rates and/or quantities are affected by influence of information or property rights, control of entry, number of sellers, sameness of product, or direct control of prices or market quantities. Involuntary exchange, as in attempts to change property rights, is antimarket behavior when it is an alternative to markets for resource allocation.

THE ARGUMENT FOR ANTIMARKET ECONOMICS

The logical argument for antimarket behavior has three facets. First, there is motive because antimarket behavior is consistent with self-interest. Second, common economic phenomena provide incentive and ability to engage in antimarket behaviors. Third, social institutions exist that allow or encourage it.

The scientific argument also includes the undeniable fact that antimarket behavior can be readily observed, and society has adopted institutions to deal with it. This fact is taken up in later chapters.

Motives and Incentives

Economic motives are the psychological drivers of economic behavior. Market and antimarket theories both presume that profit maximization of firms and utility maximization of consumers are the major drivers of economic behavior. Most of the human race wants more than they have, and the remaining few are busy protecting what they already have.

Value judgments and survival are also important motives, but they are not necessary for antimarket theory. They play supporting roles. Commonly held value judgments become social values that affect the economy in many ways. Important value judgments include altruism, ethics, and morals. Altruism acts on a value judgment concerning what is good. Altruism is important in at least two ways: (1) it provides for disposition of wealth in accordance with a variety of personal ethical and moral principles, and (2) it can result in the manipulation of government to meet altruistic goals. Property rights ethics are important in enabling market control through unique property. Morals and ethics also cause people to try to affect the economic behavior of others, typically through government. Consequently, we have laws limiting pornography, gambling, recreational drugs, and other sins even though markets for these goods might work efficiently. Value judgments tend to be expressed more and have more effect when the private means of the judge are great; the wealthy can afford to promote their value judgments more than the poor.

The belief in the right to survive is a social value, and survival is important to antimarket theory because the risk of catastrophic failure can create incentives for antimarket behaviors. The survival motive occurs when private means are too small in the short run to ensure life (for individuals) or ownership and control of property (for owners of firms and property).

Incentives are characteristics of the good and its trade which condition or allow the expression of motives. Important incentives involve the good—especially, how easily it reveals its characteristics, how mobile it is, and the nature of its property rights. Market-related incentives include risk, information, conditions for entry, number of sellers, and production and demand characteristics. The diversity of these incentives contributes to the diversity of goods, production, and exchange mechanisms. Good information, many sellers, free entry, same product and well-defined property rights are private economic incentives, not constraints.

Together, economic motives and incentives cause players to deliberately and systematically deviate from the assumptions of market theory. To what extent they succeed depends on many factors unique to each industry, good, or input involved. Some of these factors, especially institutions or technology, facilitate, promote, or even require antimarket behavior.

Sellers tend to avoid perfectly competitive markets because they have distinct disadvantages. In summary, disadvantages may include the following:

1. Freedom of entry to many sellers.
2. A high level of price and quality comparison.
3. Competitive pricing near average cost.
4. High transportation, display, and storage costs.
5. Display of unique and valuable qualities to other sellers who may be able to copy them, learn from them, or otherwise gain advantage.

Other economic problems—risk, transactions costs, market failure, imperfect goods, large sunk costs, and financial incentives—were discussed in chapters 3 through 5. These problems can also create incentives for antimarket behavior.

Investment and trade are guided by expectations, not known prices or qualities. Information problems are overcome only at a cost and are an important part of private economic incentives. Players try to change the expectations of others to advance their motives. Sellers influence consumer expectations to increase price and sales, and they influence the expectations of government to obtain favorable legislation and administration. Special interest groups try to influence public opinion by providing biased predictions of the impacts of policy alternatives. Government tries to change the expectations of taxpayers about the costs and results of its economic activities.

Downward sloping demand is a fundamental incentive for market control. Because it means that economic rents can be obtained by restricting total quantity sold. Quantity can be reduced by collusion, by eliminating competitors, or by restricted entry. Downward sloping demand creates incentive for the innovation of unique products that are highly valued and have few substitutes.

The potential for market equilibrium in free enterprise provides a substantial incentive for antimarket behavior. Market forces that would result in stable market equilibrium are constantly in conflict with antimarket forces seeking to avoid or destabilize it. Market theory sees disequilibrium as a temporary state on the way to equilibrium, but when disequilibrium is profitable, profits create incentive and perhaps the ability to maintain the disequilibrium. Market disequilibrium, as defined by market theory, can be a stable condition created by players and perhaps enabled and sustained by law.

The Means for Antimarket Behaviors

The means for antimarket trade enables the behavior. The means can be economic, institutional, and/or physical. The economic means is the economic power required and applied to engage in and sustain the antimarket exchange. The institutional means is the exchange and property rules and forums where the antimarket behavior can occur. The physical means defines how quantities can be physically controlled to create or enhance market control.

The Economic Means. When antimarket behavior is costly, economic wealth is the economic means that enables players to engage in or continue the behavior. Economic wealth can destabilize perfect markets because it provides the resources needed to help players overcome market conditions. Wealth can be used to buy competitors, to contribute to re-election campaigns, to invest in innovations, or to operate at a temporary loss to drive less wealthy competitors out of business.

Wealth is the economic means for market control, and wealth can be created by market control. If any pre-existing situation included market control, then the profit obtained from that control can provide the means to sustain or initiate more antimarket behavior. For example, the profits obtained from patented drugs are invested in the development of more drugs, and the profits obtained from farm programs become contributions to benevolent congressmen. Market control can be financially self-sustaining.

In the conventional theory with dissimilar firms, there is economic profit, or economic rent, in the long-run equilibrium. For example, some farmers earn sustained profit in market competition merely because they have exceptional climate or soils. These better situated firms can use this economic rent to finance efforts to improve on their market opportunities.

In conventional long-run market equilibrium with identical firms, producer profits are driven to zero as price is driven to average cost. Increases in demand due to increasing population or changing tastes merely increase the number of sellers, so profits remain negligible. Maximizing and successful players generally understand this result and seek to improve their lot through market control or escape. If product demand is upward-sloping, there is profit potential, but the firms are caught in a catch 22; they need resources to establish market control, but they cannot make economic rents until they have market control. They must appeal for help using institutional means—typically, government.

This type of process resulted in market control for labor. Firms were hiring labor at a wage rate that barely provided for survival. Labor had no excess wealth to buy market control, but labor was able to exert control by monopolizing, striking, and stopping entry. Early in the history of the labor movement, there was very little wealth to finance the living costs of striking labor, and survival was a real concern. Appeal to social values, the support of wealthy sympathizers, and, finally, government intervention secured the labor laws and unions now enjoyed by labor in Western mixed economies.

The Institutional Means. The institutional means for antimarket behavior include private exchange, property and production rules and conventions, and formal laws made and enforced by government.

A variety of private trade conventions define the process, forums, and rules of trade—the immediate expectations of market participants about the exchange process. Trade conventions include informal customs and traditions concerning the roles and behavior of buyers, sellers, and market managers. Typically, private markets also have formal rules to regulate conduct, protect participants, and enhance the reputation of the market. Private trade rules may explicitly require, allow, or protect market control; for example, exclusives and franchises. Players who want to participate in the trade forum must play by the rules.

Collusion is deliberate joint activity to escape or distort markets by jointly controlling exchange rates or quantities. Free enterprise societies have long recognized the need for social restraints on collusion. Assembly for group decisionmaking is an institutional means for collusion incidental to another goal: freedom of assembly. Adam Smith, a recognized founder of free market theory, said, "People of the same trade seldom meet together, even for merriment and diversions, but the conversation ends in a conspiracy against the public, or in some contrivance to raise prices."[1]

Government. Government has many purposes and roles with respect to antimarket behavior. The behavior may be illegal, regulated, allowed, ignored, subsidized, or even required. Government involvement occurs through establishment, definition, and protection of property rights, regulation of exchange or production, exemptions from and enforcement of antitrust laws, monopolies or other market control specifically granted by government, public ownership, and activities in production and consumption. Government alters exchange or property rights under public or interest group pressure or simply under the pressure of government self-interest.

Market control can be enabled by property rights, which allow their owner to limit entry. These laws are proprietary information, intellectual property, and real property laws. Product identification and diversification are protected by trademark laws that allow investments in promotion, advertising, and packaging to be protected. Government helps players enforce and protect these rights. If a competitor copies trademarks, government will help prosecute. The firm can sue its employees with the help of the state for violating noncompetition or nondisclosure agreements. Rights to privacy can also be used to facilitate market control. For example, the state can prosecute anyone who attempts to break into a firm to read customer lists or blueprints. Other federal laws create incidental market control. Farm programs increase the costs of entry to new farmers by driving up land prices. Environmental or zoning laws are used to gain competitive edge.

Many laws recognize the efficiency and equity problems caused by antimarket behaviors in free enterprise, and a substantial amount of resources is used by government to mold the economy into the perfect competition model. However, these actions often do not provide enough disincentive in terms of risks and penalties to prevent the behavior, and the very laws developed to reduce antimarket behavior can be twisted into the means that enable it (chapter 8).

The Physical Means. The physical means for antimarket behaviors involve the technology and devices used to control information or physical quantities. Locks, safes, walls, and computer access codes are the physical means for information control. Technology has greatly facilitated the flow of information about goods and markets, but it has also facilitated control of information and misinformation, mass advertising being a case in point.

Physical quantities are controlled at the point of production, storage, transportation, or sale. Storage and transportation allow for strategic manipulation of the amount sold and where it is sold, and they allow buyers more latitude in how much they purchase and where they shop. Storage can be used to control sales even when production is not controlled. For example, government-owned commodity storage is used to facilitate agricultural price support operations. Storage can also be used to avoid market control. Inventory can be used to fill orders while production labor strikes.

When there are many sellers, physical control is often used to implement a control because the institutional means are not sufficient. While all sellers presumably stand to gain from a cartel, each seller can gain even more by cheating the cartel. This problem can make the cartel unstable, so cartel agreements may allow for centrally controlled sales and monitoring to enforce the agreement.

THE RANGE OF ANTIMARKET BEHAVIOR

Some antimarket behavior is not especially interesting because it is not an issue. Either society believes that system works well enough, or the property rights and responsibilities involved are perfectly clear or inviolate. The purpose of this section is to clearly distinguish the forms of antimarket behavior that create significant social issues.

Antimarket behaviors in exchange can be organized according to the following:

1. How they operate with respect to the law. Behaviors are *legal* or *illegal*. Legal behaviors are allowed, encouraged, and/or required. Illegal behaviors are not uncommon. Their use and prevalence is affected by tolerance, ethics, risk, potential benefits and costs, and interpretation of the law. The difference between legal and illegal is often a very fine line.

For some illegal behaviors, players are able to diverge so slightly from the law that they are able to get away with it. They are either tolerated or not noticed. Two isolated gas station operators, for example, can fix gas prices so long as their prices are not far removed from average gas prices. Strictly speaking such activities are in violation of the law, but they continue by custom, silence, the burden of proof, and/or lack of resources for enforcement. A minimum divergence from perfect market conditions means that illegal behavior is harder to prove. At any rate, it is not perceived as a big problem.

2. How they are viewed by society. Most generally, they are viewed *favorably* or *unfavorably*. The significance of this distinction is that social perception affects whether the behavior may be allowed to continue and at what cost.

3. The degree of divergence from exchange under free competition. Behavior can range from *minimal* to *substantial*.

Minimal Behaviors

Antimarket behavior is a fundamental means of success in free enterprise. But the behavior does not need to be complete to be successful; it is a matter of degrees. When profit margins are measured as a few percentage points of revenue, a little influence can go a long way. Most firms are able to obtain a minimal deviation from perfect market conditions and extract profit that would be unavailable under perfect competition. Minimal behaviors represent only a small divergence from a free market condition. One or more of the assumptions of perfect competition are violated but only to a small, often inconspicuous degree. There is some control of entry, information, or more directly, prices or quantities, but the impact is not large relative to a free market condition.

Minimal behaviors may be legal or illegal and viewed favorably or unfavorably, but overall there is not a major issue. Society is so accustomed to them that we do not even consider them to be a deviation from market conditions. Their significance lies in their prevalence, not their magnitude. Product differentiation, trademarks, limited sales regions, noncompetition agreements, franchises, sales exclusives, and proprietary information are all used to obtain minimal market control. Practically all consumer products are differentiated and a variety of contracts are used to limit sales of the product. Deceptive trade practices and restraint of trade are not uncommon, often occurring in degrees that can be tolerated, undetected, or fall within the limits of the law.

Product differentiation deviates from perfect competition in that products are made slightly different or are represented as being better or different from other sellers' same products. Company or product goodwill can be used to differentiate a product and obtain a price premium. Trademarks and other name protection means that other potential entrants cannot sell the same goodwill.

Trademark protection allows the owner to obtain a price premium by control of entry into the sale of the trademarked product. Every owner of a trademark has a monopoly, but the steepness of the demand function depends on the amount of uniqueness associated with the trademark. The trademark is private property, and entry is denied. A small monopoly profit can be obtained because demand for that unique product is downward sloping. Minimal control is often characterized by elastic, but not perfectly elastic, demand. A combination of standardization, mass production, labeling and trademark protection is among the most common and successful forms of minimal market control. This combination mitigates the buyer's prediction problem, but it also enables differentiation. Hamburgers and hotels were formerly produced by many small sellers, so buyers faced large quality and taste variations. Now, near-identical hamburgers and hotels are produced in mass quantities by a handful of differentiated franchises.

Sales regions and sales exclusives authorize an exclusive right to market a certain product in a certain region. The owner of a franchise is similarly able to stop the entry of another seller of the same product into a specified region. Each franchise provides exclusive marketing rights to its representatives within a defined region, and entry to others is limited.

Some markets are created by sellers to provide a variety of different products to buyers, for example, a mall or a crafts fair. The market may limit the number of sellers of same or similar items to protect sellers. Only one seller of the same type of good, such as a shoe store or music store will be admitted, and later applicants will be denied. Competition between same products is intentionally limited, and a small amount of market control is created.

Many laws can create small or large divergence from free enterprise depending on circumstances unique to the firm or industry. Labor laws provide market control through minimum wages, collective bargaining, and other mechanisms. Labor laws provide minimum control in some cases, but more substantial control in others. Whether or not such control is minimal depends on what wages and labor conditions would exist without the labor law. Labor laws create a minimum divergence in hi-tech industries where the price of labor is unaffected by labor laws; the supply and cost of suitable labor is limited by other factors. Labor laws can create substantial divergence from perfect markets in manufacturing and other industries that use a lot of readily available labor.

Privacy of information frequently provides sellers with minimal market control by enabling control of entry. The private information may be names of buyers, prices charged, sources and prices of inputs, production details, and the exact composition of products. Some of the information might be obtained by competitors at a cost, but this cost can be a deterrent to entry.

Implications of Minimum Control. The result of legal minimum control is that society gives up some static economic efficiency for other social and economic goals or benefits. We allow proprietary information because we believe that information developed with costs and risks should be protectible, and we understand that protection is necessary to provide incentive for innovation and business development. We also allow standardization and labeling because it encourages product quality. We allow labor unions so that laborers are ensured civilized working conditions and a decent standard of living. We allow some minimum illegal controls because the cost of enforcing perfect competition is not worth the benefits.

Many industries meet the technical requirements for perfect competition, but perfect markets with identical firms can result in very small economic returns. These industries may not generate acceptable incomes given social expectations for standards of living or economic growth. Market control has frequently been allowed in these conditions, for example, airlines, trucking, and agriculture. Minimal market control can increase stability, innovation, and the personal incomes of those in the industry. Franchises, sales exclusives, and similar controls extend a degree of job security and stability and encourage loyalty, efficiency, and experience.

The implications of differentiation are a little more complicated. Firms are certainly better off, assuming they can control entry into sales of the differentiated product. But consumers buy according to their expectation of getting something better. Later, they may realize that they did not get something better. But, if consumers are fooled and are happier because of it, who's to say they are wrong? Product differentiation provides some aesthetic values through variety, even if that variety is only in packaging and in the minds of buyers.

By definition, minimum antimarket behaviors are not especially important to society in that the result is not much different from the situation without the behavior. The status quo is acceptable, if not perfect. There is not much loss of static efficiency or enormous gains in other economic goals. The significance of minimum behaviors is that so many industries have been able to capitalize on them. Most consumer goods are now sold under some protection provided by intellectual property rights, trademarks, or labeling. Western economies have been transformed by these types of property rights. The cost of this transformation has been the variety created by millions of independent small producers and retailers, but the benefit has been economic stability and reduced buyers' risk.

Substantial Antimarket Behavior

On the other end of the scale, substantial antimarket behavior operates in gross violation of the principles of market theory. Exchange occurs in ways completely unlike the free market paradigm. There is substantial control of entry, information, prices or quantities, and the result is very different from that proposed by market theory.

Illegal Substantial Controls. Illegal substantial controls are frequently characterized by deception and/or coercion. Common examples include swindles, fraud, hoaxes, racketeering, scams, extortion, bribery, graft, blackmail, payoffs, and kickbacks. Many illegal controls are involuntary. Again, there is a matter of degree. When is advertising merely deceptive and when is it fraudulent?

Free enterprise does not lead to free markets unless costs and risks restrain illegal behaviors. Culture plays an important role. Social values are important in the control of antimarket behaviors. A common ethics favoring truth, freedom, honest trade, and a belief in property rights as opposed to deception and coercion limits such behaviors.

Illegal behaviors can dominate an economy; the former Soviet Union is a case in point. A report prepared for the new Russian government claimed 70 to 80 percent of private enterprise in major cities is forced to pay a tribute of 10 to 20 percent in the form of embezzlement, kickbacks, blackmail, extortion, money laundering, bribes, and monopoly pricing.[2] Police frequently participate, so enforcement of what laws there are is limited. Russian communism was largely a system of involuntary exchange, and Russia could again become an economy dominated by coercion and deception. Still, many observers find that progress is being made.

In the United States, we have our own organized crime as a form of antimarket behavior. Arguably, a strong belief in the value and right to free trade is what keeps organized crime from becoming more influential. Economic crime makes for interesting benefit-cost analysis and stimulating reading, but most economic crime is simple in that it is unambiguously viewed as malignant, and our knowledge of it is limited only by the intelligence of the perpetrators and the diligence of the media.

More interesting illegal behaviors include those covered by antitrust and deceptive trade laws. The media plays an important role in exposing and publicizing deceptive trade. *60 Minutes*, the most popular television program for years during the 1980s, sometimes uses its own devious techniques to uncover and embarrass perpetrators before millions. Consumer groups such as Naderites are also important. Private and public services provide information that helps consumers avoid deceptive trade.

Antitrust laws were discussed in chapter 5 and are taken up in more detail in chapter 8. For the profit maximizing firm, the fact that some behaviors are illegal raises three questions: (1) do the expected benefits exceed the potential costs and penalties; (2) can we somehow be excluded from the law or avoid it; and (3) can we use it against our competitors. Penalties are normally not a constraint, and they often provide little disincentive. "It might be said that the mild, seldom imposed penalties allowed by the antitrust laws exert approximately the same impact on actual conduct as the New Testament did upon the conspirators of Watergate."[3]

Legal Substantial Behaviors. Legal substantial behaviors are among the most debated economic issues in free enterprise societies. The debate involves the proper interface between government, law, and the economy, often balancing private rights and wealth against other social goals and values. The role of government can be to allow it, support it, require it, or own it. In agriculture, for example, the government allows marketing cooperatives some exemption from Sherman Act antitrust legislation, supports commodity market control through farm program expenditures, requires grading of some food products in ways that limit the amount of fresh market sales, and owns grain storage space which can be used to control supply. Governments often own enough of a resource or good to qualify as a monopolist. The postal service, public roads and schools, and the military are examples. In some regions, the federal government owns enough of the land to exert substantial influence over prices of land and land-based natural resources.

Legal substantial behaviors can be classified by the reason for their legality. Through intellectual property law, society allows for complete but temporary control of entry to protect research investments and preserve incentives for innovation. Market failure has been used to argue for intervention or public ownership. In regulated natural monopolies, the law allows only one entity to supply a good or service, typically to a specified geographic area. Some common examples include "municipal waterworks, electrical power companies, sewage disposal systems, telephone companies, and many transportation services."[4] Prices are regulated, and entry is denied to other firms. Market control is allowed by government to transfer economic surplus to favored groups of society. Farm programs (chapter 9) have been justified by arguing that farmers as a group are disadvantaged and, therefore, deserve the help. Labor has secured market control by similar arguments. Market control in international trade is implemented to favor exporters or manufacturers under the justification that free trade conditions are otherwise violated.

Dynamic politics and public sentiment create a changing mix of laws and dynamic industrial structure. Recent deregulation of the energy, banking, airlines, trucking, and telephone industries has brought new opportunities for old-fashioned efficiency, but there have been unforeseen problems as well. Prior to 1980, the Interstate Commerce Commission regulated interstate trucking and limited entry. The Motor Carrier Act of 1980 deregulated the trucking industry. From 1979 to 1990, the number of interstate operating licenses more than doubled. By 1992, more than half of the largest trucking companies were out of business. Was this an efficient adjustment or the result of inefficient competition? The airline industry was deregulated in 1978. Nineteen ninety was the "worst financial year in American aviation history" with $3.9 billion in losses. By 1992 seven major airlines—Pan American, Eastern, Braniff, Continental, Midway, Trans World Airlines and America West Airlines—were in bankruptcy court.[5]

Regardless of the theory of efficiency and the potential cost savings to consumers, trucking and airline deregulation brought some undesirable results: unprecedented rates of entry and departure, increased pressure on employee wages and benefits, and safety issues. Some of this might be expected from market theory alone, but some also suggest long-term structural difficulties in adjusting to competitive conditions.

When should market control be made legal or illegal? What is the proper role of government? How do we know if and when the market control should be changed? Many economists argue from ideology. One group, appealing to market theory, argues that unfettered markets are the best possible solution. The other group, rationalizing from a variety of perspectives, argues that government should play a larger role in managing the economy. A more balanced view is simply that markets and governments regularly succeed and fail in their economic functions, but we need to be more aware of and concerned when they fail. Economics should be problem oriented, and each problem should be taken case by case.

Society places value judgments on market control according to whether the control is viewed favorably or unfavorably. For the purpose of our economic science, we should not say whether a control is good or bad because this is a value judgment. The importance of the distinction is that societies' opinions affect the ability of the control to be established or continue. In general, legal controls are viewed favorably, and illegal controls are viewed unfavorably. Cases in which this is not true suggest that a change to the existing condition may be considered. There is an issue.

Players invest in public opinion to create issues and to swing the balance of opinion when there is an issue. They spend money to advertise, organize, and convince the public and to convince politicians that their opinions are important to the public. The influence of government through social opinion is an important activity of business, government, and others having a large interest in government intervention.

A SUMMARY OF MARKET AND ANTIMARKET THEORIES

Economic behavior in free enterprise is a quest for something better. It is the search, development, and implementation of better options, and existing markets are just one of many options. "The word enterprise points directly to the nature of business as a venture into the unknown. Businessmen are explorers, sometimes suffering shipwreck by their bold conceptions, sometimes hitting on a path leading to revolutionary technical success."[6] The experts in applied antimarket economics are one step ahead of competitors, their customers, or the law. They are innovators of products, marketing strategies, and relations with consumers, government, and the public. They affect their destiny by reducing or eliminating market competition in the academic sense of market theory. They may create some good things along the way. The conditions and problems of free markets become opportunities, not constraints.

Antimarket theory suggests that a combination of market forces and antimarket behaviors create a dynamic and unstable economy. Innovation occurs with the expectation of profit from temporary market control. New products change patterns of complements and substitutes and increase the selection of products available to consumers. Players seek market control for existing products through control of entry and perceptions. Control of entry is obtained with proprietary information, differentiation with identity protection, or through government. In any case, the rents created by market control become the incentive for the traditional competition of market economics. Increased competition decreases economic rents and makes new antimarket behaviors a relatively favorable option.

Two fundamental results of antimarket theory are as follows:

1. *There are no set welfare implications of market or antimarket behaviors.* Market control can increase economic and social welfare through correction of market failure, innovation, diversification, and stability, and market control is sometimes consistent with other social goals such as private property rights. On the other hand, market control can also have undesirable effects through diminished allocative efficiency and conflicts with other social values. Therefore, there are no generally useful rules about the social value of market or antimarket exchange.

2. *Market/antimarket dynamics result in variety and diversity*. Economic activity is affected by many diverse circumstances and goals: information, technology and costs, exchange mechanisms and forums, and the role of government, and economic competition tends to increase diversity. Therefore, economists must understand and face the facts in each unique case before any predictions or conclusions will be valid.

A simple summary comparison of market and antimarket theories is provided in Table 6.2. Antimarket theory expands on market theory by recognizing that competition involves not just competition through the marketplace; rather, the focus of competition is manipulated, modified, or even replaced to yield the greatest possible benefit. "There are more forms of competition than those hailed by economists."[7] Economic players do not passively accept markets, market exchange, and market prices. They evaluate them, subvert them, mold them, avoid them, control them, develop new ones or destroy them, whichever way is expected to work out the best. Economics needs a broader view of free enterprise. By definition, free enterprise is a free-for-all, tempered only by the intrusion of law, ethics, and morality. Free enterprise is all about opportunism, and no economic theory should try to limit the scope of opportunities that may be devised by humans.

OTHER THEORIES OF MARKET FAILURE AND CONTROL

Antimarket theory has close ties to parts of neoclassical theory and several other economic fields and paradigms that have not been formally linked in the past. Neoclassical theories of imperfect competition and market failure; the problems of antitrust, public choice, and evolutionary economics; the theories of Schumpeter and the new growth economists; and the study of rent-seeking and capture theory have underlying similarities. They all involve economic activity that is an alternative to market exchange; they show why maximization may conflict with markets; and they can be interpreted to help explain how and why antimarket behavior develops in free enterprise. The facts of market control are recognized, but the different paradigms focus on specific types of control.

The link between theories of imperfect competition and neoclassical economics may have been forged by Adam Smith or even earlier economists, but imperfect competition became a mainstream topic with Edward Chamberlin's *The Theory of Monopolistic Competition* and Joan Robinson's *The Economics of Imperfect Competition*.[8] Neoclassical economics has fashioned the ideas of imperfect competition to fit its methods of comparative statics, deductive logic, and mathematics. The reasons for imperfect competition tend to focus on technical imperfections, such as declining average costs, or the number of sellers is taken as a given. The neoclassical view of market control is limited because it does not emphasize how and why control of entry is obtained and enforced. Product differentiation has been recognized, but the argument for differentiation has not been extended far enough to reveal the ultimate shortcomings of market

Table 6.2
A Simple Comparison of Market and Antimarket Theories

Market Theory	Antimarket Theory	Consequence
General Approach and Assumptions		
Selfish behavior constrained	Selfish behavior removes constraints. Players seek to escape or control the conditions for free markets	*A priori,* anything goes. Diversification, market control, innovation
The worth of free enterprise is static economic efficiency	The worth of free enterprise is also technical progress, freedom, responsibility, private property, etc.	Market theory largely ignores normative implications of other values
Economic competition results in equilibrium prices and quantities	Equilibrium is a relic of improper deductive reasoning	Free enterprise leads to dynamic prices and quantities
Information, Goods, and Property Rights		
Sellers make supply decisions based on known prices	Sellers usually do not know prices in time	Sellers seek to control markets and future prices
Players operating independently promote efficiency; the invisible hand	If players operate independently no one knows what anyone else is doing	Potential for inefficient supply planning
Buyers know what they are getting	Buyers frequently cannot know what they are getting	Sellers standardize and/or deceive buyers: buyers shop more
Perfect information; information is nonrival and nonexclusive	Private information; information is a rival and exclusive good	Information endogenous and is withheld as private property
Private property rights	Property rights can be affected	Property rights endogenous
Production and Trade		
Market control is a special case	Limited market control is pervasive	Much economic profit arises from market control
Short-run decisions a function of price and variable costs	Short-run decisions a function of contracts, a variety of costs, and expectations	Diverse short-run problems
Prices set by markets	Prices set by sellers or negotiation	Pricing controlled by average costs, strategy, expectations
Financial feasibility not an economic issue	Financial feasibility may control economic decisions	Financial survival may preclude short-run efficiency
Private deals in the mutual interest	Private deals often do not end in the mutual interest	Static efficiency may not follow
Static framework considers one trade option at a time	Buyers and sellers face many trade options, and they create and change trade options	Players create and select from options that differ in extent they vary from perfect competition

theory. Essentially, comparative statics can only provide a partial view of economic systems because maximization always works to disrupt a static situation.

Producer surplus created by market trade or market control is carried into future periods as wealth. In market theory, wealth becomes the initial stock of resources to be allocated by trade. In fact, profits may be used for a variety of things that have a variety of welfare implications. Profits may be invested in research, used to buy competitors, doled out as political contributions, or used to fund economic warfare. Market theory considers all dollars of producer surplus to be the same, so these potential uses and their implications are not considered.

Environmental Economics

Environmental economics has developed many important arguments regarding market failure. The field has recognized that imperfect goods with transactions costs can create inefficiency, but the debate has centered mostly on proscriptions for property rights and exchange and potential losses in static efficiency. The traditional economic view of environmental problems is that they can be fixed by making the assumptions of perfect competition hold, or that excessive transactions costs can make them inefficient to fix.

The theory of antimarket economics does not provide any result as to whether imperfections in property rights, technology, or expectations result in undesirable behaviors because there are no presumptions concerning the other assumptions (the theory of the second-best always pertains), the costs of correcting imperfections, or even the economic welfare implications of more perfect competition. Once it is admitted that the assumptions of market theory may not be true, the conventional economic theory of welfare falls apart. If imperfections can be fixed costlessly, then the fix may be a good idea. But reality is usually much more complex. New institutions developed to deal with environmental problems or other market failure often become a source of problems unforeseen at the time of their invention.

Environmental economics has developed many concepts that are valuable to antimarket economics. Especially, transactions costs and certain attributes of property rights are important to both environmental and antimarket economics. Nonexclusive rights create problems for environmental goods, but they also create problems for all property generally. Property that can be taken may be taken, and this behavior can be an alternative to market exchange. Also, nonexclusive information about how goods are made supports market behavior but discourages innovation.

Rent-seeking, Capture Theory, and Public Choice

The idea that private players seek market control through government has a long history. Notable authors in recent times include Anne Krueger, George Stigler, and James Buchanon.[9] Public choice theory has provided much documentation of antimarket behavior through government. The self-interest of firms in controlling government and restricting voluntary exchange is recognized. Chapter 8 includes more references from the public choice school. Public choice economics tends to take a free market perspective on the problems of market control caused by government intervention. For example, "I shall take as self-evident the welfare economics of free trade." Not surprisingly, then, "it may be in the direct economic interest of each group, taken in isolation and independently, to support a shift in regime toward free trade."[10] This view ignores important information and transactions costs and other factors that always provide incentive for some players to limit free trade (chapter 8).

Institutional Economics and J. K. Galbraith

Institutional and evolutionary economics are rather complex paradigms of economic study. In general, institutionalists concentrate on institutions such as law, technology, property rights or industry. The unit of analysis is often formal or informal social institutions rather than the individuals of neoclassical economics. The method of institutionalists tends to be descriptive instead of quantitative. There is great variety in the perspectives and interests of institutionalists, so it is difficult to generalize about them.[11]

Antimarket economics draws from institutional economics in its recognition of social institutions and social values. Especially, antimarket economics is concerned with how institutions enable antimarket behavior. The central emphasis, however, or point of reference of economics should involve trade and the behaviors that lead to trade. This is where the action is. Still, many institutionalists would probably agree with most of the premises and concepts of antimarket economics. "The fathers of institutionalism were intellectual rebels" and pragmatists, two brands of characters that economics might use more of.[12]

John Kenneth Galbraith was concerned with market control, especially in relation to technology and planning.[13] In his view, modern industrial technology requires planning, and planning requires control of quantities and prices. This is made possible by large firms, vertical integration, control of other firms, and forward contracts. He saw an economy planned by the needs of technology.

Chapter 4 discussed the importance of contracts in fixing prices and quantities in the short run. Antimarket theory differs from Dr. Galbraith's view in that market control is not caused by technology. Planning and contracts are part of the supply process that normally requires that supply decisions be made in advance of sales, and this problem of supply is not necessarily related to technology. Sometimes, technology reduces the need for planning because technology can reduce the time required to produce something. Technology has enabled a variety of enhanced marketing techniques, such as futures markets, that increase the availability of information, encourage efficiency, and reduce some incentives for market control. Supply, rather than technology, benefits from planning and contracts. Technology, not planning, requires market control in the form of proprietary information.

Rather than being a response to technology, market control is simply a natural consequence of the self-interest. It is one possible strategy to accumulate wealth and deal with risk, market failure, and other business problems. It is one strategy for society to promote progress, survival, or other social goals. Market control is as old as free enterprise. Many early and primitive economies had slavery and central control of their economies—the most basic forms of market control. Market and antimarket behaviors have always occurred together because they are part of the same process. Each provides incentive for the other.

Galbraith argued that firms control demand because planning requires it. In general, the idea that demand can be so completely controlled in the long run that firms can plan to simultaneously set prices and quantities is untenable because the new products and improvements being introduced by competitors will disrupt the best of plans. Still, antimarket economics agrees with Galbraith's view that demand can be and is profoundly affected by firms. Firms can affect demand merely because consumption occurs after purchase, and purchase occurs after buyers' expectations are formed. Goods differ considerably in how well they reveal their true attributes, and this affects the ability to affect demand. Firms affect demand merely to the extent that it is profitable.

Antimarket Economics in an Evolving Economy

Bionomics argues that self-interest and competition force the economy to evolve according to the rules of natural selection. "Capitalism is simply the process by which technology evolves."[14] Bionomics argues that capitalism is the natural result of economic competition.

The argument for an economy that evolves by natural selection is a good one. Firms live and die much like the living organisms of evolutionary theory. Market economics is analogous to the short-run balance of nature. Given the existing mix of technology and resources, competition selects those who can survive. Antimarket economics is more analogous to the process of species diversification. Species and economic players seek a niche where they can survive. This search may result in new niches and new species so the diversity of life and economic activity increase over time. Capitalism may be the natural result of economic competition, but capitalism also changes with competition.

There are fundamental differences between economic evolution and natural selection. Especially, the process of change is fundamentally different. Species change by mutation, survival, and reproduction, but economic players plan to change. In economic evolution, technical information and diversity is created intentionally. Human institutions may age and die, but they can also continue without death or reproduction. Human institutions, unlike species, can live, plan, and change simultaneously.

Schumpeter's Theory of Dynamic Competition

The antimarket view of innovation is similar to the process of dynamic competition as defined by Joseph Schumpeter. Schumpeter realized that innovation disturbs market equilibrium, that innovation creates temporary monopoly, and that monopoly profits created by innovation create incentive for others to enter the market. Schumpeter strongly believed that "entrepreneurial activity is the only means of access to profit under competitive assumptions."[15] Schumpeter, however, did not emphasize that economic rents created by market control are the major incentive behind innovation. He "scarcely discussed the origins of innovation."[16] Schumpeter apparently believed that the incentives for innovation were largely "the will to succeed, the joy in being creative, the urge to found a dynasty."[17] "Schumpeter seemed anxious to avoid emphasizing the pursuit of profit."[18]

As research and innovation become more the province of large institutions, profit, not individual incentives, drives innovation. Perhaps Schumpeter did not fully recognize that increased competitive pressures in markets for existing products must drive innovation because he believed that innovation was not driven primarily by profit. Still Schumpeter deserves credit for his first analysis of market/antimarket dynamics in relation to innovation and disequilibrium.

New Growth Economics

The new growth economics is concerned with a general theory of endogenous economic growth and innovation as an endogenous process. The roots of this school of thought are generally related to macroeconomic and neoclassical growth theory and early research on learning, research, and development that began in the late 1950s. In general, it is recognized that "technological advance comes from things that people do" and "temporary monopoly power is a motivating force in the innovative process."[19] The latter fact requires a growth model with imperfect competition, which was accomplished by the late 1980s. By the mid-1990s, "I am convinced that both markets and free trade are good, but the traditional answer that we give to students to explain why they are good, the one based on perfect competition and Pareto Optimality, is becoming untenable. Something more interesting and more complicated is going on here."[20]

The new growth theorists have also begun to recognize the inherent conflict between market theory and innovation. "First, efficiency dictates marginal cost pricing, but innovation requires the existence of monopoly profits. Second, efficiency demands that investment returns be fully appropriable, but the characteristics of knowledge suggest that spillovers will be prevalent."[21]

Antimarket economics differs from new growth theory in several ways. The scope of antimarket economics is larger than the scope of new growth theory. Maximization and survival motives can lead to a variety of behaviors that can potentially cause any aspect of the economy to become endogenous. The firm may choose to innovate, but it may also choose to invest in market control for existing products. Again, antimarket theory might be thought of simply as a broader perspective on the reasons, roles, and results of market control and other antimarket behaviors.

Game Theory

Game theory is not an economic theory as such, but rather, an approach to modeling of strategic problems in which "the fate of an individual . . . depends not only on his own actions, but also on the actions of the rest of the group."[22] "Players act in an environment where other players' decisions influence their payoffs."[23] Game theory has been applied to problems of imperfect competition, dominance, negotiation and bargaining, cooperation and alliances, and imperfect information, among other ideas. The field has recently grown very fast with literally hundreds of new books and a number of journals competing for the attention of economists and other social scientists.

In economic applications, there is typically a finite number of rational players, and the players have economic goals such as maximizing profit. The rules of the game involve allowable moves, strategies, coalitions, and other rules of competition, as well as assumptions about information and learning. Game theory is the logic of the procession of the game given the rules and behavioral assumptions about the players. The logic may follow the sequence of the game as each player makes his move, or reduced forms can sometimes be used to view final outcomes which are often interpreted as equilibrium.

The sequential nature of game theory has made it especially useful for the study of learning. In complete information games, every player knows information such as who the players are, all possible moves, and all potential outcomes, and each knows what the other players know. In incomplete information games, this information is somehow restricted, and models of imperfect recall can be used to consider forgetfulness.[24]

Clearly, the modeling of economic decisions and behavior in the context of a game has been useful. Real economic behavior often takes on the characteristics of a serious game, strategies are often interdependent, and sequential actions are a common problem in economics. However, game theory is, like neoclassical theory, a logical exercise. A game governed by rules can create the same types of logical problems that occur in market theory. In the real economy, the rules are endogenous and are changed according to ability, costs and benefits.

NOTES

1. Adam Smith, *Wealth of Nations,* ed. Cannon, vol. 1 (London: Methuen, 1904), p. 130.

2. *San Francisco Examiner,* 1/30/94.

3. Robert Lekachman, *Economists at Bay: Why the Experts Will Never Solve Your Problems* (New York: McGraw-Hill, 1976), p. 141.

4. C. E. Ferguson and J. P. Gould, *Microeconomic Theory* (Homewood, IL: Richard D. Irwin, 1975), p. 262.

5. Donald L. Barlett and James B. Steele, *America: What Went Wrong* (Kansas City: Andrews and McMeel, 1992), p. 111.

6. G. L. S. Shackle, *Epistemics and Economics: A Critique of Economic Doctrines* (New Brunswick, NJ: Transaction Publishers, 1992), p. xii.

7. Robert Lekachman, *Economists at Bay,* p. 168.

8. Edward Chamberlin, *The Theory of Monopolistic Competition* (Cambridge, MA: Harvard University Press, 1948) and Joan Robinson, *The Economics of Imperfect Competition* (London: MacMillan, 1933).

9. Anne Krueger, "The Political Economy of the Rent-Seeking Society." *American Economic Review* 64(3) (1974): 291-303., G. L. Stigler "The Theory of Economic Regulation." *Bell Journal of Economics* 2 (1971):3-21.

10. James M. Buchanon, *Essays on the Political Economy* (Honolulu, HI: University of Hawaii Press, 1989), p. 53.

11. A good and recent summary of institutionalist thought over time can be found in Warren J. Samuels, ed., *Institutional Economics*, volumes I–III, (Brookfield, VT: Gower, 1988).

12. Joseph Dorfman, "Background of Institutional Economics," in *Institutional Economics: Veblen, Commons and Mitchell Reconsidered,* ed. Joseph Dorfman (Berkeley, CA: University of California Press, 1963) p. 9.

13. For example, John K. Galbraith, *The New Industrial State* (New York: The New American Library, 1967).

14. Michael Rothschild, *Bionomics: The Inevitability of Capitalism* (New York: H. Holt, 1990), p. xiii.

15. Allen Oakley, *Schumpeter's Theory of Capitalist Motion: A Critical Exposition and Reassessment* (Brookfield, VT: Gower, 1990), p. 105.

16. Christopher Freeman, "Schumpeter's Business Cycles Revisited," in *Evolving Technology and Market Structure,* eds. Arnold Heertje and Mark Perlman (Ann Arbor, MI: The University of Michigan Press, 1990), p. 22.

17. Eduard Marz, *Joseph Schumpeter: Scholar, Teacher and Politician* (New Haven, CT: Yale University Press, 1991), p. 32.

18. Oakley, *Schumpeter's Theory of Capitalist Motion*, p. 105.

19. Paul M. Romer, "The Origins of Endogenous Growth," *Journal of Economic Perspectives* 8 (Winter 1994), p. 14.

20. Ibid., p. 19.

21. Gene M. Grossman and Elhanan Helpman, "Endogenous Innovation in the Theory of Growth," *Journal of Economic Perspectives* 8 (Winter 1994): 37.

22. Ken Binmore and Partha Dasgupta, "Introduction: Game Theory, A Survey," in *Economic Organizations as Games*, ed. K. Binmore and P. Dasgupta (Oxford: Basil Blackwell, 1986), p. 1.

23. Jurgen Eichberger, *Game Theory for Economists* (San Diego: Academic Press, 1993), p. 1.

24. James W. Friedman, *Game Theory with Applications to Economics* (New York: Oxford University Press, 1986), p. 9.

7

Innovation as Antimarket Behavior

The economic results of technology were entirely unforeseen by the economists of the past. The statics of market theory do not account for technological change, but now we live in an economy where change is the status quo. The market theory of Adam Smith could assume constant technology because technology in 1776 was relatively constant. Since technology was a given, economic theory did not need to be concerned about how and why technology was created, and incentives for innovation did not have to be explained.

Thomas Malthus predicted that exponential population growth with geometric food supply growth would result in starvation. In his day, any increase in agricultural productivity was so slow that it was indistinguishable from the uncontrolled variations caused by weather and crop pests. He could not imagine that agricultural productivity would grow faster than exponential population growth. From the mid-1960s to 1990, for example, U.S. population increased by 28 percent, but wheat and corn yields increased by 35 and 55 percent, respectively.[1] With genetic technologies, even greater increases in agricultural productivity could occur in the future.

Karl Marx did not foresee that labor could capture some of the profits and many of the simple pleasures of modern technology. With a minimal amount of intervention in the capitalist system, the average worker in the developed economies now lives a comfortable if not enjoyable life.

These famous theorists had good ideas for their time, but technology has diminished their relevance for the present. The present economy is characterized by (1) a large stock of diverse and complicated technology that has accumulated and evolved over time, (2) a high rate of technological change, and (3) a large share of resources devoted to innovation. Technological change is a major economic activity and it causes rapid economic change—a shifting pattern of production technology, products, complements, and substitutes.

TECHNOLOGY AS THE BASIS OF MODERN ECONOMIC WELFARE

Many of the important economic decisions modern consumers make involve technologically advanced products—electronics, appliances, and automobiles, obviously; food, energy, and shelter less obviously. Much of our food is produced with advanced plant breeding techniques, farm machinery, pesticides, and other high tech chemicals. The heat and hot water in our homes may be produced by nuclear fission or modern combustion technologies. Our homes are made from lumber and materials extracted and shaped with modern machinery and energy. The relatively simple services of modern technology often do not reveal the enormous stock of technology that went into making and delivering it.

Without a doubt, agricultural, medical, energy, and other technologies have made life possible for about 5.5 billion human beings. People can survive without perfect markets. Without modern technology, most of the human population would be dead in a month, and most of the survivors would probably wish they were.

Not only does technology sustain us; it has made life enjoyable in ways that were unthinkable in the days of Adam Smith or even a few decades ago. Once, the economy could provide only food, shelter, and a few simple pleasures. Now the economy also provides health; travel; sports; electronics; toys; art; and bigger, faster, and better pleasures—all made, enabled, or facilitated by modern technology. Modern technology, not markets, is the basis of modern economic welfare. Markets are merely one form of exchange that can be used to distribute the fruits of technology efficiently. Therefore, a modern theory of economic welfare must explain why and how technology is created, not just how it is allocated.

MOTIVES AND THE PRODUCTION OF INNOVATION

Innovation is the production of new information or products from old information. Decisions about investments in innovation are typically based on technical feasibility, expectations of cost, the amount and duration of market control, and potential demand.

The role of intellectual property rights as incentive for innovation has been debated by economists for more than a century. Early authors, including John Stuart Mill and Jeremy Bentham, generally agreed that "Inventions would actually cease if the patent system were abandoned."[2] Other economists, including Kenneth Arrow, found that innovation is under-rewarded by the patent system because of risks and "free-riding" on information that cannot be fully protected. Occasionally, economists take the view that patents provide excessive protection and unnecessary market control.

Innovation is guided by expectations, and these expectations include the degree to which control of entry can be denied to potential competitors. These expectations are often realized with intellectual or information property rights that allow their owner to legally control entry into production and sale of the innovation. When the innovator can obtain a perfect property right to the innovation, the most profit can be obtained by, first, skimming the market and, second, by monopoly pricing. If the innovator wants to sell his right to the innovation, he can maximize his return by selling it to only one buyer who then has the monopoly. Behavior to obtain market control is antimarket behavior, and the resulting technology is the basis of modern economic welfare.

The more control of entry allowed and the longer entry can be restricted, the more short-run economic incentive there is to innovate. To some extent, intellectual and information property rights must increase the pace of innovation. For example, no patent could be given to a living thing, even one that was engineered prior to 1980. In that year, research into biological technologies was given more protection by grant of a patent to an oil-eating microbe. By 1988, patents had been granted for genetically altered oysters and mice. Now, the expectation of market control has increased private investment in genetic research and applications. Biotechnology patent filings increased from about 30 in 1978 to 11,000 in 1991.[3]

Profits from monopoly can sustain monopoly by allowing the monopolist to purchase control of entry. Similarly, profits from the market control enabled by intellectual property rights are reinvested into more research and development, which results in more innovation and intellectual property rights. There is competition, but not for the market for existing goods. Instead, firms compete to be the first one to create valuable products. The winner typically takes all, so the losers are unable to obtain a return to their research investment. Free competition for intellectual property rights selects those firms that are the best and fastest innovators.

The second cause of modern economic welfare is the conventional competition of market economics. In market theory, market competition promotes economic welfare by ensuring efficient allocation of resources. Market competition also promotes economic welfare by eroding the monopoly profits of the innovator. This provides incentive to initiate new innovation, and more new products are developed as a result.

Many economists have suggested a variety of motives behind innovation. Some early institutionalists proposed that the natural curiosity of man, the glory, the "creative urge, the instinct of workmanship" are important.[4] Perhaps, the early inventors were motivated by creativity and altruism because, having achieved enough wealth to have the idle time to innovate, there was little else of value they could get with money. Perhaps profit motive for innovation has increased with the stock of technology because the desire for money is created by what can be bought with it. The more technology we have, the more there is to buy.

Free enterprise develops new products that people want, and it costs more money to buy them all. Consider the new products of just the last two decades: microwave ovens, personal computers and related products, VCRs, CD players, large screen TVs, cable TV services, roller blades, snow boards, exotic travel packages. New products increase the desire for real income to buy them, increase participation in the money economy, and increase dedication of time and effort to economic pursuits. This statement is supported by the example of product introduction into primitive societies. To acquire the new products, the primitive societies must and do learn to participate in the outside economy, and they almost always do.

In modern society, altruism and creative urges are probably decreasing in importance as motives. Realistically, innovation is driven by profit. The process of innovation has been institutionalized, and institutions thrive on money. The innovation of the solo and perhaps altruistic inventor has been replaced by the research and development process of large institutions. Now, only about one-quarter of the 100,000 patents granted annually are given to individuals. The research institution assembles the specializations necessary to innovate, arranges for the necessary capital, and provides the space necessary to apply the information, energy, and materials to the innovation process.

Modern innovation has special needs with respect to information and capital that can only be met by institutions. Innovation, like all aspects of modern production, requires information—the best and most recent information. Modern technology is a complex assemblage of old technology. In the modern technological economy, not many individuals have all or even much of the knowledge needed to innovate by themselves. Innovation has become institutionalized because no one can do it alone.

As the pace of innovation increases, so does the share of resources devoted to innovation. Especially, the increased importance of innovation in the modern economy has transformed the nature of labor. The pace, complexity, and scope of modern innovation has increased the importance of skilled labor used for innovation relative to manual and skilled labor used to produce existing goods. The earnings of this labor, and the earnings of other resources used for innovation, are also an argument of the modern economic welfare function. Jobs in research and development are some of the highest paying because scarce specializations can capture some of the economic rent created by innovation.

Sometimes, immediate survival is the mother of invention; protection of information is secondary. For example, a tailoring business recognized that, in a recession, sales of new clothing, and therefore tailoring, were declining. Survival was at stake. The business developed a practice of restyling older clothes to today's fashions. The new line of work soon made up a third of the company's business. Failure was avoided, but the business will be unable to stop other entrants from imitating its innovation. Short-run profits will be lost as soon as other restyling businesses open.

As a production process, innovation is often characterized by the most extreme temporal problem of supply. Unless the innovator is wealthy or can get buyers to pay for uninvented goods in advance, he must raise the capital to finance the costs of innovation. Given that modern technology is the most important source of economic welfare, the financing of research and development is a critical function of capital. The capital for research and development can be acquired because there is an expectation of economic rent from market control. This expectation can only be based on the expectation of demand for the new product.

The Demand for Innovations

The incentive to innovate is closely related to the expected demand function for the good. The more demand and the less responsive demand is to price, the more potential for profit from market control. Elasticity of demand is closely linked to the quality and price of substitutes and complements available. If there will be few substitutes available, and to the extent that substitutes are expensive, demand for the new good will be more inelastic and the temporary monopoly granted for the innovation will be more profitable. Goods with more inelastic demand also result in more economic surplus when they are sold competitively, all else equal.* Therefore, temporary control of entry for innovations encourages innovations that are highly valued by society.

The price and qualities of complements can affect the demand for and expected profit from the innovation. Modern innovations usually build on existing technology. Personal computers are entirely dependent on electricity, and on-line services are dependent on personal computers and communications technology. Technology increases opportunities to develop more technology. Technology builds on itself, and recent history has provided more and more to build on.

At the same time, new technologies are often substitutes for existing goods. Plastics and composites, for example, have replaced many other materials in a variety of products. VCRs and cable TV have created substitutes for network television. The dynamics of technological growth create a changing pattern of complements and substitutes, and innovation results in a dynamic economy of shifting and unstable demands and supplies. There are winners and losers, and the winners are often able to predict where new technology is going and what change means for existing and potential product demands.

The availability of substitutes, and their price and markets, are probably the most important demand-related factors in the innovation decision. An innovation that will have close substitutes already has a defined market, so the potential market size and price may be easy to estimate. For innovations used to substitute

---

* This can be shown with two linear demand functions, one being more inelastic, which intersect a conventional marginal cost function at the same point.

for existing technology in production processes, the potential revenues might be easily determined from the potential cost savings in production. Producers should be willing to pay up to their current cost plus any cost savings to acquire the less expensive production process.

When few substitutes are available, the potential demand, price, and revenues are not so easy to estimate. For life-saving drugs or medical technology, the size of the market might be determined by the number of people afflicted and the rate at which they become afflicted. The price they are willing to pay depends on how wealthy the afflicted people are as well as the availability, quality, and price of any other drugs or technologies used to treat the affliction. Once again, the survival motive must be considered. For other innovations, the market may be even less easy to judge. Who could have guessed the potential profits from Teenage Mutant Ninja Turtles[tm] or Power Rangers[tm]?

Some innovators develop and sell new products merely because buyers want new products. In art, uniqueness has a value of its own. The art industry uses many well-established media such as paint and sculpture, but artists develop new types of art based on new designs, materials, or techniques. The music business also diversifies for diversity's sake. Sometimes, aesthetically pleasing is synonymous with being different. It is the difference that is interesting.

The cost of innovation is largely fixed with respect to the quantity of the new good produced. Therefore, the average cost per unit declines with market size as population grows. Over time, increasing population increases potential demand for a new good and can help justify the investment required to invent and produce it.

PROTECTION AND ENFORCEMENT

Chapter 3 discussed the problem of information production and protection in free enterprise. Sometimes, the innovator has no potential for market control other than the fact that he started first. An intellectual property right is not always needed to substantially exclude competitors. Sometimes, the information needed to make the good is exclusive. Sometimes the product can be made so that the information is not revealed. Usually, the innovator cannot be forced to reveal the innovation to imitators. Some products are simply hard to copy.

Many innovations can be easily copied because the information is naturally nonexclusive. Competitors need merely acquire one and copy it. Since the copier does not pay the innovation cost, he can sell it for less than the innovator. At a minimum, the innovator needs to recoup his investment costs, and innovation has many unusual risks associated with costs, markets, and competitors. The innovator may fail to invent the product, the public may not accept it, or a competitor may beat the innovator to the market. Intellectual property laws and other privacy laws that allow businesses to withhold new information compensate for the costs and risks of innovation.

The federal cost of filing and obtaining a patent, if granted, is about $1,000, and costs to maintain it for seventeen years are about $3,000. The cost of a copyright registration is only $25. These costs are only a small share of the typical costs. Preparation of materials, legal fees, and enforcement costs are likely to be much larger. Once an intellectual right is granted, it must still be enforced. Government helps with enforcement, but most enforcement is left to the resources of the innovator. Most intellectual property law violations go to civil, not criminal court.

In one view, ideas are spread in one of two ways: by blueprint copying, or by idea diffusion.[5] In blueprint copying, the competitor can work with the original design. The design can be used to develop the new product. In idea diffusion, the competitor receives just the basic idea and the details must be developed without a blueprint. This distinction is useful because it distinguishes how competition can develop without or with intellectual property right protection. The mere sale of a product allows anyone to get the basic idea, but the intellectual right controls which details can be copied and which must be developed. In general, intellectual property rights cannot fully protect innovations because the law allows others to create substitutes.

Copyright law provides only limited protection for artistic innovations, which are often easy to copy because techniques can be readily determined on display. Sometimes, artistic innovations can be protected through informal enforcement. An artist who copies innovations might have a hard time finding a good market for his copies. Retail sellers would be reluctant to replace the originals with the copies even if they are less expensive. Other artists would be reluctant to provide their innovations to the retailer in the future. The retailer has his reputation at stake. The copier might be shunned by other artists. Among all, there is a certain mutual respect for each other's efforts.

Of course, copyright infringement suits are always a possibility. The threat of a copyright suit is serious business in music where innovations are especially hard to protect, many songwriters compete for similar markets, any one song may involve a lot of money, and the chance of simultaneous and similar innovations is high. Copyright protection is often invoked in music because, by precedent, limits on fair use of verse are especially stringent.

It can be difficult to enforce intellectual property rights. Illegal use of computer software is common in the United States. Rights can be even more difficult to enforce overseas. In China and Thailand, 98 percent of computer software in use is pirated.[6] In China, compact disc factories produce copies of American music without the expense of royalties. The affected industries appeal to government for help, but government conducts trade negotiations in the context of a larger economic and political agenda. Trade sanctions can be used against governments who refuse to enforce intellectual property rights, but such sanctions are not often used, and they are even less often effective.

Enforcement of intellectual property rights was a major problem in the early years of the video game industry. In 1974, sales of the first video game by Atari accounted for one-tenth of all the copies produced.[7] The initial versions of Nintendo's Donkey Kong[tm] were copied to the tune of $100 million in sales losses. In the mid-1980's Nintendo created an electronic security system in their game players which would only accept Nintendo cartridges.

The extremely popular Power Rangers[tm] have created an industry of accessories, but trademarks can only provide so much protection. Power Ranger[tm] costumes were enormously popular for Halloween 1994. Many companies can sell imitations by being careful not to violate the exact proprietary logos. But why would any parent settle for second best? "These costumes, without commercial logos, help encourage pretend play" reads a small portion of the ad.

There is a continuous test of the meaning of copyright and patent laws in the computer industry. Most major hardware and software companies have recently been involved in intellectual property rights litigation. Lotus 1-2-3[tm], the first spreadsheet software developed solely for IBM personal computers created a standard that has been emulated by many others and resulted in a lawsuit involving Quatro Pro[tm].

A California company produced a popular screen-saver program based on images of flying toasters. Another company producing similar images was quickly brought into a copyright suit, which was eventually settled out of court. But then, the rock group Jefferson Airplane claimed the first company was violating their copyright; one of their albums also had flying toasters on the cover. A U.S. District judge eventually decided that the group's copyright covered just the music, not the cover. In the competition for exclusive rights, even pictures of flying toasters are worth fighting over.

Innovation in computer technology raised many new issues in innovation and intellectual property rights. Early spreadsheet programs were not patentable because they were not machines; their developers accepted copyrights instead, and the difference was probably worth several hundred million dollars.[8] The first software patent was not obtained until 1981, and the software involved turned out to be unsuccessful.

IBM went into the personal computer business in early 1981 using standard parts and technology. IBM developed ROM-BIOS to link their hardware to Microsoft's operating system. PC clones were made possible because IBM's copyright on the ROM-BIOS could protect only lines of computer code, not the functions they perform. The cloners merely had to acquire "programmers who could prove they have never been exposed to IBM's ROM-BIOS code" to reverse-engineer the ROM-BIOS functions.[9] Competitors were forced to demonstrate that they were not copying blueprints, merely building on ideas. Then, these programmers wrote their own code, which exactly duplicated what IBM's code did.

IBM did not anticipate that competitors could copy the PC and undercut their price and sales so rapidly. "In the absence of such competition, IBM would have done nothing" but faced with the extreme competition of cheap clones, IBM set about developing a series of personal computers that were all copied or rejected by buyers in short order.[10] The threat of competition was the incentive for additional innovation.

IBM used information control techniques to keep competitors as far behind as possible, but with little success. They announced proposed innovations for others to try to imitate which they themselves had little intention of completing. They promised new products just when competitors were just starting to ship new clones in the hopes that buyers would wait. The increased competition from many new entrants caused IBM to continue innovation for a time, but IBM eventually lost control of the personal computer market because they could not control entry. IBM also made several strategic errors that allowed rivals to capture the market. With personal computers, the world got the innovation under the expectation of market control, but customers quickly benefitted from lower prices and more innovation through the creation of close substitutes and market competition.[11]

Patents create and sustain minimal market control in the automobile industry. Cars made by different companies are similar but not identical partly because each make includes some patented components. Japan's big four companies were granted 1,263 patents in 1987 as compared to 622 for General Motors, Ford, and Chrysler.[12] But by 1993, U.S. manufacturers caught up. Ford alone spent nearly $5 billion on research in 1993, up from $2 billion a decade earlier. Each patent, marketed as a unique attribute of the patent owner's car, provides a protectable degree of diversification, profit, and, hopefully, quality.

THE PUBLIC ROLE

Government research has been an important part of the innovation process in many ways. Government often subsidizes basic research that is the foundation for future inventions. Government subsidizes research directly through public research institutions, universities, science programs, and private grants. Important research subsidies occur in the energy, agricultural, and medical industries. Technical give-aways of space and military technology are important. Much medical research is subsidized because of the strong social value associated with survival.

With a few minor modifications, private players can often obtain intellectual property rights to technology and information developed in the public sector. For example, a computer software producer can acquire a publicly developed computer algorithm, produce software to make the algorithm user friendly, and copyright the software. Copyrighted versions of government data are sold privately.

Sometimes, applications of new technology can start only with government subsidies. The passenger airline business of the 1920s and 1930s operated only with subsidies provided by the U.S. mail. The airlines recognized that their long-term survival depended on designing an airplane that could carry more passengers. The DC-2 and DC-3 were developed in response to this expectation. The innovation was a direct response to the unprofitability of airlines given the current technology.

There are many other arguments for a public role in innovation. First, society gains from public research when it is provided for public use without intellectual property rights protection because the inefficiency created by a temporary monopoly is avoided. Second, there is an equity issue. Private innovation tends to direct resources to products that will be most wanted by the rich. Therefore, the public role should emphasize research that will benefit the poor. Also, there is the social value associated with survival. The inelasticity of demand that makes medical patents so valuable occurs precisely because the new products reduce suffering and increase survival. The merits of the patent system for medical innovations is frequently debated. The American Medical Association (AMA), for example, has criticized patents because they restrict access to medical knowledge and harm patients.

Third, there is a property problem. Private innovation directs resources to innovations that have perfect property rights. Innovations that cannot be protected by intellectual property laws and innovation of nonexclusive goods might not ever happen if left to the private sector.

On the other hand, government does not face the same incentives as private innovators to produce the most valuable innovations. Research subsidies are sometimes driven by politics, not profit. Any argument against government intervention based on a history of inefficiency and favoritism would apply as much to innovation as to any other activity.

Government's most important role in innovation is the legal protection provided for intellectual property, and the proper scope and duration of intellectual property rights is an important social issue. Intellectual property laws must balance incentives for innovation against temporary monopoly. Intuitively, the optimal duration of protection should vary according to the type of product involved. If a shorter period of protection is known to be sufficient to encourage the innovation, then society should grant only the shorter period. Later, more economic benefits in the form of static efficiencies will be obtained. But in other cases, the seventeen-year period of protection may be too short to justify the research investment, and a good invention will never happen. In this case, society might grant an even longer period of protection.

SUMMARY

The drive for change is the recognition of the possible against the background of existing opportunities. By definition, market opportunities are always available. Anyone can play, but market control in existing markets can be hard to come by. Innovation, either with or without the protection and enforcement of property rights is one legal way to get market control, and the innovation later becomes the stock of technology that is the basis for modern economic welfare. Therefore, technological change induced by the expectation of market control makes the neoclassical models of competition and welfare untenable. Market/antimarket dynamics foster creation and variety as well as allocative efficiency.

The practice of economics is just beginning to understand the profound implications and diverse problems of technological change. The issues of innovation and intellectual property should receive more attention from economics because the pace of innovation has increased and a larger share of goods are sold with intellectual property rights protection. Innovation and intellectual property raise a large number of policy issues including (1) the role of government in innovation and enforcement of intellectual property rights, (2) trade-offs between the pace of innovation and efficiency, and (3) tradeoffs between property rights and other social values.

NOTES

1. U.S. Department of Agriculture, *Agricultural Statistics* (Washington, D.C.: U.S. Government Printing Office, 1982), pp. 30,1; Ibid., 1990, pp. 31,1; and U.S. Department of Commerce, Bureau of the Census, *Statistical Abstract of the United States 1992,* 112th Edition (Washington, D.C.: U.S. Government Printing Office, 1992), p. 7.

2. Ward S. Bowman Jr., *Patent and Antitrust Law: A Legal and Economic Appraisal* (Chicago: The University of Chicago Press, 1973), p. 18.

3. Gale R. Peterson, "Introduction" in G. R. Peterson, ed., *Understanding Biotechnology Law, Protection, Licensing and Intellectual Property Policies* (New York: Marcel Dekker, 1993), p. 8.

4. As briefly summarized by Todd G. Buchholz, *New Ideas from Dead Economists: An Introduction to Modern Economic Thought* (New York: Dutton, 1989), p. 176.

5. Jared Diamond, "Blueprints, Bloody Ships, and Borrowed Letters," *Natural History* 104(3) (March 1995): 16–21.

6. "Making War on China's Pirates," *The Economist,* February 11, 1995, p. 33–34.

7. Roy Gardner, *Games for Business and Economics* (New York: John Wiley, 1995), p. 229.

8. Robert X. Cringely, *Accidental Empires: How the Boys of Silicon Valley Make Their Millions, Battle Foreign Competition, and Still Get a Date* (Reading, MA: Addison-Wesley, 1992), p. 150.

9. Ibid., p. 171.

10. Ibid., pp. 272–277.

11. The history of the struggle for profits in the personal computer market is told in several other books, including Paul Carroll, *Big Blues: The Unmaking of IBM* (New York: Crown, 1993); and Charles H. Ferguson and Charles R. Morris, *Computer Wars: How the West Can Win in a Post-IBM World* (New York: Random House, 1993).

12. The source for these figures is an article appearing in *The Marin Independent Journal,* "U.S. Winning Auto Patent War," October 23, 1994.

8

Government Failure and Roles in Antimarket Behavior

Market failure is the inability of private enterprise to provide goods and services efficiently in the public interest. Similarly, government failure means that government has failed to accomplish its economic purposes in the public interest. When government fails to define or protect public and private property, economic players may try to take that property. Sometimes, government fails in its roles, such as antitrust or consumer protection, to promote efficient market competition. This often happens as an accidental result of poor legal or administrative process.

In other cases, government failure is no mistake. The emphasis of this chapter is government failure from allowing or promoting substantial antimarket behaviors. Government's economic activity is frequently biased against the public toward the interests of elected representatives, public employees, or select powerful interest groups. Many established government activities do not promote efficiency or any other social goal for that matter; they are simultaneously unjust and inefficient.

Government economic activity often generates unusual economic profit or rent by creating market control, by charging low prices for public products or services, or by paying high prices for goods and services it purchases. The static inefficiency created by government intervention and sale of public resources is a standard topic of conventional economics, but this loss may only be the tip of the iceberg. Government intervention can also reduce economic welfare by disrupting market/antimarket dynamics. Intervention can lead to market control that creates and sustains economic rents in existing products. This discourages innovation by keeping resources dedicated to the existing product, by discouraging the invention of substitutes, and by consuming resources in activities such as lobbying and political pay-offs used to sustain the intervention. Antimarket behavior in free enterprise can create economic benefit through innovation, but sustained market control enabled by government often creates incentives for inefficiency and technical stagnation.

FAILURE TO DEFINE OR ENFORCE PROPERTY RIGHTS

Market theory presumes that rights to goods are perfect, and rights are easily transferred with the good in trade. Imperfect property rights mean that the rights associated with a good are uncertain or costly to enforce. It is costly to maintain rights to a naturally nonexclusive good. Most goods are actually somewhat nonexclusive. Someone must pay to enforce the property right. Property rights are enforced by a common belief in the values and the letter of the property laws and, if that fails, by public or private threat of force.

One of the most fundamental economic roles of government is the definition and enforcement of property rights, but the efficient amount of enforcement is frequently not provided. Government, the final arbitrator and enforcer of property rights is unwilling or unable to fulfill one of its most important economic functions. Consequently, taking of property remains a significant way to void the assumptions of economic theory.

White collar crimes cost Americans more than $100 billion annually.[1] By comparison, only $15 billion of property was reported stolen in 1991.[2] Convicted white collar offenders "generally receive light sentences" and "aren't compelled to pay back what they have stolen." The government is apparently unable even to collect outstanding fines of about $4.5 billion. In one case, a defendant robbed persons of tens of millions of dollars; was convicted five times, and enjoined from violations of securities laws seven times, yet spent no time in jail; had $11.5 million in outstanding fines and judgments; and received probation in his most recent conviction. Apparently, white collar crime gets little real attention from the criminal justice system.

Government has assumed exceptional management and enforcement costs for some nonexclusive goods, such as fisheries. A mix of federal agencies define and enforce ocean fishing laws within 200 miles of any U.S. territory, including small islands. The process of setting rights and rules is very political, and the resulting rules often respond to special interests, not efficiency or the public. The government grants fishing rights to foreign nations in exchange for other favors. Fishermen and fish consumers pay the price of misguided politics and poor management.

Residency is a type of property valued for the benefits of the place of residence. The U.S. government was recently sued by California for failure to enforce the U.S. border with Mexico. California is not allowed to defend the border, yet it is forced to pay a share of social costs for illegal immigrants who have rights to health and education services. The children of illegal immigrants born in the United States are automatic citizens entitled to all the benefits that follow. These incentives are partially responsible for the hundreds of thousands of illegal immigrants entering the United States every year. Not only has government failed to enforce its citizens' rights to a secure border, but it provides incentive for illegal immigrants to violate that border.

Sometimes, property rights are unclear because the rights are disputed in litigation. Much of the practice of civil law boils down to disputes over property rights. If property rights are uncertain because they are in dispute, efficient allocation through markets cannot occur until the dispute is resolved. Government creates an inefficient situation to the extent that the legal process cannot expeditiously determine the assignment of property rights.

Laws that allow players to claim the property of others enable antimarket behavior. Clearly, damages are often not the real reason for lawsuits, and the amount of the claim has little to do with the real amount of damages. Rather, the process is a way to obtain economic rents by appeal to a small sample of social values called a jury. Litigants consider the juries' preconceptions about justice and equity in relation to the parties involved.

Sometimes, government decides to consider a change in the system of property rights, and ownership becomes uncertain. Rights to use of land, water, and other natural resources are sometimes changed by legislative and judicial decisions. Users of these resources invest to defend their accustomed rights, and to change the extent, duration, and assignment of rights in their favor. The resources are "bought" with expenses for persuasion, and market efficiency in the sense of economic theory cannot occur until property rights are clarified.

In most western states, property rights to water are assigned according to the doctrine of prior appropriation: in case of shortage (drought), he who used the water first in history now has first priority. The priority of the right affects its value, since low-priority water is not available in dry years. While the appropriation doctrine has its problems, legal uncertainty is not one of them. The amount of uncertainty is largely limited to the unavoidable uncertainty of weather.

Some states, such as California, have more complex systems for assigning property rights to water. Riparian, appropriation, pueblo, basin of origin, and public trust doctrines compete as a basis for water law. Changing legal interpretations about the priorities between and relationships among the doctrines lead to uncertain and changing property rights.

The public trust doctrine was established by court precedent. This precedent now requires water allocation in California to consider public trust uses such as fish and wildlife. The courts, however, provided little guidance to the state as to how the allocation of responsibility, meaning the reduction of established water uses, to provide water for public trust uses should be accomplished. The courts have only said that such allocation should be reasonable. Water users have consistently stated that uncertainty in water allocation is their single largest concern, but they can only plead their case before the responsible state board. Faced with administrative allocation and the uncertainty of the outcome, water users invest in advocacy to increase the quantity and decrease the risk associated with their allocation. The lack of clear rights has made the process completely political; the economics of water are the expenses for speakers, consultants, lawyers and quasi-judicial hearings.

Recently, federal reserved rights to water have received much attention in the western United States. Federal reserved rights, by court precedent, are assigned to federal lands. The reserved rights doctrine, first confirmed in 1908, states that the federal government implicitly reserved water to meet the purpose for which the federal land was set aside, but the government has rarely gotten around to deciding how much water was set aside. The reserved water rights doctrine, like the Endangered Species Act (ESA) and public trust doctrine, creates uncertainty in property rights and results in substantial expenditure to reassign or defend water rights.

The extent of property rights to land is also debated and changed through the legislative and judicial branches. In the United States, government may not take property without just compensation, but the definition of "take" is frequently uncertain because the extent of property rights prior to the take was uncertain. For example, the ESA has resulted in land development restrictions where endangered species are found. Land owners claim that these restrictions are takings, while wildlife advocates claim that the wildlife resources residing on the land were never the private owners' property to begin with. In the advocates' view, the state always owned the wildlife resources residing on the land, and the state is just now exerting its right to the protection of these resources.

The ESA allows local governments to develop land use plans which allow planned development to continue when approved by the responsible agencies. However, this certainty lasts only until another species is listed. Then, local plans can be forced to be redrawn from scratch. In southern California, land use plans approved for Stephen's kangaroo rat were essentially disapproved following listing of the California gnat catcher. Again, the ESA created substantial uncertainty in property rights.

In all of these cases, the change in property rights or accustomed uses occurs outside of the market system. Property rights change hands not through the market, but through influence of the assignment of property rights in courts or by government decree. The value of the exchange is reflected in the expenditures of players who hope to affect the outcome. Opportunities for antimarket behaviors are created when government allows players to influence the process of assigning or changing property rights. Such influence must be allowed as a matter of economic justice, but influence is often conducted for economic gain when the expected benefits exceed the costs. The costs of resources used for influence reflects a loss of these resources for other, possibly more productive activities.

FAILURES OF PUBLIC OWNERSHIP AND RESPONSIBILITY

Economists have analyzed government as a selfish interest for decades. The selfish interests of the government involve a bureaucracy, which wants to increase budgets and salaries, and politicians, who want to increase votes, political contributions, and personal wealth. When economic rent in public resources is created, contributions and votes follow. One common way to create economic rent is to charge a low price for the public resource. The price can be lower than would be charged by a private owner because costs can be subsidized by other funds such as tax revenues.

Many analyses of federally owned resources have found that government tends to provide for its own interests, rather than that the public. The Department of the Interior and the Forest Service together manage about 30 percent of the land area of the United States. One author finds that "the Interior Department has continually influenced land policy to advance its administrative and regulatory role."[3] Public resource prices, where they exist, are frequently set at levels below market rates.[4] Grazing rights are sold for a fraction of local private prices. Under a nineteenth-century law, federal lands are sold for less than $5 an acre for mining. The Forest Service has been criticized for years for selling timber at a price much less than the cost of roads and infrastructure required to provide access to it. The U.S. Bureau of Reclamation, a federal owner of water works, sells water at a cost far below its original cost to taxpayers. These subsidies are sustained by the influence and political contributions of regional mining, forest, and water interests.

An especially expensive case of government failure involved the savings and loan (S&L) scandal. The federal government and the states deregulated the S&L industry by allowing more entry, more S&L investments in real estate and other risky ventures, increasing federal insurance coverage on deposits, and allowing a sole person to own an S&L. The S&L lobby was understandably supportive. Any loss due to unprofitable or illegal S&L diversions would be covered by the federal government. Depositors were insured, so depositors had no incentive to make sure their deposits were being well spent. However, the federal government clearly did not look after the insured deposits either. They did not enforce the public trust in federally insured money. Numerous swindlers "realized they could have access to all the money they ever wanted."[5] The result will cost every U.S. citizen about $1,000.

One of the most important functions of private lenders is to constrain the overzealous aspirations of entrepreneurs. Private money will not be leant unless payment of principal and interest is quite certain. The federal government lends money to special interests. Students, small businesses, and disadvantaged groups, such as minority owners and farmers, can receive loans on terms not available to others. Failure rates for government loans are often substantially higher than for private lending. These failures, through taxation, subtract from the capital used to finance private innovation and other more efficient investments. Efficiency and innovation is sacrificed for equity, but the meaning of equity is, after all, a value judgment.

REGULATION, CAPTURE THEORY, AND PUBLIC CHOICE

The regulatory process tends to favor those groups or businesses that can most influence the process in their own interest.

Council of Economic Advisors, *Economic Report of the President*, 1993[6]

Market controls are often initiated with good intentions. Society sometimes decides that unfettered free enterprise is not for the best, so intervention is established to enhance the public interest. But then, rational players seek to control the regulators. Government intervention often fails to achieve a fair or efficient provision of goods and services because private and related government players are able to manipulate the intervention in their self-interest. Eventually, the intervention becomes a vested interest for some of the private and public players involved, and the original reason for intervention often becomes a rationale for a substantial market control.

This problem has been discussed extensively in *rent-seeking*, *capture theory*, and *public choice* theory. Rent-seeking is perhaps the most general term of the three. "Restrictions upon economic activity give rise to rents of a variety of forms and people often compete for the rents."[7] Capture theory is more specific in the role of government and the methods of private players. The regulated industry captures and controls the regulating agency.[8] Many authors have proposed and confirmed that regulation is often intended "to restrict competition in ways that involve wealth transfers from one group (often consumers) to another (often specific economic sectors)."[9]

Regulation is frequently sought by government for its own economic benefit. One author states that "the creation of monopolies is one of the government's major preoccupations." The Civil Aeronautics Board and the Interstate Commerce Commission made cartels out of their respective industries, and the government "sponsored the creation of monopolies of labor, ocean shipping, and oil and gas. A large part of government activity is devoted to generating particular benefits for small groups of people."[10]

Another proposes that "antitrust is designed to benefit special-interest groups" as opposed to the public interest. "Efficiency has no strong politically active constituency."[11] A third study found that Federal Trade Commission (FTC) case dismissals tended "to be nonrandomly concentrated on firms headquartered in the home districts of those members of the House of Representatives who are on committees and subcommittees with budgetary and oversight responsibilities over the FTC." The FTC's actions are characterized as "antitrust pork barrel."[12] Another study found that FTC investigations are seldom in the public interest and are undertaken for reasons such as "shifting costs of litigation to taxpayers or harassing competitors."[13] Appointed commissioners seeking to maximize their own opportunities provide benefits to the dominant interest group.

The Federal Communications Commission (FCC) regulates the telecommunications industry. Communications interests try to affect the FCC to enhance their own interests and harm others. The Senate Commerce Committee has found that the regulatory process enabled firms to impede competitors and delay new services. One observer saw the FCC as serving "as sort of an institutionalized cartel manager" for "the purpose of preventing companies from committing competition."[14] Until the 1970s, AT&T was a monopoly protected from competition by the FCC. As the FCC began to let in more competitors, AT&T defended its position to the public by claiming that it would have to raise rates as it lost business. Eventually, AT&T was required to divest of its operating companies and was allowed to enter other lines of business.

State and local laws are similarly used for private gain. Local insurance companies can lobby state governments for special treatment, and states can use insurance regulation to favor companies based in their state. In the banking industry, one insider found that "to an unusual degree, banking sets the terms of its own regulation and stays clear of effective independent review. The power of the banks rests on an intricate political and financial structure: political contributions, the power to make loans, a highly sophisticated lobbying effort, and a close similarity of interest" with other powerful groups.[15]

Households are strongly dependent on the value of their real estate holdings for wealth, so households sometimes work together (collude) to restrict growth and increase the value of their holdings. This collusion is conducted through zoning, open space programs, and other residential development restrictions enabled by government. Sometimes, this control is conducted with the implicit goal of inhibiting entry. One analysis found that "the politics of planning and zoning have become the politics of exclusion."[16] In a 1995 case, a successful campaign to deny the zoning application of a hardware outlet was allegedly financed by a rival chain.[17]

Iron Triangles and Artificial Transactions Costs

Legal antimarket controls can involve complex relationships between government, regulators, industry, and public perception. The players seeking control must expect it will be profitable, some degree of public acceptance of the rationale is helpful, and a system of rewards to players in government who have the power to create and administer the intervention must be possible.

One general arrangement for administering substantial antimarket controls has been called an *iron triangle*. A conventional iron triangle is an economic exchange involving three groups: private beneficiaries, legislative representatives, and a bureaucracy. The private beneficiary and bureaucracy obtain public funds, and the legislative representatives obtain contributions from the private beneficiaries. Private beneficiaries buy continuing support through established patterns of reward to legislators, lobbies, political contributions, insider tips, the potential for future favors, and so forth. Personal gain provides a substantial incentive to continue the control, and the system is "iron" because the concentration of wealth and power that results can be very hard to change. A simple representation of an iron triangle is provided in Figure 8.1.

The government's role involves politicians, who receive money for their legislative support, and a bureaucracy, who administers the money received from taxpayers. In exchange for the favorable administration and rationalization of the control, bureaucrats receive advancement and the possibility of future rewards. "Protected by social security, as well as civil service, government jobs are a species of property," which are protected and enhanced by participation in the iron triangle.[18]

The theory of iron triangles can be extended to publicly supported market control, the only difference being that the system is driven by unusual profits paid by consumers instead of taxpayers, and the bureaucracy protects the market control instead of distributing subsidies. "Government brings about excess profits through restrictive licensing through setting up or permitting cartels and monopolies or through import controls. All of these measures restrict the amount of goods sold and hence raise their price and the profits of the producers." In one view, government imposes or allows market control simply to obtain a share of the excess economic rent through taxation. "Government joins in the exploitation of the consumer by maintaining the circumstances which provide the excess profit and then taxing it."[19]

An iron triangle typically requires some degree of taxpayer acceptance or, in the case of market control, consumer acceptance. The beneficiaries and government often obtain public acceptance by arguing that the original benign purpose of the intervention or program is still being served. All three of the participants typically help support the triangle by providing rationales to the public. The rationales appeal to a variety of social values, but efficiency and equity are normally part of the mix. The degree of effort and cost needed to obtain public approval depends on the incentives and abilities of the public to uncover and correct the situation. Substantial control through general taxation and spending is one of the most successful forms because each taxpayer has a small stake and is too far removed from the action to understand the truth and demand change. The beneficiaries create an information problem that requires a transactions cost to overcome.

The problem is similar to the public (nonrival and nonexclusive) goods problem. For public goods, such as a scenic tree, many people obtain a small scenic benefit, but the collection of payment from these many people requires larger transactions costs. Therefore, trees are directed to uses such as lumber that have lower transactions costs even though the total benefit of the tree as lumber may be less. For substantial controls, each consumer or taxpayer, through taxation or prices, pays only a small cost of each control, so each individual has little incentive to overcome transactions costs and correct the problem. For each individual, the costs of overcoming misinformation exceeds the potential benefit. In the case of public goods, the nature of the thing leads

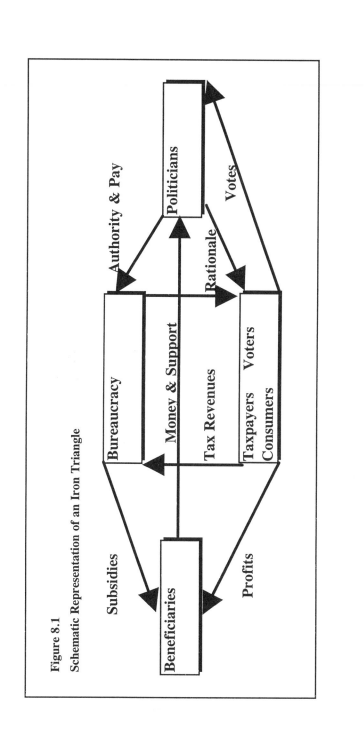

Figure 8.1
Schematic Representation of an Iron Triangle

to an inefficiency. In the case of iron triangles, the beneficiaries create transactions costs by control of information. In both cases, the small costs to each of many become the large benefits for a few. As in the case of monopoly, concentration of wealth provides the incentive and capability to continue.

Iron triangles can persist in part because many of the participants believe in the rationales and purposes of the arrangement. Often, the private and government interests involved believe that the system operates in the public interest. Believers are believable, and their beliefs mean that iron triangles are a social issue, not a matter of conspiracy. Legislators and bureaucrats who believe in the system are especially well qualified to be paid by it. Some individuals involved may even argue against it. Frequently, there are bureaucrats who take up the opposing point of view, and sometimes they are successful in bringing about improvements.

GOVERNMENT WASTE AND THE DEBT

> When the world was quiet the errors of economists were trivial matters. Our days are different and more dangerous.
>
>   R. Lekachman, *Economists at Bay: Why the Experts
>   Will Never Solve Your Problems* [20]

The problem of government waste has recently received increased attention in the popular press. One book on the topic even made the *New York Times'* bestseller list.[21] Government waste is the stuff of legends, but it is still appropriate to put it in the context of antimarket behavior.

Pork barrel politics refers to a tendency of representatives to support wasteful projects that benefit regional or special interests. A federal project that has major regional benefits can generate substantial political and financial support for regional representatives, but the project will not be funded without the support of a majority of representatives in Congress. When such a project is not in the national interest, the only way to secure the number of votes required for passage is to combine a large number of similar projects or programs into one bill. Logrolling provides a means to implement substantial market control, where legislative approval is required. Each program or policy in the bill may be obviously inefficient, but passage is ensured by the collusion of a majority. The resulting legislation includes many wasteful projects with no economic but great political value. Each representative has brought home the bacon to his constituents. Often, the bacon is taxpayers' money concentrated into the hands of a smaller number of recipients who will return a share to government via political support and contributions.

The federal government is currently about $5.5 trillion in debt. The debt continues to grow at a rate of about $300 billion annually; roughly 20 percent of federal expenditure is borrowed money. Currently, 15 to 20 percent of federal tax revenue goes just to pay interest on the debt. The federal debt was created and is sustained by short-sighted government and economic logic. On the political side, it is a reflection of the short-run survival problem of political players. No administration wants to deal with it in the present. The fear of worse economic conditions is a major factor increasing chance of re-election.

Economic theory has usually not helped. The "Ricardian vision" finds that "substituting debt issuing for taxation does not make any difference for the real state and development of the economy," while the Keynesian view finds that "a properly timed budget deficit is thus seen to enlarge both current and future well-being."[22] Both of these views ignore the real potential for government default such as occurred in this century in Argentina, Germany, and China. Default is not an immediate threat, but debt crowds out private-sector investment, increases the risk of inflation, and America's aging population will increase costs of social programs substantially in the next twenty years.

The deficit increased dramatically during the mid-1970s and again during the Reagan administration. The 1980s saw a surge in private economic activity. This was expected by Keynesian macroeconomists and common sense; reduced taxes left more money in private hands, while the federal spending stimulus to the economy continued unabated. In one view, larger interest payments on the accumulated debt now cancel the stimulus provided by deficit spending, so continued deficit spending occurs alongside a sluggish economy.

The fiscalist view of the economy ignores the impacts of government expenditure in creating and sustaining inefficiency and in disrupting market/antimarket dynamics. Not only does government create inefficiency, but intervention can inhibit technological change. A recent comparison of industrialized economies found that "as a general rule, those economies with the lowest rise in public spending since 1960 seem to be more efficient and more innovative. They boast lower unemployment and a higher level of registered patents."[23]

Government intervention inhibits progress and economic growth by taxing or borrowing capital that would be used for investment and innovation, by dedicating resources to nonproductive activities, and by supporting the status quo through the structure of intervention. If government could cull out practices and programs that create inefficiency and hinder progress, these improvements might mitigate or even compensate for the reduced fiscal stimulus of deficit spending. But, of course, government does not recognize that its spending could create inefficiency, much less technical stagnation. Keynesian macroeconomics, the concept of economic multipliers, and other rationales have sustained the belief in government that government spending helps sustain the economy.

John Maynard Keynes said, "The political problem of mankind is to combine three things: economic efficiency, social justice and individual liberty."[24] While having great intuitive appeal, the problem with this lofty statement is that it suggests there must be trade-offs. Conventional economic theory often implies such trade-offs: trade-offs between efficiency, equity, and justice; between groups of players; and between current economic conditions and deficit reduction. This type of thinking plays into the hands of a selfish government which must rationalize inaction by claim of losses.

Government programs are often simultaneously inefficient, unjust, and inequitable. Government has a hard time being an unbiased advocate for the public. Instead, government favors regional and special interests at the expense of taxpayers and consumers. The reason for this is simple. Programs that provide dispersed public benefits do not generate a strong constituency, even if they are in the national interest. Inefficient programs that provide concentrated benefits to small groups of society create wealthy constituencies, and these constituencies fund election campaigns and the personal campaign for early retirement. Similarly, government has little incentive to reduce costs, since there is a limited reward system for cost savings. Savings are disbursed, but the benefits from continued spending are concentrated.

SUMMARY

It is of serious interest to the country that the people at large should have no lobby and be voiceless in these matters, while great bodies of astute men seek to create an artificial opinion and to overcome the interests of the public for their private profit. Only public opinion can check and destroy it.[25]

There is a pervasive feeling that the federal government is out of control, especially with respect to wasteful programs and the federal debt. Somehow, when money is involved, the system of checks and balances does not work as well as it should. For two decades, there has been an obvious lack of common-sense fiscal responsibility. To finance its short-term political agenda, the federal government can borrow indefinitely against the future of the nation.

The budget debate rages as this book is being completed. Although the debate is ostensibly a matter of public interest, it is perhaps more a matter of self-interest and special interests than is generally recognized. A better solution to the crisis must eliminate the incentives for wasteful government. Private interests can have undue influence on government because the law allows them to, and selfish interests make sure that these laws are maintained. "The government rule book has become a catalogue of special interest provisions" and the same goes for government programs.[26] Political Action Committee money, "nonfederal funds," "24E" money, and numerous election law loopholes enable iron triangles and government capture.

Previous sections have shown that private actors and government often use public resources and laws for their own interests. These activities are obviously antimarket when they work directly to control market competition. The sale of public resources at a price far below cost or market value is antimarket in that inefficient quantities are bought and private market sales of the same resource are adversely affected. With these and other forms of subsidy, private players become involved in rent-seeking rather than rent-creating activities. Both government and private players expend resources to maintain the status quo as opposed to seeking efficient or innovative solutions to real problems.

NOTES

1. John R. Emshwiller, "Easy Pickings: How Career Swindlers Run Rings Around SEC and Prosecutors," *Wall Street Journal,* May 12, 1995, p. 1.

2. *1993 Information Please Almanac* 40th edition, Ed. Otto Johnson (Boston: Houghton Mifflin, 1993), p. 854.

3. Gary D. Libecap, *Locking up the Range; Federal Land Conflicts and Grazing* Pacific Studies in Public Policy (San Francisco: Pacific Institute, 1991), p. 4.

4. For example, see R. L. Stroup and J. A. Baden, *Natural Resources: Bureaucratic Myths and Environmental Management* (San Francisco, CA: Pacific Institute for Public Policy Research, 1983).

5. Stephen Pizzo, Mary Fricker, and Paul Muolo. *Inside Job: The Looting of America's Savings and Loans* (New York: McGraw-Hill, 1989), p. 14.

6. Council of Economic Advisors, *Economic Report of the President,* Chapter 5. Markets and Regulatory Reform. Transmitted to Congress, January 1993. (Washington: U.S. Government Printing Office, 1993).

7. Anne Krueger, "The Political Economy of the Rent-Seeking Society," *American Economic Review* 64(3) (1974): p. 291.

8. The idea of capture theory has often been attributed to G. L. Stigler, "The Theory of Economic Regulation," *Bell Journal of Economics* 2 (1971): 3–21.

9. Bruce L. Benson and M. L. Greenhut, "Special Interests, Bureaucrats and Antitrust: An Explanation of the Antitrust Paradox," in *Antitrust and Regulation*, ed. R. E. Grieson (Lexington, MA: Lexington Books, D.C. Heath, 1986), p. 54.

10. Gordon Tolluck, "Concluding Thoughts on the Politics of Regulation," in *Public Choice and Regulation: A View from Inside the Federal Trade Commission,* eds. R. J. Mackay, J. C. Miller, and B. Yandle (Stanford, CA: Hoover Institution Press, 1987), p. 340.

11. Benson and Greenhut, in "Special Interests, Bureaucrats and Antitrust," p. 54.

12. Roger L. Faith, Donald R. Leavens, and Robert D. Tollison, "Antitrust Pork Barrel," in *Public Choice and Regulation: A View from Inside the Federal Trade Commission*, eds. R. J. Mackay, J. C. Miller and B. Yandle (Stanford, CA: Hoover Institution Press, 1987), pp. 15–28.

13. Benson and Greenhut, in "Special Interests, Bureaucrats and Antitrust," p. 54.

14. Bernard Wunder, "Department of Commerce National Telecommunications and Information Administration," in *Telecommunications in Crisis: The First Amendment, Technology and Deregulation*, eds. Edwin Diamond, Norman Sandler, and Milton Mueller (Washington, D.C.: Cato Institute, 1983), p. 6.

15. Carol S. Greenwald, *Banks Are Dangerous to Your Wealth* (Englewood Cliffs, NJ: Prentice-Hall, 1980), p. 218.

16. Michael N. Danielson, *The Politics of Exclusion* (New York: Columbia University Press, 1976). Quoted in J. A. Gardiner and T. R. Lyman, *Decisions for Sale: Corruption and Reform in Land Use and Building Regulation* (New York: Praeger Publishers, 1978), p. 19.

17. Eleena De Lisser and Anita Sharpe, "Stealth Warfare: Home Depot Charges a Rival Drummed Up Opposition to Stores," *Wall Street Journal*, August 18, 1995, p. 1.

18. Robert Lekachman, *Economists at Bay: Why the Experts Will Never Solve Your Problems* (New York: McGraw-Hill, 1976), p. 136.

19. Rodney Atkinson, *Government Against the People: The Economics of Political Exploitation* (Southampton, England: The Camelot Press, 1986), p. 141.

20. R. Lekachman, *Economists at Bay,* p. 136.

21. Martin L. Gross, *The Government Racket: Washington Waste from A to Z* (New York: Ballentine Books, 1993).

22. Harrie A. A. Verbon and A. A. M. Van Winden, *The Political Economy of Government Debt*. Contributions to Economic Analysis 219 (Amsterdam: North-Holland, 1993), pp. 8, 14.

23. "The Withering Away of the State," *The Economist* April 6, 1996, p. 82. The article is based on V. Tanzi and L. Schuknecht "The Growth of Government and the Reform of the State in Industrial Countries," International Monetary Fund Working Paper, December 1995.

24. Quote is from Robert Kuttner, *The Economic Illusion: False Choices Between Prosperity and Social Justice* (Boston: Houghton Mifflin, 1984), p. 1.

25. This quote by Woodrow Wilson is from D. L. Barlett and James B. Steele, *America: What Went Wrong* (Kansas City, MO: Andrews and McMeel, 1991), p. 219.

26. Ibid. p. 216.

9

Government Intervention in Agriculture and Water

The problem of substantial market control by influence of government is illustrated by the recent activities of two federal agencies. The U.S. Department of Agriculture (USDA) administers several of the oldest and most extensive market control systems in the United States. For some fruits, nuts, and vegetables, the USDA oversees a system that allows privately managed market control exercised through quantity and quality restrictions. For some other agricultural commodities, the federal government has subsidized production, supported prices and incomes, and restricted quantities produced. The USDA also uses taxpayers' money to reduce production through several direct acreage control provisions. The Federal Agriculture Improvement and Reform Act of 1996 has reduced the scope of these activities, but this change may be temporary and occurred only because it was in the best short-term economic interest of the agricultural interests involved.

On the other hand, the Department of Interior has developed water supplies for irrigation in the western United States through the Bureau of Reclamation (USBR). Taxpayers paid to develop millions of acres of highly productive irrigated land with public money. The two departments, Agriculture and Interior, simultaneously spent public money to fallow and develop agricultural land, frequently in the same region and sometimes on the same farm. Land developed by the USBR was often fallowed by farm programs. The two agencies interacted through markets even when they did not operate on the same land. The actions of each agency have served to cancel the actions of the other, and taxpayers have paid twice to obtain no net result.

To advocate their programs, the two departments and their interest groups have provided opposite rationales to the public. Farm program advocates have argued that farmers overproduce. The USBR has rationalized its expenditure by arguing that more cropland was a good investment. The beneficiaries of USBR and USDA expenditures have frequently benefitted from both programs, and economic rents created by the two subsidies have been used to sustain support in Congress.

FARM PROGRAMS

Federal farm programs have existed in some form since the 1930s. The original intent of these programs were "to protect the family farm, to support prices and farm income to conserve natural resources" and to "ensure the orderly distribution" of commodities.[1] A new farm bill typically becomes law about every five years: the Agriculture and Food Act of 1981 (PL 97-98), the Food Security Act of 1985 (PL 99-198), and the Food, Agriculture, Conservation and Trade Act of 1990 (PL 101-624); and most recently, the Federal Agriculture Improvement and Reform Act (FAIRA) of 1996.

Commodity Programs

The example of substantial market control is most clearly shown in the case of commodity programs. Program commodities include feed grains (sorghum, corn, oats, barley), wheat, rice, and upland cotton. The land area participating in commodity programs was recently about the size of Texas.[2] Only farmers with a history of production of program commodities could participate in commodity programs. If an eligible producer decided to participate, he could, and still can, obtain a nonrecourse loan from the government based on a loan rate per unit crop and his expected production. If, after harvest, crop price falls below the loan rate, the government has no recourse but to assume ownership of the crop in repayment of the loan. That is, the commodity is collateral, and the farmer may default without penalty regardless of what the value of his collateral turns out to be. Since many farmers turn their crops over to the government when market price falls below the loan rate, and the government then holds this crop off the market, the loan rate acts as a support price. Nonparticipating farmers also benefit because the entire market is affected by these price support operations. The higher prices are passed on to consumers, especially through meat products that use large amounts of feed grains.

Until the mid-1990s, support prices were often higher than world market prices, which made our commodities too expensive for foreign buyers. Marketing loan and export enhancement provisions allowed producers to sell for export and repay their loans at a price less than the loan rate, or exports were directly subsidized. Export enhancement provisions targeted export subsidies to international markets lost to "unfair competition," which is largely anyone who has the same types of agricultural policies that we do. The agricultural lobby has used trade negotiations "to justify larger rather than smaller export subsidies" by arguing that the United States must increase subsidies to bring these unfair competitors to the bargaining table.[3] Commodity prices were also increased by USDA open market purchases.

Until 1996, farmers who participated in commodity programs could also receive deficiency payments. Deficiency payments were a check direct from U.S. taxpayers to the farmer. Payments were based on the difference between a target price per unit crop and the market price or the loan rate, whichever difference was smaller. Target prices were frozen by Congress in 1990 for five years, and deficiency payments were cut 15 percent. Still, rice and cotton growers recently obtained a quarter to a half of their gross income from deficiency payments, nonrecourse loans, marketing loans, and other subsidies.

Farm policy has many provisions that subsidize agriculture to increase production. Research, soil conservation, and subsidized on-farm improvements increase productivity, and the USDA's extension service provides free information on new technologies developed with taxpayer dollars. If the support prices, deficiency payments, and production subsidies were provided without production controls, government storage would quickly overflow with agricultural goods, and this has happened from time to time.

To obtain some semblance of balance between supply and demand, farm programs had to restrict the quantity of commodities produced. Until 1996, farmers who wanted commodity program benefits had to reduce their planted acreage by an acreage reduction percentage (ARP). The ARP for each commodity was determined each year according to stocks and projected use. In 1985, the USDA began to adopt more voluntary measures to reduce commodity supplies. The 0/92 and 50/92 provisions allowed farmers to receive 92 percent of their deficiency payments even with one-half or more of their land idled. Beginning in 1990, flex acreage provisions allowed up to 25% of acreage to be planted to some other crop.

The USDA removes agricultural land from production for longer terms using leases. The Conservation Reserve Program (CRP) has used ten to fifteen-year leases to idle 36 million acres of farmland—an area the size of Iowa—between 1985 and 1993. Although the CRP is legally targeted to highly erodible lands, it is generally recognized that it was administered partially to obtain a reduction in commodity production. Over one-quarter of the enrolled acreage was not highly erodible. At a minimum, lease programs demonstrate that the federal government is willing to reduce acreage and production even for extended periods. All together, ARPs, voluntary reduction provisions, and long-term fallow programs idled a maximum of about 80 million acres in the continental United States in 1987—an area the size of Iowa and Illinois combined. Total land fallow under the CRP and farm program provisions declined to roughly 50 million acres in the early 1990s.

While commodity programs are the single largest USDA intervention in terms of direct expense, many other programs control production and markets for other agricultural goods. Programs for dairy, sugar, tobacco, and peanuts and oilseeds recently supported prices, controlled production, and increased costs to consumers. Recent estimates of producer subsidy equivalents suggest that sugar and dairy are much more subsidized than other commodities.[4]

The 1996 Farm Bill: How To Get It Both Ways

The Federal Agriculture Improvement and Reform Act (FAIRA) became law in April of 1996. The system of program commodity deficiency payments based on target and market prices has been replaced with a system of fixed payments per acre, called market transition payments. The payments are roughly the same amount as deficiency payments were under the old system, but they are no longer dependent on market prices. Instead, payments are based on a fixed annual budget. The fewer participants, the more payment per acre, and total payments will decline over time until 2002 when FAIRA expires. Total expenditure on the transition payments is limited to $5.57 billion in 1996 declining to $4.01 billion in 2002.[5] Any acreage certified as base acreage in the last five years is eligible for the seven-year market transition contracts, and any crop except fruit and vegetables can be grown on the contract acreage. Participants are free to grow nothing at all and still receive the payment, and there will be no acreage reduction requirement.

The new farm bill retains most important conservation, promotion and nutrition programs. The CRP has been reauthorized with up to 36.4 million acres enrolled at any one time. Some existing CRP leases can be voided at the landowners' discretion and the land can receive the market transition payments if it was eligible base prior to enrollment in the CRP.

FAIRA represents a substantial change in the direction and methods of farm policy. The initial reasons for the change were a desire for budget savings and a more market-oriented agriculture. As might be expected, farm program advocates were at first very concerned about this new direction. Two events occurred that made the new farm bill politically feasible.

First, commodity crop prices rose to unprecedented levels, and high prices are expected to continue for some time. The index of prices received for food grains, feed grains and hay, and cotton increased 50, 38 and 40 percent, respectively, between 1993 and January of 1996. The 1996 market prices of wheat, barley, oats, and cotton are expected to exceed the target prices under the 1990 farm legislation.[6] Therefore, producers of these commodities would have received no deficiency payments under the old system. Under FAIRA, they will receive the market transition payments. In the short run at least, FAIRA represents an improvement over the previous farm program for most commodity farmers. "Farmers would benefit from continuation of sizable payments from the government *on top of* the higher market prices, plus enhanced profitability from the efficiency gains brought about be deregulation."[7] The farm legislation which started as a budget-cutting measure will actually cost taxpayers more in the short term than the legislation it replaces.

The second factor that allowed FAIRA to become law was that the 1949 authorization for support programs is retained, and these programs can be continued after 2002 if political and economic conditions warrant. If market prices fall, the farm lobby will probably argue for a return to the old method of price-based subsidies. If prices remain high, the new method of fixed payments is likely to retain favor.

Marketing Orders

Section 6 of the Clayton Act and the Capper-Volstead Act provide agricultural cooperatives with limited protection from antitrust limitations on combinations in restraint of trade as outlawed by the Sherman Act. Marketing orders, a form of market control, are authorized by additional laws and a vote of the majority of growers for many fruits and vegetables. They are applied most effectively to fresh oranges, lemons, and some other tree fruits. Prices are supported by weekly marketing volume restrictions. Recommendations on volume controls are made weekly by administrative committees to the USDA who routinely approves them.

While industry advocates claim that marketing orders promote efficient marketing to the benefit of growers and consumers alike, others claim that they promote monopoly pricing, distort international trade and processed fruit markets, alter regional production patterns, and increase prices throughout the United States. The controls are frequently administered by a small group of the largest growers who have used their power to drive other growers out of business. Marketing orders allow growers to "outlaw competition, to force growers to abandon much of their crop, to prohibit new entries" and to effectively ban new technology.[8]

The USDA announced in late 1992 that weekly volume controls for navel oranges and lemons would not be approved for the remainder of the 1992-93 year. This decision was based on USDA guidelines that were encouraging industries to shift their marketing focus toward marketing rather than volume controls, and on the moratorium on new regulations that President George Bush announced in January 1992. Sunkist Growers, Inc., is the agricultural cooperative representing California and Arizona citrus producers and is represented on the administrative committees. Sunkist obtained a temporary restraining order for two weeks, but the USDA decision was upheld by a U.S. District Court.

Reasons, Real and Contrived

The case of agricultural intervention is an example of antimarket exchange in the form of both substantial market control and transfers from taxpayers. The iron triangle involves farm lobbies, the USDA, and Congress. The farm lobby, supported by payments from farmers, works with Congress to ensure continued subsidies or direct market controls. Mutual support and vote trading among commodity groups allows farm program legislation to have broad-based support in Congress.[9] The addition of the food stamp program to USDA activities even brought the urban poor into the coalition.

The three main participants provide a self-reinforcing economic mechanism in which all work together for mutual benefit. Farmers get the direct payments or market control, and farm state representatives get re-elected with the contributions of their agricultural supporters. The USDA administers the programs and sometimes provides rationales, but farm state representatives do most of the rationalizing for farm programs.

The cost of farm programs to taxpayers only, and only that share paid by the Commodity Credit Corporation, recently ranged from $7 to $25 billion annually.[10] This cost does not include conservation programs such as the CRP, which currently costs about $2 billion annually, and most USDA research and administrative costs. Consumers as a group also pay more for food and clothing costs when prices are supported and production curtailed. Many farmers are also hurt by USDA programs. Marketing orders favor some farmers and commodity programs drive up livestock feed costs.

Congress often based its five-year farm program bill on inaccurate predictions. In the late 1970s, the government improperly calculated that world markets for crops would continue to expand, but they did not. The result was that taxpayers paid farmers to fallow land that had been brought into production by subsides. In the early 1980s, the government surmised that the inflation of the late 1970s would continue, and support prices and loan rates were indexed upward. Since inflation did not continue, U.S. commodities were soon priced out of the world market, farmer's share of income from the government increased, and more farmers were drawn into the farm programs. The costs of farm programs have usually turned out to be much higher than predicted.[11]

Farm programs continue because of politics, not economics, and political support is sustained by numerous rationales, which have little basis in fact. These rationales, and the opposing perspective, are as follows:

1. *Farmers are poor.* The farmers who receive much of USDA subsidies are, on average, wealthier than average Americans. The median income of farm families passed the average families' median income in about 1964. In 1989, the average farm household had a net worth of $381,000. In 1984, 70 percent of farm program dollars went to the largest 15 percent of farms—people who are clearly much wealthier than most. Still, total farm program subsidies could be as high as $250,000 per person per year.[12,13,14,15]

2. *Farm programs help the family farmer.* Despite continuing claims that the USDA programs support family farms, a third of farm production now comes from less than 2 percent of farms. Subsidies become capitalized into land values, and this makes land prices less affordable for new family farmers.

3. *Farms need public support.* Most public support goes to farmers who don't need it, or farmers who bought land at prices inflated by farm programs then needed the programs to pay the land off.

4. *Farm programs benefit consumers* by increasing production and keeping food prices down. This rationale is very doubtful since a major purpose of farm programs has been to increase prices at the national level.

These rationales have been supported by agricultural interests, farm state representatives, and, sometimes, federal research and publications. Farm advocacy groups told the public that they were supporting the rights of farmers to compete fairly in free markets, while at the same time, their representatives lobbied Congress to get support for the next farm bill.

Experts do not agree if there ever was a farm problem that could justify farm programs, or on the original cause of the farm problem if there was one. In one school of thought, agriculture suffers from excess productive capacity. "The national farm economy simply has not been able to make the rapid resource adjustment required by the rapid inflow of new and improved capital and practices."[16] In this school, agriculture produced too much, so intervention was required to reduce production and increase prices. "Assuming that there were no farm programs in operation to support farm prices and protect farm incomes—that is, no programs to control production and no programs to dispose of products, the price and income consequences to American farmers would be disastrous."[17]

Farm program advocates have never emphasized the fact that the entire problem of overproduction is government-induced. Government not only created the excess capacity, but farm policy virtually ensures that resources will be kept in agriculture. The homestead laws required that owners reside on the land for years before title could be obtained. This caused settlers to stay on the land at almost any cost, so economic survival forced overproduction. Now, the government subsidizes increased production through prices, research, low interest loans, development of new acreage, and technical giveaways. At best, government policies to expand cultivation and increase productivity aggravate an imperfect market. At worst, these policies caused the problem. In this view, a problem of government-induced overabundance masquerades as chronic market failure.

Farm program advocates argue that the programs are needed to sustain a healthy agricultural sector. Farm programs have not promoted long-run food security because they have contributed to a loss of nonrenewable agricultural resources. Farm programs are responsible for sustaining intensive agricultural production on highly erodible lands. They have contributed to depletion and pollution of ground water resources in the Midwest and the salinization of cotton lands in the Southwest. Many pests have become resistant to pesticides used to sustain crop yields for farm programs. While proponents argue that programs help family farmers, others argue that they lead to larger farms and fewer farmers. Even the experts cannot agree whether food prices would be lower or higher if the programs were ended.

What seems clear is that United States agriculture is currently capable of producing far more food than the United States needs, and the rest of the world will not pay the price our special interests believe farmers should receive. Everyone involved in agriculture—farmers, government, and industry—is quick to take credit for America's agricultural productivity. In truth, the United States is endowed with some of the best agricultural land and climate in the world, and technical innovation has allowed this resource base to be used with remarkable productivity. Some combination of private and public effort has resulted in this productivity, but the role and contribution of each is debatable.

Now, there is little reason to believe that modern farmers would produce too much without farm programs. Many agricultural goods are produced largely free of government influence, and these farmers get along fine without them. With modern forward contracts and futures and options markets, commodity producers can obtain annual price guarantees in advance of production. These markets effectively coordinate the plans of thousands of farmers, so there is little potential for an expectations problem now. Agriculture is not the homogenous industry of the theory of production in which many identical producers drive profits to zero. Variations in land and climate mean that long-term profits in agriculture can sustained by free markets. Only the most inefficient farmers and the least productive land would be taken out of production. In contrast, the ARP system removed a fixed percentage of every participating farmers' land from production regardless of its productivity.

In the long term, there is little evidence to support continuing programs and lots of evidence that suggests potential for substantial gains. The increased freedom to select crops and elimination of ARPs under the 1996 Act will encourage efficiency in production as farms adjust to their true comparative advantage. Farmers will adjust resource use to levels justified by market price. Quantitative studies using general equilibrium models find that commodity prices fall without farm programs, but the elimination of farm programs might increase economic welfare by restoring market/antimarket dynamics. Commodity programs all but eliminated incentives to produce new crops on commodity acreage.* Some share of agricultural profits and resources are diverted to political activities that sustain market control. Free enterprise will encourage development of new marketing mechanisms, new production techniques, and new varieties and types of crops.

---

* The "flex" acreage provisions in the 1990 farm bill allowed farmers to plant up to 25 percent of their commodity acreage base to some alternative crops without loss of base acreage protection. Farmers responded by experimenting with new crops and varieties.

It is important to note that many farmers did not like the traditional commodity programs, especially those who produce livestock and crops sold in free markets. Even farmers who produce program commodities sometimes wish that the intervention would be eliminated. A survey conducted by the USDA found that two out of five farmers favored phasing deficiency payments out, and most supported flexibility to plant any crop they wanted on base acreage.[18] Similarly, many USDA employees have provided evidence unfavorable to farm programs, and even those who support the programs are usually well intentioned.

Despite the exclusions and qualifications, the point remains the same. A substantial share of U.S. agricultural production and trade has not occurred through free markets. Government has controlled the exchange or allowed others to control it. The beneficiaries have usually been relatively wealthy landowners, legislators, and a bureaucracy. Outdated rationales, perpetrated and defended by the beneficiaries, have sustained the public support needed to maintain the system. Resources have been dedicated to the production of traditional crops, and incentives to develop new crops or new markets were reduced. Welfare has been reduced not only by static inefficiency, but also by a lack of progress.

FEDERAL IRRIGATION DEVELOPMENT

The federal government subsidizes water supply development for irrigation of crops, hydropower, navigation, flood control, and other purposes through several bureaucracies. The Army Corps of Engineers, Tennessee Valley Authority, and Bonneville Power Administration are important, depending on location. This section concentrates on the Department of Interior's Bureau of Reclamation (USBR), whose primary mission has been to develop irrigated land. The USBR has recently been the subject of some substantial critiques.[19]

In summary, the USBR was driven to develop irrigated land by pork barrel politics, agricultural ideology, and a system of subsidies that virtually ensured the support of local beneficiaries. USBR land development can be characterized as antimarket because much of the developed land would never have been irrigated if left to market forces. The costs often exceeded the benefits by a wide margin, but optimistic forecasting and biased benefit-cost analysis were used to rationalize USBR projects while disregarding past economic failures (chapter 10).

The USBR currently provides partial or full water supplies for irrigation of about ten million acres. Taxpayers paid most of the cost of the facilities to develop this irrigated land. This subsidy was allowed largely because farmers' liability to repay irrigation development is limited by law to their "ability to pay." When the Bureau of Reclamation was established in 1902, beneficiaries were required to repay their share of project costs in ten years, interest free. The Reclamation Extension Act of 1914 extended the repayment period to twenty years. Repayment was first tied to ability to pay in 1924, the repayment period for what can be paid was extended to forty years in 1926, a ten-year repayment deferral was authorized in 1939, and variable repayment was authorized by 1958.[20]

Several techniques are available for the USBR to finance project costs when beneficiaries are found to be unable to pay them. First, when a water supply project serves multiple purposes, some of the project cost can be shifted to other purposes, such as flood control, which by law does not have to repay its costs. Second, the USBR can use hydropower revenues to pay for the projects. Large dams such as Glen Canyon on the Colorado River generate power, and the revenues are used to finance irrigation development elsewhere. Of course, the USBR can go to Congress and request more money. This happened frequently in the past.

The ability-to-pay law has resulted in rent-seeking behavior by landowners and regional interests who stand to gain from the projects. One article called this "willingness to play" in contrast to the "willingness to pay" doctrine of market economics.[21] First, beneficiaries realize the economic windfall they stand to gain from getting subsidized water from the USBR. Their total benefit is much less than the cost to taxpayers, but the share of cost they must pay is less than the benefits by design. So naturally, the beneficiaries work with their representatives to get the project authorized and built. Once a project is built, local efforts shift to getting the water for an even lower cost. This is possible because farmers' repayment of capital costs can be reduced to zero under the ability-to-pay law. The net result is that the land receiving water pays for only a small share of project costs. One study found that irrigation components of nineteen projects, which had originally been allocated costs of $1.4 billion, were expected to eventually repay only $73 million or 5 percent of their cost, largely due to ability-to-pay provisions.[22]

The Animas-La Plata Project, in Colorado and New Mexico, has had a long planning history. The project was authorized, but not funded, in 1968. The half-billion dollar project would provide water to second-class land with a 120-day growing season requiring irrigation water pump lift of up to 800 feet. Even in the best of conditions, farmers rarely pump water 800 feet for irrigation. The land can only be irrigated because the USBR will also subsidize the electricity required to pump the water.

The project stalled in Congress for many years until it became a pivotal player in the reserved water rights claims of the Colorado Ute Indian tribes. While settlement of Indian water rights claims seems a noble purpose, less than 10 percent of the irrigated land and about one-third of the water developed by the project would be for the tribes. As one observer noted, the best way to get subsidized federal water development past today's Congress is to "wrap it in an Indian blanket."

Local property taxes can be used repay a part of the small share of project costs paid by the region, further reducing the costs to the direct beneficiaries. Reclamation law requires an election in the project service area to approve a contract for repayment of project costs covered by local tax revenues. Figure 9.1 shows a flyer used by proponents to support their cause. The contract election was approved by voters.

Not only is the cost of development subsidized, but the USBR also subsidizes operating costs through subsidized hydropower. USBR dams often produce hydropower, and the law allows farmers to receive the power required to move water at below-market prices. The law requires that power be allocated first to USBR projects, meaning irrigated agriculture; second to preference customers, such as the federal government and irrigation districts; and finally to the citizens who paid for it.

The USBR continued to develop irrigated land at the same time the USDA was paying farmers to fallow similar land in the same region. New land and more commodity production meant that, to maintain prices at the support price, the USDA had to stop an equivalent amount of production elsewhere. Once the USBR built a project, much of the new irrigated land could produce commodities for USDA programs, which meant that some of it had to be fallowed by the ARPs. In 1989, about 36 percent of harvested acreage on USBR projects was program commodities or sugar beets.[23]

The economic arrangement for federal water development and pricing is similar to that for agriculture. The main players are a bureaucracy, Congress, and local interests, especially land owners. The system was rationalized by a myth concerning the need and value of additional agriculture. The myth stated that since population and export markets were growing, we needed more agricultural land. This was not true since crop yields per acre were growing faster than population, and foreign agriculture was also increasing their productivity faster than population growth. Rural and regional development provided another rationale.

Like the USDA, the USBR is now changing. Rather than develop new irrigated land, the USBR is now concentrating more on management of existing projects, especially for environmental purposes. Recent new project legislation even included a requirement for surcharges on water delivered to grow surplus agricultural commodities. Nonetheless, the USBR and local interests continue to press for new or expanded irrigation projects in several locations around the nation, and land owners on existing projects work to undermine or overturn laws that would increase their water costs.

SUMMARY

The USDA rationalized price supports, direct payments to farmers, and the reduction of agricultural acreage on the basis that farmers were producing too much. The USBR rationalized the expensive development of more land for highly productive irrigated agriculture based on the value of more agricultural production. The actions of both agencies were based on outdated rationales. Commodities may have been overproduced in the past because of an expecta-

Figure 9.1
Election Flyer, Animas-La Plata Project Repayment Election

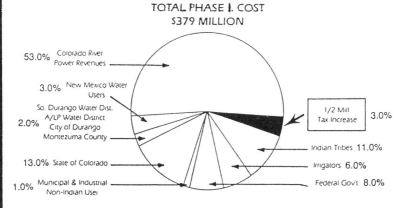

WHY WE SHOULD SUPPORT THE ANIMAS - LA PLATA PROJECT.

REASON #7:

...BECAUSE SOMEONE ELSE IS PAYING MOST OF THE TAB!

We get the water. We get the reservoir. They pay the bill.

TOTAL PHASE I. COST
$379 MILLION

53.0% Colorado River Power Revenues

3.0% New Mexico Water Users

So. Durango Water Dist.
A/LP Water District
2.0% City of Durango
Montezuma County

13.0% State of Colorado

1.0% Municipal & Industrial Non-Indian User

1/2 Mill Tax Increase 3.0%

Indian Tribes 11.0%

Irrigators 6.0%

Federal Gov't 8.0%

SUPPORT
ANIMAS - LA PLATA
VOTE ☑ YES
TUESDAY, DECEMBER 8

PAID FOR BY TAXPAYERS FOR WATER & ECONOMIC DEVELOPMENT
JEFF MORRISSEY - TREASURER

tions problem or because the federal government subsidized the development of new agricultural land.

Now, farmers can work with futures and options markets to control price risk. There is little new land development occurring and productivity growth has slowed. The USBR's irrigation development was based on the idea that a growing population needs more food, but this need has been met with improved productivity. Now, the farm economy might perform quite efficiently for farmers and consumers without any subsidies or intervention.

The economic exchange that drove both systems always had little to do with the public welfare; rather, their real reason and effect was to distribute economic rents to landowners, politicians, and bureaucrats. A small number of beneficiaries provided substantial payments to their representatives in the form of campaign contributions, political support, and other favors, the representatives sustained the bureaucracy, and taxpayers and citizens paid in the form of higher taxes, higher prices, reduced efficiency, and a loss of technical improvement. The 1996 FAIRA represents, at a minimum, a temporary improvement in farm policy, and the USBR now has its hands full trying to maintain the irrigation projects it already has. Still, agricultural policy and federal development initiatives may always respond to economic incentives made possible by market control, misguided legislation, and biased economics.

NOTES

1. S. Langley and H. Baumes, "Evolution of U.S. Agricultural Policy in the 1980's," in *Agriculture-Food Policy Review: U.S. Agricultural Policies in a Changing World*, Agricultural Economic Report Number 620 (Washington, D.C.: U.S. Department of Agriculture Economic Research Service, 1989), p. 8.

2. Enrolled base was 166.6 and 165.5 million acres in 1990 and 1992, respectively. U.S. Department of Agriculture, Office of Public Affairs, "USDA Announces Final Compliance Figures for 1990 Acreage Reduction Program" (Washington, D.C.: USDA) p. 1. By comparison, Texas is about 262,015 square miles, or about 168 million acres.

3. Robert L. Paarlberg, "Does the GATT Agreement Promote Export Subsidies?" *Choices The Magazine of Food Farm and Resource Issues* (Fourth Quarter 1995): 9–12.

4. F. J. Nelson, M. Simone, and C. Valdes, "Agricultural Subsidies in Canada, Mexico and the United States, 1982–1991," *Choices The Magazine of Food, Farm and Resource Issues* (First Quarter 1994): 22–25.

5. John Otte and Sally Schuff, "Freedom to Farm. Phaseout of Price-Based Subsidies Begins as New Farm Bill Passes." *California Farmer* 279(8), May 1996 p. 12

6. Economic Research Service, U.S Department of Agriculture, *Agricultural Outlook* (Washington, D.C.: USDA., 1996) March, 1996, pp. 32, 6, 43.

7. David Orden, Robert Paarlberg, and Terry Roe, "Can Farm Policy be Reformed? Challenge of the Freedom to Farm Act." *Choices The Magazine of Food, Farm and Resource Issues* (First Quarter 1996) p. 39.

8. James Bovard, *The Farm Fiasco* (San Francisco: ICS Press, 1989), p. 180.

9. David G. Abler, "Vote Trading on Farm Legislation in the U.S. House," *American Journal of Agricultural Economics* 71(3) (August 1989): 583–591.

10. U.S. Department of Commerce, Bureau of the Census. *Statistical Abstract of the United States* (Washington, D.C.: U.S. Government Printing Office, 1990), Table 1131, 1982 to 1989 data, p. 652.

11. Bovard, *The Farm Fiasco*, p. 255.

12. Ibid., p. 49.

13. U.S. Department of Agriculture, *U.S. Agricultural Statistics* (Washington, D.C.: U.S. Government Printing Office, 1990), pp. 364, 357.

14. Osha G. Davidson, *Broken Heartland: The Rise of America's Rural Ghetto* (New York: Maxwell Macmillan International, 1990), p. 167.

15. U.S. Department of Agriculture, Economic Research Service, *Provisions of the Food, Conservation and Trade Act of 1990.* Agriculture Information Bulletin Number 614. (Washington, D.C.: 1991), p. 36.

16. Willard W. Cochrane, *The City Man's Guide to the Farm Problem* (Minneapolis, MN: University of Minnesota Press, 1965), p. 111.

17. Ibid., p. 117.

18. "Of Wheat and Welfare," *The Economist*, February 11, 1995, p. 26.

19. For example see Marc Reisner, *Cadillac Desert: The American West and Its Disappearing Water* (New York, Viking, 1986); and Doris Ostrander Dawdy, *Congress in Its Wisdom: The Bureau of Reclamation and the Public Interest,* Studies in Water Policy and Management No. 13 (Boulder, CO: Westview Press, 1989).

20. Joseph L. Sax, *Federal Reclamation Law. Volume II.: Water and Water Rights* (New York: Allen Smith Company, 1967).

21. William E. Martin, H. Ingram, and N. K. Laney, "A Willingness to Play: Analysis of Water Resources Development," *Western Journal of Agricultural Economics* 7(1) (1982): 133–139.

22. Douglas R. Franklin and R. K. Hagemann, "Cost-sharing with Irrigated Agriculture: Promise Versus Performance," *Water Resources Research* 20(8) (August 1984): 1047–1051.

23. U.S. Department of the Interior, Bureau of Reclamation, "1989 Summary Statistics: Water, Land and Related Data" (Washington, D.C.: 1989), p. 18.

10

Quantitative Analysis and the Role of Economics in Rationalization

Several applications of quantitative analysis demonstrate a lack of empiricism in economics as well as the role economics sometimes plays in rationalizing substantial antimarket behaviors. For purposes here, quantitative economic analysis is the application of economic theories and data to provide predictions or estimates of the economic impacts of alternative actions. Sometimes, the purpose of quantitative economics is to provide good predictions. When properly confirmed, many quantitative applications demonstrate predictive value.

On the other hand, many applications are undertaken without adhering to good scientific principles and produce results that are not or cannot be confirmed by facts. To make things worse, economists are often paid by public and private advocates. Interest groups create a large demand for dollar estimates of impacts of new laws, regulations, or public projects, and many such studies are required by law. The buyers of the services of economists want results, the limits of the theory, data, or methods notwithstanding. Quantitative analysis, unchecked by the principle of validation, is easily manipulated to support preconceptions or the propaganda needs of one's financial supporters.

Economists, like anyone else, have personal values and beliefs. Personal beliefs affect the choice and conduct of research, decisions on what results are factually right or wrong, and even who economists work for. An advocate can usually find an economist with the right beliefs for the job. Preconceptions, ideology, and the demand for rationales, not science, are often used to select the right model and the right economist.

Government, like most groups of people, is a self-advocate, and many economists work for government. One function of economics is the justification or rationalization of economic expenditure or intervention for government and the public. Congress occasionally uses independent commissions or other impartial bodies to develop methodologies for this research, but economic analysis is often conducted by agencies who have a strong money interest in the outcome. A lack of scientific protocols to check results combined with self-interest and preconception results in biased economics.

These problems are shown by analysis and examples of three quantitative techniques. Benefit-cost studies of some types of major federal projects and regulations are required to demonstrate to Congress that the proposed change is in the public interest. When the federal interest has already decided that the expenditure or regulation should occur, the economic research can become part of the rationale provided to the public and other parts of government. Without application of sound methods for confirmation of results, "the most significant factor in evaluating a benefit-cost study is the name of the sponsor."[1]

Contingent valuation (CV) is a relatively new economic technique developed to estimate economic benefits of unpriced resources. Although numerous studies have found that CV can be used to produce biased results, the method is commonly used to rationalize public expenditures and regulations related to the environment.

Input-output analysis is another method that has been extensively used to rationalize government as well as private actions. Input-output analysis does not adhere to even the most fundamental principles of economics. Furthermore, the method fails a logical test of what it is supposed to do. However, it does provide dependably inflated dollar values to help rationalize public development and expenditure initiatives.

All of these examples show why and how bad science in economics is sustained by a demand for rationales and by a lack of concern for scientific process. The common denominator of all of these techniques is that assumptions and results are not usually confirmed or verified by reference to independent facts, which are often available. The degree of manipulation becomes apparent only when alternative analyses compete openly in public or when predictions are checked against actual results.

BENEFIT-COST ANALYSIS

Estimation of benefits and/or costs is required for several types of federal actions. Economic analysis of critical habitat designation is required under the Endangered Species Act. Regulatory impact assessments (RIAs) are required by executive order to provide information about the benefits and costs of major federal regulations. Natural Resource Damage Assessments (NRDAs) are used to support claims of damages to state, federal and tribal natural resources. Recent executive orders and initiatives have proposed more use of benefit-cost analysis in implementing federal regulations.

Perhaps the oldest and most formalized .application of benefit-cost analysis is in the evaluation of water resource development projects. The most recent principles for project evaluation were provided in 1983.[2] Presumably, the benefit-cost analyses would identify projects with unfavorable economics, and Congress would not appropriate the money to build them. However, the responsible agencies always conducted their own benefit-cost analyses, and these studies almost always found proposed projects to be economical. The economic research then became part of an advocacy effort aimed at ensuring local, regional, congressional, and public support. Campen calls the efforts of the Army Corps of Engineers and USBR to attain favorable results "legendary."[3] Even the precise procedures used to manipulate benefit-cost analyses have been discussed in hearings before Congress.

Repayment analyses must also be conducted as part of USBR project planning to determine what farmers should pay for irrigation water. By law, farmers must only repay what they are able to pay. The less farmers must pay for a project, the more rents generated to be distributed for beneficiaries and the more the beneficiaries will support the project through their representatives. From the beneficiaries' perspective, the benefit-cost analysis should show that farmers will make more money, but the repayment analysis should show they can make less. To obtain the desired results, two economic analyses with different projections and assumptions are conducted. Sometimes, both are displayed in the same document. The benefit-cost analysis shows that the inflated national benefits can cover the understated costs, while the repayment analysis shows that the beneficiaries can only afford a small percent of the cost.

Studies conducted for the Animas-La Plata Project demonstrate this disparity. The benefit-cost analysis for most land served by the project found an annual per-farm income almost double expenses, an unlikely result even for the best corn land in Iowa. The repayment analysis for the project calculated a net return per acre of $77; the benefit-cost analysis calculated a net return of $137. The difference was mostly due to larger crop yields assumed in the benefit-cost analysis, for example, 5.8 tons of alfalfa per acre instead of 4.8 tons used in the repayment analysis. Then, the repayment analysis reduced total net revenue for a family living allowance of $15,000 per farm to obtain an ability to pay per acre of $25. Finally, the net benefit used to rationalize the project ($137 per acre) was more than five times what the USBR claimed farmers should pay for the water ($25).

The ability-to-pay provisions and family living allowance ensure that the federally developed irrigated land will be farmed. USBR projects were reimbursed with public revenues to cover the costs of agricultural job creation even as the USDA reduced agricultural employment by idling land. The USBR's family living allowance clearly favors federal development over private. Private investors do not get reimbursed for the costs of wages they pay, but the family living allowance requires taxpayers to pay farmers' living expenses.

The Animas-La Plata benefit-cost analysis ignored several economic benefits that would be lost if the project were built. These benefits included hydropower generated by the water on its way downstream, the value of the water in reducing salinity, and the use of the water for water supply downstream. The latter two external costs of the project were completely ignored, but a rationale for excluding adverse salinity impacts of the project was provided. "The negative externalities from the salt-concentrating effects of the project stream depletion have not been included . . . since it is believed that the rights to divert and deplete streamflows . . . are associated with a corresponding right to concentrate the salt of the stream without penalty."[4] The unfavorable facts, where they must be recognized, are dismissed on the basis of a legal technicality. The federal government also spent millions to reduce salinity from its irrigation projects in the Colorado River Basin Salinity Control Program, but even these costs were not considered.

Irrigation benefit-cost analyses frequently presumed much more irrigated land than turns out to be the case once water deliveries begin. The more acres, the more benefits. One ex-post study of seventeen projects found that 82 percent of planned acreage was irrigated.[5] On some projects, only a fraction of the planned acreage is ever irrigated. The land or climate is so unfavorable that it does not pay to farm even with subsidies.

All of this has not been completely ignored by responsible members of government. The Carter administration sought to have some of the least economical proposed projects, including Animas-La Plata, deauthorized. The Reagan administration succeeded in forcing water resource benefit-cost analysis to use the nominal federal cost of funds as the real interest rate.* Since the cost of funds is not adjusted for inflation, it discounts the future benefits more than they should be, a sort of second-best method for reducing inflated estimates of future benefits.

The Animas-La Plata story continues in 1995. Environmental groups forced a reconsideration of project environmental compliance after endangered fish were found downstream. Three new benefit-cost analyses were conducted; one under the original rules, one under Water Resource Council 1983 rules that included hydropower and salinity losses and the low discount rate, and one using the nominal interest rate as currently required.[6] The analysis under the original rules still finds the project to be economical (benefit/cost ratio equal to 1.41), but analyses under the new rules find the project to be substantially uneconomical (B/C ratios of 0.40 and 0.36).

None of the analyses include the value of the water consumed by the project even though the Colorado River is oversubscribed. Allocations of Colorado River water among water users assumed more water than the hydrologic evidence now indicates will be available. Water from the river rarely reaches the ocean even though several states have not yet used their full allocation. Hydrologic and economic analyses notwithstanding, the 1995 Congress

---

* The real interest rate, or discount rate, is the rate of interest used to compare future constant-dollar (no inflation) to current construction costs. The higher the discount rate, the less economical irrigation projects appear.

appropriated $5 million to begin project construction.

Benefit-cost analysis of irrigation development has frequently been faulted for not considering the influence of USDA programs. USBR land that would be enrolled in USDA programs and then fallowed by acreage reduction requirements was not considered, and the crop prices used in the USBR's benefit analyses reflected some of the USDA's price support and acreage reduction operations. In 1987, the Natural Resources and Environment Committee of Congress agreed to use a comprehensive supply-demand analysis "to remove the influence of government programs on market prices" for purposes of analysis. The estimated prices were substantially lower than prices the USBR had previously used to calculate crop production benefits. This set off a round of re-evaluations, which found that some projects would indeed appear uneconomical with the new prices. Current procedures, formalized by Section 632 of Public Law 100-460, require that "market clearing prices without government crop support programs will no longer be reported" much less used.[7,8,9]

A policy to require program-adjusted prices would help, but the fact that every unit of commodity crop brought into production resulted in an equivalent decrease in production elsewhere was still ignored. The USDA adjusted acreage reduction requirements according to a set stocks-to-use ratio. Therefore, a benefit of more irrigated commodity production can only occur if the commodity can be produced at a higher profit than the average profit on land taken out of production by the USDA. Given that USBR water service typically costs more per acre than the best irrigated land in California, this seems unlikely, and even this approach would allow the inefficiency created by USDA land-idling programs to justify development of new land because the idle land increases crop prices and profits.

Some Other Benefit-Cost Studies

Economists have estimated the benefits society places on clean air, endangered species, human life, and just about every phenomena capable of being imagined in dollar terms.[10] Economic studies are frequently solicited for an identified need, as when particular interest groups are interested in the outcome of legislation or for big economic changes, such as trade agreements.

Campen tells of many other biased federal benefit-cost studies; for example, six different benefit-cost studies of the Concorde each achieving the result to rationalize the preconceived position of each of six federal agencies or agencies systematically ignoring one side of the issue in an RIA. Sometimes, economic benefit estimates are required for legal proceedings; for example, when NRDAs result in damage claims, and the guilty party brings to court its own estimate of dollar damages. In one case, the defendant and plaintiff estimated total damages of $240,000 and $65,000,000, respectively. In another case, the two claims were about $500,000 and $100,000,000.[11] In another comparison, which includes four additional cases, damage estimates differ by a factor of 4 to 50.[12]

The disparity of these estimates suggests the range of possible outcomes when economic analysis for advocates is unchecked by confirmation.

Benefit-cost analysis often plays a role in defending or attacking environmental programs. The Delaney clause of the Food, Drug, and Cosmetic Act requires zero-tolerance of suspected carcinogenic pesticides or other additives in food. A court decision found that the government must enforce this clause literally even as the detectable amounts of pesticides have fallen to minuscule amounts. An EPA official testified that "we are confident we can reduce pesticide use and pesticide risk without any decrease in the quality of our product or the output of our farms."[13] The American Farm Bureau Research Foundation hired some economists who started with two assumptions: (1) either no more pesticide use, or (2) a 50 percent reduction in the number of applications. They then surveyed university experts about how much production loss they thought might result from these assumptions and conducted their economic analysis based on the survey results.

This example demonstrates a lack of scientific principles on both sides. First, consider the official's statement. The entire statement does not answer any useful questions. Which pesticides? Are these the carcinogenic ones? How much would they be reduced? Would they be reduced enough to meet the requirements of the Delaney clause? The Farm Bureau's researchers made the same types of mistakes, but with the opposite bias. Neither one answered the appropriate questions given the issue at hand.

Some Prescriptions

Federal benefit-cost analysis should (1) show why efficiency improvements are possible from the national perspective, (2) show why private enterprise is not doing the job, (3) consider the full effects of additional taxation, and (4) be constrained to use real data when available, especially information from past experience with similar projects and programs.

Benefit-cost analysis is an outgrowth of the concept of static economic efficiency. If a proposed action has a positive net benefit, then some people can be made better off without making anyone else worse off. A positive net benefit, therefore, implies that there was something wrong with the economy to start with. For some reason, free trade was unable to realize some good deals. Conventional benefit-cost analysis does not require a showing that there was any problem to start with. Benefit-cost analysis should be forced to investigate and show that market failure exists, and the reason why free enterprise does not fix the problem by itself should be provided. This type of analysis might reveal ways to encourage free enterprise to correct the problem at a lower cost to the public.

All economic analysis of federal expenditure should consider and display the incremental effects of more taxation using the same methods as allowed for project benefits. There has been a tendency to assign a variety of economic and social benefits to federal programs without considering the corresponding effects of taxation or deficit spending. The effects of taxation must be readily comparable with the effects of the expenditure—how efficiency is impaired or improved, how local economies will be affected, the distribution of direct payments and taxes in terms of the wealth and status of the affected groups. The taxation aspect of federal analysis is relatively simple compared to the expenditure side because expenditures vary considerably in terms of place and types of impacts, but the structure of general taxation is relatively constant as between projects.

Economic analysis should be constrained to use real and current data collected by independent and unbiased techniques. Frequently, the purpose of quantitative analysis is to predict conditions in the future. This opens the door for the analyst to use optimistic projections to obtain the favorable result. These forecasts cannot be validated, so they cannot be directly refuted. For example, irrigation benefit-cost procedures allow detailed prediction of future farm prices and crop yields to determine benefits. Historically, crop yields have increased and real crop prices have fallen over time, but some benefit-cost studies have embraced the former fact while ignoring the latter. The use of predictions involving a favorable change in relative prices should be allowed only after the closest of scrutiny.

Irrigation project analysis was often justified by predictions of benefits and costs that turned out to be optimistic, but this information was never used in later benefit-cost studies. Actual results and data from comparable projects and ex-post studies of previous projects would be less open to manipulation than price predictions.

Benefit-cost analysis should be forced to use obvious and simple tests of economic feasibility when possible. Federal guidelines allow benefit-cost analysis to use the price of comparable irrigated land in the region as a measure of benefit. If the price of development is far in excess of the value of land, the development is obviously not economical. More use of this approach in the past would have revealed some very uneconomical projects.

Benefit-cost procedures have been criticized for not considering the distribution of benefits and costs. Benefit-cost is based on the principle of a potential Pareto-improvement. An action is deemed worthy if the total benefits exceed the costs even if the beneficiary does not have to pay the costs. To benefit-cost analysis, a project that costs 1,000,000 taxpayers $1 and provides a rich beneficiary with $1,000,001 is a good project.

By not considering the distributional effects, benefit-cost analysis favors antimarket relationships, in which wealthy players gain at the expense of common citizens. The concept of potential Pareto-improvement allows that the 1,000,000 taxpayers who pay for an "efficient" project do not have to be compensated for their costs, and this is precisely what happens. Federal investments are frequently undertaken without any requirement or plan for the beneficiaries to repay the government at all. In some cases, this may be economically efficient. For example, the transactions costs of collecting from many beneficiaries may be too high. But in many cases, there is no reason why the government could not collect; the beneficiaries are large, private players who could easily be charged for the government's services.

ENVIRONMENTAL ECONOMICS AND CONTINGENT VALUATION

The roles and powers of advocates change often in Washington, and this has changed the role of economics in justifying government activities. Especially, the environmental movement gained enormous influence during the 1970s and 1980s. Environmental economics was originally concerned with the problem and correction of pollution; this was the environmental issue of the day. Later, the field responded to public concern about unpriced resources and environmental amenities such as scenery and endangered species. The field developed several concepts: bequest value, existence value, and option value to explain why people apparently value species and natural resources they will never see or use.

Contingent valuation (CV) is a technique used to value natural resources that are not priced. Surveys are used to ask people how much they would be willing to pay for, or accept in compensation for damages to a natural resource.[14] CV was developing into a prized tool of federal environmental and wildlife agencies until the Exxon Valdez oil spill. Exxon then convened a group of economists who evaluated the method using theory and a variety of empirical applications and found it to be "not a suitable source of information on values for benefit-cost analysis" and "not suitable to measure compensatory damages."[15]

Many of the arguments against CV are compelling. First, there is a matter of experimental evidence related to stated versus actual willingness to pay (WTP).* In one case, people were asked to provide their WTP for membership in an environmental organization. Those who stated a value above the true membership cost were then invited to join. Less than one-tenth of those invited actually did. In another case, 6 and 15 percent of a sample of Montana resident and nonresident respondents stated they would pay for habitat acquisition, but only 1 and 6 percent of another sample actually did. In another study, many persons who said they would buy certain products declined to do so when faced with the real choice.[16] In short, people often will not "put their money where their mouth is."

Second, there are several types of tests of theoretical and internal consistency that have failed. Stated values are often responsive to the format of the survey, the order and types of other questions provided, and other cues inadvertently given concerning the "right" response. In one experiment a hypothetical

---

* Economic value in demand is willingness to pay less what is actually paid, and this is also a common measure of economic benefit to consumers. The demand function defines marginal willingness to pay for the good.

referendum format was compared to open-ended queries of WTP.* Mean and median WTP values from the referendum question were ten and four times, respectively, the values obtained from open-ended questioning.[17]

Results from CV studies are often independent of the scale of the resource that people are asked to value. In one study of wilderness areas, results suggested that the value of protecting three areas was not different from the value of protecting one area. In another study, the value of preventing a decline in fish populations in a small region was not different from the value for a much larger region. In another, the stated value of saving 2,000; 20,000; or 200,000 birds was not different.

Third, there is a matter of common sense. Total contributions to environmental and wildlife causes in 1990 was estimated to be $2.3 billion. CV studies have estimated that U.S. citizens would be willing to pay up to $28 billion annually to avert the extinction of whooping cranes, $14 billion to protect the northern spotted owl and its habitat, and $3.5 billion to restore just one river for salmon and steelhead trout habitat on the Olympic Peninsula.[18] This latter study assumed that fish population would increase by 300,000. Therefore, the estimated value works out to $10,000 per fish. Public safety agencies use economic estimates of the value of life to satisfy federal benefit-cost requirements. Values of $1.1 million to $8 million per statistical life have been used, but a consensus value of less than $2 million per life has been suggested as a median.[19] At this rate, we should be willing to sacrifice up to 1,750 lives to restore that one Olympic Peninsula river for anadromous fish.

Despite these and numerous other criticisms, qualified approval of contingent valuation was recently provided by a panel of eminent economists.[20] CV studies have played a role in justifying other environmental programs and have even been applied to estimate values of priced goods. Two CV studies in California estimated costs of urban water shortage even though urban water is priced and more reliable empirical demand studies are possible and even available.[21]

CV studies are not necessarily biased. One study compared numerous studies, each comparing CV with other methods, and found no systematic bias in relation to the other methods.[22] Still, survey techniques can be used to create bias, or bias can be unintentionally created by the content or format of the survey or by inadvertent cues given by the surveyor. The potential for error in CV studies can be substantially diminished by use of a bias sample. The sample, which is a subset of the respondents to the hypothetical questioning, is somehow provided with a real opportunity to pay for and receive the good. The difference between results for the bias sample and the larger set of hypothetical responses is used to correct results from the hypothetical responses for the bias revealed

---

* The hypothetical referendum typically asks if the respondent would vote for an initiative that would increase taxes by some given amount; the open-ended format merely asks the respondent to state their WTP.

by the sample.

INPUT-OUTPUT ANALYSIS

Sometimes, local support is required to obtain government funding for a local project, or local interests wish to defend their economy from government actions, such as military base closures or regulations. In such cases, an economic rationale must be developed to bolster local support, appease or discredit local detractors, and persuade external interests who might have a say in the outcome.

Input-output analysis (IO) is a quantitative method frequently used to predict the local economic stimulus provided by proposed actions. The method is relatively simple to understand and apply, but this simplicity comes at the expense of realism. IO has no basis in economic theory and is premised on many unlikely assumptions that are routinely ignored. Many recent studies have criticized IO applications for regional economic policy analysis, but it is fair to say that these studies are largely ignored in the face of public and private demands for low-cost economic rationalization.[23]

Often, the true purpose of IO is to increase the dollar figure associated with a direct impact and to convince regional economic interests that everyone has a similar stake in the project or action. IO transforms direct effects into bigger and more diffuse total impacts, and everyone in the economy is affected in the same direction. Government or other well-heeled interests frequently call on IO analysis because of these economic multiplier effects. These changes in income, output, or employment then provide economic rationale for the proposed actions. In short, IO provides the perfect rationale for pork barrel spending.

As a prelude to an article about IO, an economist recently wrote the following:

Politics often motivates undertaking studies on the size and importance of agriculture in a state or region. State and federal departments of agriculture and state-supported colleges of agriculture use this information to lobby either on budgeting or policy issues by touting the importance of agriculture to the economy. Agricultural economists have a responsibility to make sure that such studies follow acceptable procedures in economic accounting.[24]

A more pertinent question is whether economic accounting, or IO, can be an appropriate tool at all. The method, even more than conventional theory, completely ignores many real economic phenomena that affect economic activity. The method presumes that there are no fixed or sunk costs, no substitution among inputs in production, no price changes, no economies of scale and no resource constraints.[25] Still, it is obvious that new basic industries, a big project, or an increase in government expenditure result in many regional economic effects through trade linkages with the directly affected sectors of the economy (those first affected by the project). Increased output in one industry increases demands for goods from other regional industries, and respending of increased personal incomes results in induced spending effects.

However, it is argued here that under the assumptions of regional IO models there can be no change in incomes paid to regional factors of production unless there is pervasive involuntary unemployment, an unusual condition in modern economies. Few IO studies, however, concern themselves with regional employment and production constraints. Much of the increased regional incomes that IO estimates are typically paid to imported factors, such as labor, that were not part of the regional economy before the project or action.

The recognized assumptions required for use of IO methods are as follows:

1. Technical coefficients are fixed; they do not change with final demands.[*]
2. Supply increases with constant returns to scale, and there are no fixed costs.
3. Prices are fixed.

If the regional economy does not meet these assumptions for the change to be analyzed, use of IO methods will lead to inaccurate conclusions. Because it is only data, the gross flows matrix does not provide the information required to determine if the economy meets these assumptions, so independent analysis would be needed to confirm that the assumptions are not grossly violated. Such studies are rarely if ever conducted.

IO is sometimes used to predict the impact of reductions in final demand. If resources become unemployed by such a reduction, they may have limited alternative opportunities in the short run. Therefore, if all of the other IO assumptions were actually true, IO might be used as a short-run predictive device for reductions in economic activity. However, the assumption of no fixed costs becomes suspect in the short run. It is hard to reduce costs in the short run for the same reasons that it is hard for unemployed resources to find work in the short run. If some costs are actually fixed, then Assumption 2 is violated. Several problems with the application of IO are most obvious in a situation of increasing final demands, and the following discussion assumes this type of application.

While the assumption of constant returns to scale in production allows the application of IO methods, it also rules out one type of increase in economic benefits that could accrue to owners of regional industries following an increase in final demands. Increasing returns to scale would imply declining marginal and average costs, so profits could increase with final demand. If there were fixed costs, then average costs might decline with production. However, these are not options given the listed assumptions.

---

* Final demands are generally exports or any other purchase of goods and services from the region that are not affected by incomes in the region. Technical coefficients are the shares of expenses of each industry from each other industry in the region.

Since prices are fixed, increased prices cannot provide the incentive to increase production. Therefore, why would industries want to increase production at all? The only reason regional industries would increase production consistent with the other assumptions is if:

4. Industries are ready, willing, and able to increase output at the fixed prices, but production is limited by a lack of demand.

That is, the method presumes that industries want to and can produce and sell more output given current prices, but the demand just is not there.

Next, consider regional inputs of production such as labor.* In an IO analysis, an increase in final demand results in all linked industries having output larger than before, so an increase in total use of labor in the regional economy must follow. There are four possible methods for supplying this labor:

a. Regional labor is underemployed and can be used more intensively.
b. Labor imports can increase (more people commute into or move into the region).
c. Labor previously exported from the region, like out-commuters, can switch jobs and decide to work within the regional economy.
d. Labor can be made available by decreasing some other final demand. Production of other goods could be decreased and the labor transferred to the new employment.

Consideration of methods c and d are possible, but manual manipulation of final demands would be required to reallocate regional inputs among regional industries. Again, this is rarely if ever done. IO presumes that methods a and b both occur, but only according to the pre-existing fixed expenditure shares (technical coefficients) for regional and imported labor. In IO, regional labor use changes only according to the fixed expenditure share for labor. The only way that an increase in final demand can be filled without decreasing production in some other regional industry or violating the assumptions is by also assuming the following:

5. Unemployed productive inputs (labor) in the regional economy are ready, willing, and able to work more at current input prices (wages).

Assumption 5 means that the method presumes enough involuntary unemployment of the right kinds of labor to meet the new direct and indirect demand. From the new assumptions 4 and 5, an IO application to increased final demand must fail as a predictive device, unless there is willingness but inability to produce more at current prices, and regional factors such as labor are

---

* To help the noneconomist escape the jargon, I have substituted "labor" for "factor" or "input" in the following discussion, and the term "unemployment" also refers to nonuse of any factor of production.

involuntarily unemployed at current prices. The fixed technical coefficients and prices for regional and imported factors are inconsistent with full employment. In fact, resources in a modern regional economy typically exhibit close to full employment. Most inputs in the region are either employed or unqualified for the new work. When final demand increases significantly in comparison to the size of the regional economy, most of the required labor and resources must be imported from elsewhere. Therefore, the new work and increased incomes go to nonresidents, not residents, and much of the economic rationale provided by IO is not true. The new incomes will be paid from within the region, but they will not be paid to people who now live in the region.

The economic history of regional development shows that regional development initiatives can have substantial regional benefits. The true benefits more frequently involve direct payments to property owners, technological and structural change, lower average costs per unit sold and other economies of scale, price changes, and incomes paid to immigrants, not reduced local unemployment or use of idle capacity. IO is incapable of modeling the former impacts and subsequently provides totally inaccurate measures of economic impacts and benefits. But the purpose of input-output is often not accurate measurement, it is advocacy.

In fact, new projects typically harm some regional residents. The price changes ignored by IO can be a detriment or a benefit to local people. Direct and indirect increases in regional activity caused by the expenditures of immigrants may increase local prices, such as housing. This benefits some home owners, but residents who have no plans to sell their homes are faced with higher assessed valuation and property taxes, and tenants must pay more for rent. Irrigation projects can reduce local crop prices by expanding production so some local farmers are harmed. Often, big projects have detrimental social effects, such as crowding of schools and highways and social conflicts with newcomers. Businesses who sell their products within the region may benefit, but those who export can be harmed because wage rates and other input prices are increased by the increased local demands initiated by the project. In contrast, IO predicts that everyone in the regional economy will be better off than before.

But even more disturbing is the fact that regional development studies normally ignore indirect economic losses elsewhere caused by the taxation needed to fund regional development. With IO, government expenditure is shown to have multiplier effects in the regional economy. But if that money had remained in private hands, the same types of multiplier effects would occur somewhere else. This effect is usually ignored in IO because the small region under study contributes only a small share of the taxes for a project. But all small regions contribute all of the money spent by government everywhere. Regional impact studies are undertaken in many regions without considering the loss in economic activity in each region due to the taxation of all. The practice of IO contributes to government spending that concentrates benefits and disperses costs.

Recently there has been a proliferation of computer software and databases to develop and apply IO models. Some of these were originally developed by government agencies. The very popular IMPLAN was developed by the Forest Service.[26] IMPLAN, and some other commercial IO databases, have empirical problems above and beyond the theoretical problems of IO. IMPLAN uses county-level total output data with technical coefficients developed from national data. That is, the analyst can apply national-level average industrial structure to estimate county-level impacts without consideration of the actual local economic structure.

Common IO applications show a complete disregard for factual information. Real local conditions can be completely ignored; the analyst can provide economic multipliers without ever observing or accounting for the facts. If IO studies of government spending must be conducted, the analyst should determine if economic conditions assumed by the method—no fixed costs, constant returns to scale, idle capacity and resources, fixed prices, and fixed technical coefficients—actually exist. If not, then IO should not be applied. Real information about the structure of an economy should be obtained before applying a model that merely assumes a highly unlikely economic structure.

The assumptions of IO suggest it should be used only under very specific economic circumstances, but this has not reduced its misapplication. Local developers use IO to support arguments for subsidized development initiatives, such as business parks, ignoring the fact that the facilities mostly attract businesses from across town and drive down rents. A new baseball stadium may create jobs, but most of the money spent there by locals would have been spent somewhere else in town. The new airport will add construction jobs, but many of the workers may be brought in from outside of the region.

The concept of the economic multiplier has its parallel in the macroeconomic government spending multiplier of Keynesian theory. Here too, the use of the concept can be and has been used to support bad economic policy. One author makes many of the same points with respect to that multiplier as have been discussed with respect to IO here.[27] The macroeconomic multiplier skews economic policy toward spending as opposed to saving and toward government spending as opposed to private spending. Generally, the multiplier principle ignores the private spending or other use of money that would have occurred if government had not taken the money to begin with.

SUMMARY

These examples have demonstrated that quantitative methods are often biased, and bias is often enabled by a lack of confirmation of underlying premises. Often, the purpose of quantitative economics is selective advocacy, not objective research. Frequently, the role of economists is not to support free enterprise or provide objective research but, rather, to help selected players control markets or obtain public subsidies. This help is provided by supplying economic rationales that find market control or government enterprise to be in the public and/or local interest. This role results in an ironic situation in that economists, trained in the virtues of free competition and market forces, work against these very markets.

Campen finds that "there is a tendency for BCA (benefit-cost) to become one more means by which those with wealth and power are able to influence governmental decision making in their favor."[28] Persons who have much to gain are able to call on economists to help rationalize their activities, but each taxpayer with a small stake has little incentive to hire an opposing perspective. Economists are frequently the first to criticize other economists for biased research, and society invariably depends on other economists to provide the opposing point of view. But frequently, there are no economists representing the public. If there are, they are often underfunded, too late, or they lack the legal authority to have the analysis reconsidered.

Again, it must be remembered that the agencies and economists involved are often well intentioned, but preconceptions are unchecked by facts. The prevailing ideologies in an agency influence the conduct and results of analyses, often to a substantial and obvious degree. "Problem-solving techniques are dangerously open to the covert influences of individual and agency ideologies. Ideology is invariably buried in techniques of analysis, however neutral they appear to be."[29]

Finally, we are back to where we started, which is a disregard for scientific methods. Positivism in economics has come to mean the application of numerical methods. Many numerical procedures merely assume that an economic theory or structure is valid, develop quantitative models accordingly, and do not bother with confirmation. There is rarely an attempt to confirm the underlying premises or results of quantitative models by reference to facts. In the case of benefit-cost, contingent valuation, and IO, confirmation and ex-post analysis would have revealed the errors and bias of these techniques, perhaps saving billions of dollars in pork-barrel spending and unjustified costs of intervention. If the practice of economics were more scientific, perhaps economics would have contributed to better economic policy instead of providing biased rationales for poorly conceived initiatives.

NOTES

1. Quotation from James T. Campen, *Benefit, Cost and Beyond: The Political Economy of Benefit-Cost Analysis* (Cambridge, MA: Ballinger, 1986), p. 55.

2. Water Resources Council, *Economic and Environmental Principles and Guidelines for Water and Related Land Resources Implementation Studies.* (Washington, D.C.: 1983).

3. Campen, *Benefit, Cost and Beyond*, p. 53.

4. U.S. Department of the Interior, Water and Power Resources Service, "Animas-La Plata Project Colorado-New Mexico Definite Plan Report" (Salt Lake City, UT: Upper Colorado Region, 1979), p. 146.

5. Douglas R. Franklin and R. K. Hagemann, "Cost-sharing with Irrigated Agriculture: Promise Versus Performance," *Water Resources Research* 20(8) (August 1984): 1047–1051.

6. U.S. Department of the Interior, Bureau of Reclamation, "Animas-La Plata Project Colorado-New Mexico Economic and Financial Analyses Update" (Denver, CO: U.S. Department of the Interior, 1995).

7. John E. Lee, "Subject: 1986 Normalized Prices Free of Government Programs." Administrator, U.S.D.A., E.R.S. To: George Dunlop, Assistant Secretary for Natural Resources and the Environment. March 30, 1987.

8. "Briefing Paper. Change in Administration's Procedures for Evaluating Federal Water Projects." Dated June 2, 1987.

9. U.S. Department of the Army, U.S. Army Corps of Engineers, "Policy and Planning: Guidance for Conducting Civil Works Planning Studies." ER 1105-2-100 (December 28, 1990), p. 6–146.

10. M. W. Jones Lee, *The Value of Life: An Economic Analysis.* (Chicago: The University of Chicago Press, 1976).

11. Raymond Kopp and V. Kerry Smith, "Benefit Estimation Goes to Court: The Case of Natural Resource Damage Assessments." *Journal Policy Analysis and Management* 8(4) (Fall 1989): 593–612.

12. William W. Wade, "Natural Resource Damage Assessment: A Path Through the Pitfalls of Evolving Regulations," in *Litigation Economics*, eds. Patrick A. Gaughan and Robert J. Thornton. Contemporary Studies in Economic and Financial Analysis, Volume 74 (Greenwich, CT: JAI Press, 1993).

13. Ronald D. Knutson, C. Hall, E .G. Smith, S. Cotner, and J. W. Miller. "Yield and Cost Impacts of Reduced Pesticide Use on Fruits and Vegetables," *Choices The Magazine of Food, Farm and Resourse Issue* (First Quarter, 1994): 14–18.

14. The premier textbook on the practice of contingent valuation is probably Robert Cameron Mitchell and Richard T. Carson, *Using Surveys to Value Public Goods: The Contingent Valuation Method* (Washington, D.C.: Resources for the Future, 1989).

15. Peter A. Diamond and Jerry A. Hausman. "CV Measurement of Nonuse Values," in *Contingent Valuation: A Critical Assessment,* ed. Jerry A. Hausman. Contributions to Economic Analysis 220 (Amsterdam: North-Holland, 1993).

16. McKinley Blackburn, G. W. Harrison, and E. E. Rutstrom, "Statistical Bias Functions and Informative Hypothetical Surveys," *American Journal of Agricultural Economics* 76(5) (December 1994): 1084–1088.

17. Daniel McFadden, "Contingent Valuation and Social Choice," *American Journal of Agricultural Economics* 76(4) (November 1994): 689–708.

18. John B. Loomis, "Measuring the Economic Benefits of Removing Dams and Restoring the Elwha River: Results of a Contingent Evaluation Survey." *Water Resources Research* 32(2) (February 1996): 441–447.

19. Federal Emergency Management Agency, "A Benefit-Cost Model for the Seismic Rehabilitation of Buildings." Volume 1: A User's Manual.   Earthquake Hazards Reduction Series 62. FEMA 227. (April 1992), pp. 3–13.

20. Kenneth Arrow, R. Solow, P. R. Portney, E. E. Leamer, R. Radner and H. Schuman. *Report of the NOAA Panel on Contingent Valuation* (Washington, D.C.: Resources for the Future, 1993).

21. Richard T. Carson and R. C. Mitchell, "Economic Value of Reliable Water Supplies for Residential Water Users in the State Water Project Service Area." (Palo Alto, CA: QED Research, 1987); and Barakat and Chamberlin, Inc., "The Value of Water Supply Reliability: Results of a Contingent Value Survey" (Oakland, CA: 1994).

22. Richard T. Carson, Nicholas E. Flores, Kerry M. Martin and Jennifer L. Wright, "Contingent Valuation and Revealed Preference Methodologies: Comparing the Estimates for Quasi-Public Goods," *Land Economics* 72(1) (February 1996): 80–99.

23. For example, Robert A. Young and S. L. Gray, "Input-Output Models, Economic Surplus and the Evaluation of State or Regional Water Plans," *Water Resources Research* 21 (December 1985): 1819–1823.

24. Julie Leones, G. Schluter, and G. Goldman, "Redefining Agriculture in Interindustry Analysis," *American Journal of Agricultural Economics* 76(5) (December 1994): 1123–1129.

25. The input-output method can be summarized as follows. First, a square matrix of money flows that represents the financial side of trade among industries or other economic entities must be obtained. An example is provided in Table 10.1.

Table 10.1
Example of a Gross Flows Matrix

		Columns of expenses				
		Industry 1	Industry 2	More Indus- tries	Regional House- holds	Final Demands
Rows	Industry 1	$	$	$	$	$
of	Industry 2	$	$	$	$	$
sales						
receipts	More Industries	$	$	$	$	$
	Regional House- holds	$	$	$	$	$
	Value Added	$	$	$	$	$
	Imports	$	$	$	$	$

Each row of numbers in this matrix of data represents money receipts from sales by one industry to all industries in the region, and additional rows of "final payments" consist of value added and imports. Value added typically includes wages, profit, taxes, proprietor's income, and rental income. Each column of the gross flows matrix represents expenditures by an industry for goods and services purchased. Additional "final demands" are sales to buyers outside of the region or to buyers whose incomes are otherwise independent of the regional economy.

Then, a matrix of technical coefficients is calculated. Each dollar amount in a column is divided by total industry expenditure, equal to the sum of the column. The input-output multipliers are then derived. Multipliers express the direct plus indirect effects as a proportion of the direct effect. A household income multiplier of 3, for example, suggests that each direct (exogenous) dollar increase of household income will eventually generate two more dollars of household income. The technical coefficients are also used to simulate the impacts of changes in final demands with the same result.

26. Gregory S. Alward, "IMPLAN 2.0 Progress Report" (Fort Collins, CO: USDA, Forest Service, Systems Application Unit, 1985).

27. Mark Skousen, *Economics on Trial: Lies, Myths and Realities* (Homewood, IL: Business One Irvin, 1991), pp. 66–69.

28. Campen, *Benefit, Cost and Beyond,* p. 101.

29. Robert Lekachman, *Economists at Bay: Why the Experts Will Never Solve Your Problems* (New York: McGraw-Hill, 1976), p. 132.

11

Toward Better Economics

The practices and theories of neoclassical economics provide an inadequate basis for an economic science. The market model is a description of conditions required for static economic efficiency, not a theory based on fact, and it is not a good generalization of the fundamentals of modern free enterprise. Previous chapters have shown that economic competition occurs in many forums outside of free markets. There is great diversity in production and trade and in the mechanisms players use to compete and stay ahead. Production for sale in competitive markets is just one of many possible options in free enterprise, and all options are evaluated by the selfish without prejudice.

It is the variety and complexity of the modern economic experience that diminishes the worth of neoclassical economics. The unchanging attribute of economies in the last century has been continuous change in the form of creation, diversification, and specialization. More goods are relatively new and are sold with some degree of market control, and more resources are now dedicated to innovation than ever before. As the economy has changed, the static theories of economic competition have remained relatively constant, unaltered by the facts of change and self-justified by their internal but ultimately faulty logic. The dominant theory of economics has changed little over time because logic cannot observe how times have changed. Until and unless the economy becomes static, economists should spend more time monitoring and learning and less time trying to rationalize a very small and old theory by appeal to select facts.

Previous chapters have shown that the basic problem of quantitative and theoretical economics is that they emphasize theory and logic at the expense of the empirical methods of observation and confirmation. Essentially, economic logic is not science, and numerical analysis as practiced by most economists is not a complete empiricism. The practice and logic of comparative statics largely ignores dynamics, and the practice of quantitative economics is frequently a mere extension of theory, sometimes positivist but rarely empirical. Empiricists are positivists who "avoid the use of theory while trying to concentrate wholly on knowledge acquired from direct observation."[1] By this definition, neoclassical economics has little useful empirical content or direction.

Observation is not the only scientific method that is underutilized in economics. Economics could be substantially improved by utilizing a better balance of basic scientific and research methods. These other methods, somewhat related to observation, are classification and taxonomy, confirmation and replication, opportunism and creativity, and realism.

EMPIRICISM

The practice of economics should utilize more direct and systematic observation of the economic process of interest to formulate and confirm theories. Science is an iterative process between observation and theory. Thinking about observations generates theories, and thinking about theories should generate more observation in the form of confirmation. Logical thinking should be a link between observation and theory, not the theory itself.

I propose that the practice of economics should change to (1) observe real economic actions and processes, (2) determine the reason for these actions, and (3) confirm any economic theories about human behavior by the observation of that behavior. This means the observation of people in action and an understanding of their reasons for their actions.

An empirical approach to economic practice is based on two generalizations about economic behavior that makes the empirical approach possible. First, economic actions are inherently observable; they involve the movement of physical things or human beings. Second, economic actions are the result of conscious, intentional thought, and therefore, people can explain the reasons for their economic actions.

Actions are economic behaviors as well as the events that may influence them. For example, what happens to generate an interest in buying a good or initiating production? What steps are taken to plan and acquire information? What actions are taken to produce, sell, and move goods and services? Economic *process* is a sequence of actions: the acquisition and interpretation of information, the decision-making process, the decisions made, the process of planning based on these decisions, the negotiation of terms and implementation of trade, and, finally, the results of these actions in terms of production, prices, or trade.

Most economic data only provide information about the last of these steps. Economic data, such as prices and quantities, are not economic actions. Prices and quantities are merely the footprint of economic process, the result of actions, and they are economic signals that people respond to. They are generated by economic process as the process goes along. They merely happen to be the results of the process that are most interesting to economists and policymakers. To develop a good theory that can be tested by quantitative data, the analyst must first understand the process that leads to the data, and this requires observation.

Many sciences use controlled experiments to isolate and observe the influence of many factors. Experimental economics offers the potential for unbiased observation and measurement in controlled experimental conditions.[2] People, however, do not like to be experimented on, especially when their money is at stake, and methods such as contingent valuation have demonstrated some limitations of the use of hypothetical situations in experiments. Therefore, economists are somewhat limited in the potential scope of applications of experimental principles. Real data about the economy is not generated by experimental design, so economists must become better observers and analysts of real-world economic actions. Players are often unwilling to be observed, and they often will not provide the desired information when asked. Better research techniques to obtain unbiased information about real-world economic actions and their reasons are required.

Still, many types of economic phenomena are readily available for observation. Much economic activity, especially trade, occurs in public places, but much important economic behavior, especially production and consumption, occurs behind closed doors. There is much secondary information about economic process and behavior available for economists because the economy generates enormous amounts of secondary information. Useful information is found in books written by insiders, in technical writings, and in business and trade journals and newspapers. There are trade shows, conventions, and other meetings that economists might participate in to a greater extent.

The study of economic behavior and process should not only determine what people do; it must determine why they do it. Particularly, there is a great need for better understanding of the behavioral processes that result in economic phenomena. Economic behavior involves conscious choices and decisions. Therefore, people can explain why they do things. Part of the study of economic process must reveal the conscious reasons for people's economic choices.

Economists need to reach out more to the players they are concerned with, not in to the theory and data they have readily available. This may be more difficult and expensive than logical thinking, but it will be much more rewarding. If this approach seems hard, consider the plight of the natural biologist. His subjects usually run away terrified. A field biologist may spend months just finding and getting close to his subject. People are somewhat more accessible, and they can explain using language, but they are more complex. They are usually willing to give facts and opinions, but facts are selected and opinions biased toward one's self-interest. People seek to understand and benefit from the observer.

Part of the observation of economic process must involve the environment in which it occurs. The economic environment includes not just other players, but all of the resources, technology, and institutions that influence that behavior. Economics is largely psychology with respect to material things, and these things are the human environment.

The conventional economic theory of production and other common production models (input-output, especially) have had a tendency to ignore the real and unique facts of production. When an economic issue involves technical relationships, the underlying technology and cost structure must be determined by observation or some other reliable technique, not assumed. Some of the pertinent information may be gleaned from the applied technical science appropriate to the problem at hand. Still, there is no good starting-point substitute for an unbiased expert description of the process of production. Production is a product of willful and intelligent creation and it can be explained.

The product of observation is mostly description. Most actions cannot be quantified, but they can be described. Observation, properly conducted, generates a description of how things work in terms of actions and process. With proper questioning, the economic players have provided some description of the reasons and purposes of their actions. These observations lead to a general understanding of the economic process or problem. With multiple observations, there is more potential for quantitative analysis in the form of classification and statistics. Then analysis, conjecture, and logical thinking can be used to develop hypotheses, and more selective observation can be conducted to clarify and isolate critical or uncertain parts of the hypotheses. When a theory is confirmed by observation, it may be good enough to justify analysis using quantitative models.

This chapter has not discussed econometrics, the application of statistics to economic data. Many economists will argue that econometrics has made economics a positivist and even an empirical science. Econometrics has made many valuable contributions to economics, but the limitations of statistics generally must be recognized. Essentially, the empirical value of econometrics is limited by the economic and probability theories that underlie it. The statistics of econometrics is largely the probability theory of association, and the potential for error from false cause is always there. Always, it must be recognized that quantities and prices are the result of economic behavior, not the behavior itself. Positivism by statistics is inherently different from observation.

CLASSIFICATION AND TAXONOMY

Classification is used to make order from multiple disorganized economic observations. Sometimes, economic phenomena appear chaotic. Economists are generally good statisticians, well trained in statistical methods of classification, but descriptions of economic actions and reasons are generally qualitative. Often, economic facts must be organized around qualitative classifications, and numerous observations over many players generate data.

Observation unguided by preconception will generate disorganized and possibly irrelevant facts. Conventional economics tries to explain it all by appeal to several stylized categories, for example, the two types of costs or the stylized production inputs of land, capital, and labor. It is useful to try to organize things in different ways; it reveals more about their character. Classification reveals the need for more or different categories, and the recognition of more categories leads to different hypotheses about different processes.

A taxonomy is a formal classification. The taxonomy is useful if it relates to the problem at hand—in this case, economic behavior. A good taxonomy is mutually exclusive as between categories, and users of the taxonomy should be able to easily sort items into one of the categories. The taxonomy, taken together, should be all encompassing. Economics has a taxonomy for market structure that has proved its worth. This book has suggested taxonomies involving types of costs and types of exchange. Other possible taxonomies might involve factors of production, price-setting mechanisms, and types of contract terms.

Economic perspective, which defines whose economic impacts or benefits are to be counted, is anther important classification problem in economics. National benefit-cost studies often do not explicitly consider the share of economic benefits paid to foreigners, and regional IO studies do not adequately consider the share of regional incomes paid to nonresidents. In the modern economy, incomes paid in a region are often not paid to regional residents.

CONFIRMATION AND REPLICATION

Economic theories and models must be confirmed by reference to real economic actions whenever possible. Validation is the process of making a model legitimate; it implies social acceptance. In economics, professional validation often involves the internal logic and mathematics of the model, but logical proficiency does not demonstrate factual accuracy. Economics needs a higher standard of empiricism to judge the worth of economic models.

Truth is a relative concept in quantitative economics. Verification is simply not a practical standard for economic models for several reasons. First, dollars and quantities are continuous variables. It is not realistic to hope that economic models can predict to the last unit. Second, all economic systems except the world economy are open. Third, economic models are simplifications of complex systems. Fourth, aggregate economic data are inherently stochastic. No economic model can be verified, so a different concept is needed.

In quantitative models, worth is largely a function of predictive or explanatory ability judged impartially. Models must exhibit the ability to predict not just general economic behavior in line with theory, as current validation frequently finds, but they must provide useful information for the problem at hand. Frequently, useful means a better prediction than other available predictions. The validated model or theory should be the one that predicts best.

Confirmation is the process of measuring a theory or model's predictive accuracy by using the theory or model to predict numbers or other phenomena that were not used to develop the theory or model. We can measure how closely a model predicts with statistical methods, and we can compare this result to other predictions, explanations, or models with the same statistics. To argue that a model should be validated (accepted), it is not enough to say merely that it predicts with an accuracy shown by so many statistics. Rather, these statistics should be compared across predictions.

If a model can be confirmed by cross-prediction comparisons in many situations, then perhaps it will become validated. At least, many independent confirmations show the degree of error that may be expected in applying the model to new situations. This is a form of replication. The continuous retesting of a model or theory by confirmation provides an updated and more complete understanding of its worth.

In some cases, the model may be the only one available. The sole model may be so inaccurate that informed judgment may be the better predictor, the costs of using the model may exceed any potential benefit from using it, or the inaccurate conclusion may lead to poorly conceived actions. No information is often better than the damage done by bad information. All of these situations are common for economic models, and they often suggest situations in which more observation is needed to improve the theoretical basis of the model.

OPPORTUNISM AND CREATIVITY

Creativity is the art of producing through imaginative skill. Imagination and creativity are not terms often associated with economics, but they should be. Economic practice needs new ways of testing theories and conducting observation and confirmation. Creative research should better utilize new and existing technology to obtain information. For example, cameras in places of public trade could be used to obtain more information on behavior. The internet provides a new opportunity to solicit information about reasons for economic behavior.

Economists need to be opportunistic by using unforseen situations to gather information. Sometimes, events occur that provide a chance to observe important economic phenomena. For example, a sudden shortage or surplus caused by an unforeseen event provides an opportunity to learn about demand in a different range of quantity. The entry or loss of a large business in a regional economy might provide information about the economic impacts of regional development. A price-cut in a sale provides an opportunity to learn about elasticity of demand.

Economics typically makes little use of case studies and past experience to validate and improve models. Where possible, similar projects or situations should be observed, and data kept and made available for later use. When a series of analyses and actions have already been conducted and completed, ex-post analysis should be used to confirm the analytic techniques used. Extrapolation from a good case study will often provide information that can improve economic models. For example, the USBR frequently developed irrigation benefit-cost analyses that turned out to be overly optimistic in terms of costs, crop production, and prices.[3] These past projects should have served as models for benefit-cost analyses of new projects, but this opportunity was never embraced by benefit-cost practitioners.

REALISM

Webster's defines *realism* as "concern for fact or reality and rejection of the impractical and visionary."[4] Realism in economics means a concern for empiricism. For a particular problem, it means concern for the facts of the case. It also means a concern for the applicability of economic methods in relation to the economic problem and situation at hand.

Economics often tries to use available techniques or data that have little applicability to the problem at hand. Economists sometimes investigate economic problems using quantitative models that are not appropriate given the scope of the problem at hand, much less the facts of the case. Scope involves the nature of the problem, program, or impact: the range of the economy that will be affected, when it will be affected, whose economic measures should be counted, and, finally, what economic measures are appropriate. The worth of a quantitative model for a particular problem is related to its coverage as well as its predictive ability. Issues of problem and scope should guide models and analysis, not vice versa.

TEACHING AND THE MULTIDISCIPLINARY NATURE OF ECONOMICS

To improve economics, we must train better economists. Above all, economics needs to become more aware of and teach the importance of scientific method. Students need to be taught how to observe, how to obtain and process information, how to get the pertinent facts, and how to tell which facts are pertinent. The teaching of economics should replace logic with information on where to get real economic information, how to determine if its good and applicable information, and how to get new information if needed. Scientific process should probably be a general requirement of any undergraduate curriculum. The scientific process also includes experimentation, research strategies, adaptation, imagination, and intuition. The teaching of economics, especially at the undergraduate level, typically does not utilize these concepts.

Given the limited utility of economic theories at this time, what should be taught under the title of economics? Undergraduate economics is taught to many students who have no intention of becoming economists, and the agenda must be responsive to their needs. One author outlines an undergraduate agenda that includes economic history and statistics; the facts of production, consumption, work, and finance; and political economy.[5] Everyone should be taught about the economic facts that affect them as consumers, taxpayers, and workers: the causes and significance of inflation, interest rates, the instruments of financial and stock markets, public finance and expenditure, and economic and trade laws. There is a history of economic activity and an enormous world economy that students need to be aware of. There are economic concepts of relevance to everyone, such as alternative and opportunity costs, substitutes and complements, risk and expectations, and trends in production, trade and employment.

Economics should be a multidisciplinary study in teaching and practice. Many of the multiple concerns of economics are the single concerns of other disciplines. Economics is the study of human behavior in relation to the material world. Sometimes, behavior can only be understood in a social context. Therefore, economists should study psychology and sociology and the relevant concepts should be isolated. The economic theory of production, which really boils down to the assumption of diminishing returns, is too general to be accurate. Therefore, economics students should study production process and techniques, and production economics should emphasize empiricism. In more advanced economics classes, the study of production might involve engineering, manufacturing processes, biology, agronomy, auto mechanics, construction —whatever applies given the students' specialized interests.

Economics needs to consider finance and management, so finance and business courses should be part of the curriculum. The economy is the dominant concern of government, so political economy and government are also important. Business management has obvious applications. Economics should draw on these fields and selectively teach those aspects most relevant to the observed economy.

The evolution of organizations is important, so the teaching of economics should include the relevant aspects of the theory of biological evolution. The theory of evolution provides a useful analog for a theory of economic change. The similarity of biological and social evolution are not mere analogies. Economic growth and technological change is part of the evolution of the human species.

Fortunately, economics should not be merely a collection of other disciplines. Aspects of economic phenomena that are unique to the study and practice of economics are (1) voluntary exchange and (2) the psychology of information and expectations that leads to economic decisions.

Economics students should study real trade where exchange actually occurs. Students should observe trade in action, not just the data generated by trade. Exchange includes negotiation, contracting, and the obligations of buyers and sellers. Economists should focus on the timing of these components of exchange and how expectations, prices, and terms are set. They should study contracts; contract law; the disposition of production; how goods are moved; and the services of transportation, storage, and marketing. They should be taught trade, contract, and antitrust laws and the role of government in exchange. They should study patterns of exchange outside of free markets: the involuntary exchange of civil law, taxation, public utilities and regulated monopoly, and the laws of intellectual property and other property rights. They should be taught the reasons for regulation and the history of private-public relationships that have forged the mixed economy of today. They need to understand the economic problems of mixed enterprise: when and why markets and government may fail.

Information problems are central to economic problems, so economics students need to learn more about information processes. How is information developed, revealed, transferred, and protected? What are the laws of information? Production and purchase decisions are fundamentally guided by expectations. The search for better information on which to base expectations is, to say the least, an important economic activity.

Economics students need to be brought up to date so they can go out and begin to contribute to the detailed world of business and government. They need to understand the potential as well as the substantial limitations of research tools such as statistics, simulation and operations research. Computer training needs to become more sensitive to the potential for abuse of this technology. Students need to understand the limits and proper roles of mathematical techniques within the scientific process. Essentially, mathematics is logic and should be treated as such.

THE CONTENT OF A BETTER ECONOMICS

Part of the problem of neoclassical economics is the generality of its models. Perhaps, economics should have a lot of economic theories that are smaller in scope. There could be an economic theory just for agriculture and, perhaps, just for oranges, wheat, or onions. There could be a theory for automobiles, or maybe one just for tires. Each theory would be clearly dated, so the user would be well advised as to when it should be revalidated or thrown out. Each theory must clearly reference the facts on which it is based, so when the facts are no longer true, the theory could be changed accordingly.

In truth, there are a lot of smaller theories displayed in the scores of economic and scientific journals and trade magazines that cater to specialized economic and business research. Unfortunately, this enormous body of knowledge has not trickled down to change the basic content of economics.

Market theory, neoclassical economics and other logical methods have their place. Market theory shows the conditions required for free enterprise to lead to static economic efficiency, and the theories of imperfect competition also show what may follow from the given assumptions. Economics students must be taught that market theory is a partial logical argument, not a factual description of real economic process. They need to be shown why the theory is faulty as a logical device, and why it fails to describe the modern economy. It shows *one* of the good things that *may* follow from free enterprise. It shows that private economic incentives *might* result in production of *some* kinds of things people want. If interpreted properly, it can suggest why there *may* be a reason for government intervention. Once students are taught these things, they should be taught about the importance of economic facts, and how to acquire and interpret facts, with equal emphasis.

Antimarket theory augments market theory as a general description of the forces that guide modern economic behavior and exchange. Together with market theory, it provides a general description of what competition may do in free enterprise. Economic students should be taught how and why economic players control and escape markets and how and why economic exchange occurs outside of markets. There is incentive, economic means, and opportunities allowed or created by law. Antimarket behavior is fundamental to the process of change and technological innovation. It explains many important activities of private and public players and is the root of some of the most common foibles and values of free enterprise.

NOTES

1. Glenn C. Johnson, *Research Methodology for Economists* (New York: Macmillan, 1986), p. 22.

2. See, for example, Daniel Friedman and Shyam Sunder, *Experimental Methods: A Primer for Economists* (Cambridge: Cambridge University Press, 1994).

3. Douglas Franklin and R. K. Hageman, "Cost Sharing with Irrigated Agriculture: Promise Versus Performance," *Water Resources Research* 20(8) (August 1984): 1047–1051.

4. *Websters' New Collegiate Dictionary* (Springfield, MA: Merriam, 1981), p. 964.

5. Guy Routh, "What to Teach Undergraduates," in *Economics in Disarray,* eds. P. Wiles and G. Routh (New York: Basil Blackwell, 1984), p. 241.

Selected Bibliography

Abler, David G. "Vote Trading on Farm Legislation in the U.S. House." *American Journal of Agricultural Economics* 71(3), (August 1989): 583–591.

Arrow, Kenneth, R. Solow, P. R. Portney, E. E. Leamer, R. Radner, and H. Schuman. *Report of the NOAA Panel on Contingent Valuation.* Washington D.C.: Resource for the Future, 1993.

Atkinson, Rodney. *Government Against the People. The Economics of Political Exploitation.* Southampton, England: The Camelot Press, 1986.

Barlett, Donald L., and James B. Steele. *America: What Went Wrong.* Kansas City MO: Andrews and McMeel, 1992.

Beveridge, W. I. B. *The Art of Scientific Investigation.* New York: Vintage Books, 1950.

Binmore, Ken and Partha Dasgupta, eds. *Economic Organizations as Games.* Oxford: Basil Blackwell, 1986.

Blackburn, McKinley, G. W. Harrison, and E. E. Rutstrom. "Statistical Bias Functions and Informative Hypothetical Surveys." *American Journal of Agricultural Economics* 76(5), (December 1994): 1084–1088.

Blackhouse, Roger E., ed. *New Directions in Economic Methodology.* London: Routledge, 1994.

Blaug, Mark. *Economic Theory in Retrospect.* Third Edition. Cambridge: Cambridge University Press, 1978.

Blaug, Mark. *The Methodology of Economics or How Economists Explain.* Cambridge: Cambridge University Press, 1982.

Blaug, Mark. *Economic Theories: True or False?* Essays in the History and Methodology of Economics. London: Edward Elger, 1990.

Boland, J. C. *Wall Street's Insiders: How You Can Profit with the Smart Money.* New York: William Morrow, 1985.

Bovard, James. *The Farm Fiasco.* San Francisco: ICS Press, 1989.

Bowman, Ward S. *Patent and Antitrust Law: A Legal and Economic Appraisal*. Chicago: University of Chicago Press, 1973.

Braudel, Fernand. *The Perspective of the World*. New York: Harper and Row, 1986.

Buchanan, James M. *Essays on the Political Economy*. Honolulu, HI: University of Hawaii Press, 1989.

Buchholz, Todd G. *New Ideas from Dead Economists: An Introduction to Modern Economic Thought*. New York: Dutton, 1989.

Campen, James T. *Benefit, Cost and Beyond: The Political Economy of Benefit-Cost Analysis*. Cambridge, MA: Ballinger, 1986.

Carroll, Paul. *Big Blues: The Unmaking of IBM*. New York: Crown Publishers, 1993.

Carson, Richard T., Nicholas E. Flores, Kerry M. Martin and Jennifer L. Wright. "Contingent Valuation and Revealed Preference Methodologies: Comparing the Estimates for Quasi-Public Goods." *Land Economics* 72(1), (February 1996): 80–99.

Chapman, Dudley H. *Molting Time for Anti-Trust: Market Realities, Economic Fallacies and European Innovations*. New York: Praeger Press, 1991.

Cochrane, Willard W. *The City Man's Guide to the Farm Problem*. Minneapolis, MN: University of Minnesota Press, 1965.

Council of Economic Advisors. *Economic Report of the President*. Chapter 5. Markets and Regulatory Reform. Transmitted to Congress January 1993. United States Government Printing Office, 1993.

Cringely, Robert X. *Accidental Empires: How the Boys of Silicon Valley Make Their Millions, Battle Foreign Competition, and Still Get a Date*. Reading, MA: Addison-Wesley Publishing, 1992.

Davidson, Osha G. *Broken Heartland: The Rise of America's Rural Ghetto*. New York: Maxwell Macmillan International, 1990.

Dawdy, Doris Ostrander. *Congress in its Wisdom: The Bureau of Reclamation and the Public Interest*. Studies in Water Policy and Management, No. 13. Boulder, CO: Westview Press, 1989.

Diamond, Edwin, Norman Sandler, and Milton Mueller, eds. *Telecommunications in Crisis: The First Amendment, Technology and Deregulation*. Washington, D.C.: Cato Institute, 1983.

Diamond, Jared. "Blueprints, Bloody Ships, and Borrowed Letters." *Natural History* 104(3), (March 1995): 16–21.

Dorfman, Joseph, ed. *Institutional Economics: Veblen, Commons and Mitchell Reconsidered*. Berkeley, CA: University of California Press, 1963.

Eichberger, Jurgen. *Game Theory for Economists*. San Diego, CA: Academic Press, 1993.

Ethridge, Don. *Research Methodology in Applied Economics: Organizing, Planning and Conducting Economic Research*. Ames, IA: Iowa State University Press, 1995.

Ferguson, C. E., and J. P. Gould. *Microeconomic Theory*. Fourth Edition. Homewood, IL: Richard D. Irwin, 1975.

Ferguson, Charles H., and Charles R. Morris. *Computer Wars: How the West Can Win in a Post-IBM World*. New York: Random House, 1993.

Franklin, Douglas R., and R. K. Hagemann. "Cost-sharing with Irrigated Agriculture: Promise Versus Performance." *Water Resources Research* 20(8), (August 1984): 1047–1051.

Friedman, Daniel, and Shyam Sunder. *Experimental Methods: A Primer for Economists*. Cambridge: Cambridge University Press, 1994.

Friedman, James W. *Game Theory with Applications to Economics*. New York: Oxford
   University Press, 1986.
Galbraith, John K. *The New Industrial State*. New York: Houghton Mifflin, 1968.
Gardiner, J. A., and T. R. Lyman. *Decisions for Sale: Corruption and Reform in Land
   Use and Building Regulation*. Praeger Special Studies. New York: Praeger
   Publishers, 1978.
Gardner, Roy. *Games for Business and Economics*. New York: John Wiley, 1995.
Gaughan, Patrick A., and Robert J. Thornton, eds. *Litigation Economics*. Contemporary
   Studies in Economic and Financial Analysis, Vol. 74. Greenwich, CT: JAI Press,
   1993.
Greenwald, Carol S. *Banks Are Dangerous to Your Wealth*. Englewood Cliffs, NJ:
   Prentice-Hall, 1980.
Grieson, R. E., ed. *Antitrust and Regulation*. Lexington, MA: Lexington Books, D.C.
   Heath, 1986.
Gross, Martin L. *The Government Racket: Washington Waste from A to Z*. New York:
   Ballentine Books, 1993.
Grossman, Gene M., and Elhanan Helpman. "Endogenous Innovation in the Theory of
   Growth." *Journal of Economic Perspectives* 8 (Winter 1994): 23–44.
Hausman, Daniel M., ed. *The Philosophy of Economics: An Anthology*. Cambridge:
   Cambridge University Press, 1994.
Hausman, Jerry A., ed. *Contingent Valuation: A Critical Assessment*. Contributions to
   Economic Analysis 220. Amsterdam: North-Holland, 1993.
Heertje, Arnold, and Mark Perlman, eds. *Evolving Technology and Market Structure*.
   Ann Arbor, MI: The University of Michigan Press, 1990.
Hotelling, Harold. "The General Welfare in Relation to Problems of Taxation and of
   Railway and Utility Rates." *Econometrica* (July 1938): 242–269.
Johnson, Glenn L. *Research Methodology for Economists Philosophy and Practice*. New
   York: Macmillan, 1986.
Kaldor, Nicholas. *Economics Without Equilibrium*. The Arthur M. Okun Memorial
   Lecture Series, Yale University. Armonk, NY: M. E. Sharpe, 1985.
Kaplan, A. D. H., Joel B. Dirlam, and Robert F. Lanzillotti. *Pricing in Big Business:
   A Case Approach*. Washington, D.C.: The Brookings Institution, 1958.
Knutson, Ronald D., C. Hall, E. G. Smith, S. Cotner, and J. W. Miller. "Yield and
   Cost Impacts of Reduced Pesticide Use on Fruits and Vegetables." *Choices: The
   Magazine of Food Farm and Resource Issues* (First Quarter 1994): 14–18.
Kopp, Raymond, and V. Kerry Smith. "Benefit Estimation Goes to Court: The Case of
   Natural Resource Damage Assessments." *Journal Policy Analysis and Manage-
   ment* 8(4), (Fall 1989): 593–612.
Krueger, Anne. "The Political Economy of the Rent-Seeking Society." *American
   Economic Review* 64(3) (1974): 291-303.
Kuttner, Robert. *The Economic Illusion: False Choices Between Prosperity and Social
   Justice*. Boston: Houghton Mifflin, 1984.
Langley, S., and H. Baumes. "Evolution of U.S. Agricultural Policy in the 1980s." In
   Agriculture-Food Policy Review: U.S. Agricultural Policies in a Changing World,
   Agricultural Economic Report Number 620. Washington, D.C.: U.S. Department
   of Agriculture Economic Research Service, 1989.
Lee, M. W. Jones. *The Value of Life: An Economic Analysis*. Chicago: The University
   of Chicago Press, 1976.

Lekachman, Robert. *Economists at Bay: Why the Experts Will Never Solve Your Problems*. New York: McGraw-Hill, 1976.

Leones, Julie, G. Schluter, and G. Goldman. "Redefining Agriculture in Interindustry Analysis." *American Journal of Agricultural Economics* 76(5), (December 1994): 1123–1129.

Libecap, Gary D. *Locking up the Range: Federal Land Conflicts and Grazing*. Pacific Studies in Public Policy. San Francisco: Pacific Institute for Public Policy Research, 1991.

Mackay, R. J., J. C. Miller, and B. Yandle, eds. *Public Choice and Regulation: A View from Inside the Federal Trade Commission*. Stanford, CA: Hoover Institution Press, Stanford University, 1987.

Mansfield, Edwin. *Microeconomics Theory and Applications*. Third Edition. New York: W. W. Norton, 1979.

Martin, William E., H. Ingram, and N. K. Laney. "A Willingness to Play: Analysis of Water Resources Development." *Western Journal of Agricultural Economics* 7(1), (1982): 133–139.

Marz, Eduard. *Joseph Schumpeter: Scholar, Teacher and Politician*. New Haven, CT: Yale University Press, 1991.

McFadden, Daniel. "Contingent Valuation and Social Choice." *American Journal of Agricultural Economics* 76(4), (November 1994): 689–708.

Mitchell, Robert Cameron, and Richard T. Carson. *Using Surveys to Value Public Goods: The Contingent Valuation Method*. Washington, D.C.: Resources for the Future, 1989.

Nelson, F. J., M. Simone, and C. Valdes. "Agricultural Subsidies in Canada, Mexico and the United States, 1982–1991." *Choices: The Magazine of Food Farm and Resource Issues* (First Quarter 1994): 22–25.

Oakley, Allen. *Schumpeter's Theory of Capitalist Motion: A Critical Exposition and Reassessment*. Brookfield, VT: Gower, 1990.

Oreskes, Naomi, Kristin Shrader-Frechette, and Kenneth Blitz. "Verification, Validation and Confirmation of Numerical Models in the Earth Sciences." *Science* 263, (February 1994): 641–646.

Paarlberg, Don. "Economic Pathology, Six Cases." *Choices: The Magazine of Food Farm and Resource Issues* (Third Quarter 1994): 17.

Paarlberg, Robert L. "Does the GATT Agreement Promote Export Subsidies?" *Choices: The Magazine of Food Farm and Resource Issues* (Fourth Quarter 1995): 9–12.

Pizzo, Stephen, Mary Fricker, and Paul Muolo. *Inside Job: The Looting of America's Savings and Loans*. New York: McGraw-Hill, 1989.

Randall, Alan. "The Problem of Market Failure." *Natural Resources Journal* 23, (1983): 131–148.

Reisner, Marc. *Cadillac Desert: The American West and Its Disappearing Water*. New York: Viking, 1986.

Romer, Paul M. "The Origins of Endogenous Growth." *Journal of Economic Perspectives* 8, (Winter 1994): 3–22.

Rosenberg, Alexander. *Economics: Mathematical Politics or Science of Diminishing Returns*. Chicago: University of Chicago Press, 1992.

Rothschild, Michael. *Bionomics: The Inevitability of Capitalism*. New York: H. Holt, 1990.

Samuels, Warren J., ed. *Institutional Economics.* Vol. I to III. Brookfield, VT: Gower
    Publishing, 1988.
Sax, Joseph L. *Federal Reclamation Law. Volume II: Water and Water Rights.* New
    York: Allen Smith, 1967.
Shackle, G. L. S. *Epistemics and Economics: A Critique of Economic Doctrines.* New
    Brunswick, NJ: Transaction Publishers, 1992.
Silk, Leonard. *Economics in the Real World.* New York: Simon and Schuster, 1984.
Skousen, Mark. *Economics on Trial: Lies, Myths and Realities.* Homewood, IL: Business
    One Irvin, 1991.
Smith, Adam. *Wealth of Nations.* Cannon ed. London: Methuen, 1904.
Stigler, G. L. "The Theory of Economic Regulation." *Bell Journal of Economics* 2,
    (1971): 3–21.
Stroup, R. L. and J. A. Baden. *Natural Resources: Bureaucratic Myths and Environmen-
    tal Management.* San Francisco: Pacific Institute for Public Policy Research,
    1983.
U.S. Department of Agriculture, Economic Research Service. *Provisions of the Food,
    Conservation and Trade Act of 1990.* Agriculture Information Bulletin, No. 614.
    Washington, D.C.: 1991.
U.S. Department of the Army, Army Corps of Engineers. "Policy and Planning:
    Guidance for Conducting Civil Works Planning Studies." ER 1105-2-100.
    December 28, 1990.
U.S. Department of the Interior, Bureau of Reclamation. "Animas-La Plata Project
    Colorado-New Mexico Economic and Financial Analyses Update." Denver, CO:
    U.S. Department of the Interior, 1995.
U.S. Department of the Interior, Water and Power Resources Service. "Animas-La Plata
    Project Colorado-New Mexico Definite Plan Report." Salt Lake City, UT: Upper
    Colorado Region, 1979.
U.S. Federal Emergency Management Agency. "A Benefit-Cost Model for the Seismic
    Rehabilitation of Buildings." Vol. 1: "A User's Manual." Earthquake Hazards
    Reduction Series 62. FEMA 227. Washington, D.C.: April, 1992.
Verbon, Harrie A. A., and A. A. M. Van Winden. *The Political Economy of Govern-
    ment Debt.* Contributions to Economic Analysis 219. Amsterdam: North-Holland,
    1993.
Water Resources Council. *Economic and Environmental Principles and Guidelines for
    Water and Related Land Resources Implementation Studies.* Washington, D.C.,
    1983.
Wiles, P., and G. Routh, eds. *Economics in Disarray.* New York: Basil Blackwell,
    1984.
Young, Robert A., and S. L. Gray. "Input-Output Models, Economic Surplus and the
    Evaluation of State or Regional Water Plans." *Water Resources Research* 21,
    (December 1985): 1819–1823.

Index

About the Author

ROGER MANN is an agricultural and resource economist specializing in microeconomic theory, natural resource policy, and quantitative methods. He currently works in private practice for government, utilities, and private corporations and has contributed to several books and journals.

ISBN 0-275-95466-8

90000>

EAN

9 780275 954666

HARDCOVER BAR CODE